Suffer and Be Still

WOMEN IN THE VICTORIAN AGE

Suffer and Be Still

WOMEN IN THE VICTORIAN AGE

Edited by Martha Vicinus

A woman's "highest duty is so often to
suffer and be still."
— Mrs. Sarah Stickney Ellis (1845)

Indiana University Press   Bloomington & London

Contents

Acknowledgments

For permission to reproduce the paintings, acknowledgment is given to the Tate Gallery, London, for Plates 2, 8, 9, and 10; to the Victoria and Albert Museum, for Plates 1 and 4; to the Hon. Keith Mason, D. F. C., for Plate 3; the Courtauld Institute, for Plate 5; The Royal Academy of Arts, for Plate 6; The Wilmington Society of Fine Arts, for Plate 7.

The editor would like to thank Michael Philp, former Managing Editor of *Victorian Studies* (1969-1971), for his assistance at every stage in the preparation of this book.

M. V.

Introduction

The Perfect Victorian Lady

THE WOMEN'S LIBERATION MOVEMENT HAS BROUGHT BACK TO LIFE, IF NOT academic respectability, the study of women. Yet, much of the material currently being published covers the familiar ground of the rise of feminism and emancipation, or male attitudes toward women. As with Black studies, there has been widespread distrust in the new field of women studies. Some argue that it lacks academic depth and rigor, or that there is not enough material to study, while others say that we must maintain our loyalty to a particular discipline lest we lose ourselves in an ill-defined area without "acceptable" criteria of research or clear academic standards. The most common criticism has been against research that might be biased, trivial or, worst of all, trendy. The simplest answer to such critics is that the failure to study the position of women in society and in history is equally biased — and to date no standard nineteenth-century history text gives the women's movement more than token space (see p. 77). With the widespread publication of books about women, past and present, and the growing acceptance of courses on women, many of these fears will be silenced. Nevertheless, the financing of women studies and research remains minimal — in part because of financial cutbacks in higher education, but primarily because of the continued refusal to take seriously the study of women as a paramount, and not merely legitimate, field of study.

Only a cursory look at Dr. Kanner's bibliography indicates how little secondary work has been done on the nineteenth-century British woman in the context of wider social change. Even fewer comparative studies have been done, although historians have long recognized the importance of nineteenth-century Britain as the first industrializing nation. As Kanner says in her introduction, "There are few systematic, historically oriented studies that relate changes in English women's status to national socioeconomic phenomena in terms of time, place and circumstances. . . . Still wanting are . . . investigations concerning the position of women of the various social classes in categories of inquiry such as national education, administrative and institutional developments, law amendments, technology, politics and social service." The essays which follow are a beginning — they do not encompass all those areas mentioned, but I believe, they point the way to further study and research.

In the autumn of 1969 *Victorian Studies* advertised a special issue on the theme of the Victorian woman; we requested that articles submitted be interdisciplinary in outlook and offer either new material or a new approach to familiar subject matter. The success of the September 1970 issue led to the commissioning and submission of further essays, out of which come the following nine chapters and annotated bibliography. A number of important subjects are missing, which hopefully could result in a second volume. Emigration, inevitably recommended by Victorian commentators when confronted with the statistics showing the disproportionate number of women to men, needs further study. The attitudes and situations of women who emigrated, both before and after they left Great Britain, are but sketchily known. The many legal disabilities from which women suffered, both at home and at work, have been examined largely from the point of safety legislation or the headline divorce and child custody cases. The growth of women's education at school, college and university levels needs further exploration. Historians have frequently defined the nineteenth-century women's movement as essentially middle class, yet the *Northern Star* carried regular reports of the doings of Female Radical Clubs. Their disappearance is yet to be explained. The petty bourgeoisie is a forgotten class. One wonders how many wives, having assisted in the management of a corner store, took over the business after the death of their husbands. What was the legal position of a middle-aged woman running a shop? A number of excellent literary studies have been published focusing on the portrayal of the heroine in novels written either by women or men. Women's magazines, annuals and other popular literature should now be examined. While men made their opinions widely known as to the rightness or wrongness of the feminist movement, what were the opinions of women from every class? Why and how did attitudes toward women, held by both women and men, change?

In planning this anthology I began with no overall scheme except to give priority to those essays which opened new fields in the study and teaching of the Victorian period. Each chapter offers an interpretation of Victorian attitudes toward women in a particular sphere, or an analysis of the objective conditions of women. The authors analyze the changes in the behavior and beliefs of Victorian women and men in regard to a model of femininity, the "perfect lady."[1] Prior to and at the beginning of the nineteenth century the ideal had been the "perfect wife." The perfect wife was an active participant in the family, fulfilling a number of vital tasks, the first of which was childbearing. She was expected in the lower classes to contribute to the family income. In the middle classes she provided indirect economic support through the care of her children, the purchasing and preparation of food and the making of clothes. This model gave way to an ideal which had little connection with any functional and responsible role in society. Precisely why and how this change took place cannot be completely explained in one anthology, but each author contributes at least a partial answer to the making and dissolution of the "perfect lady" as a Victorian ideal.

This ideal was most fully developed in the upper middle class. Before marriage a young girl was brought up to be perfectly innocent and sexually ignorant. The predominant ideology of the age insisted that she have little sexual feeling at all, although family affection and the desire for motherhood were considered innate. Morally she was left untested, and kept under the watchful eye of her mother in her father's home. Milton's lofty notion of tried virtue rather than blank virtue would have met few responsive chords in the hearts of Victorian men looking for an ideal helpmate. Once married, the perfect lady did not work; she had servants. She was mother only at set times of the day, even of the year; she left the heirs in the hands of nannies and governesses. Her social and intellectual growth was confined to the family and close friends. Her status was totally dependent upon the economic position of her father and then her husband. In her most perfect form, the lady combined total sexual innocence, conspicuous consumption and the worship of the family hearth.

The perfect lady, in turn, gave way to the "perfect woman," or as she is sometimes called, "the new woman," who continued to hold chastity as an ideal, but made it equally applicable to men as to women. Moreover, through a variety of economic and social changes her sphere of action became greatly enlarged. The new woman worked, sought education and fought for legal and political rights. While few lower-class women immediately benefited from the gains made by upper-class women in these fields, the process of change to an ideal more closely modeled on social and psychological reality could not be halted. Emancipation once begun was inexorable.

Throughout the Victorian period the perfect lady as an ideal of femininity was tenacious and all-pervasive, in spite of its distance from the objective situations of countless women. Indeed, its strength can be measured by examining, as Dr. Conway does, the biological metaphors employed by early social scientists in describing the innate character- istics of men and women. The main difficulty with the perfect lady as a model of behavior even in the middle classes (and it came to be ac- cepted, in an altered form, in other classes) was the narrowness of the definition. Few women could afford to pursue the course laid out for them, either economically, socially or psychologically.

The cornerstone of Victorian society was the family; the perfect lady's sole function was marriage and procreation (the two, needless to say, were considered as one). All her education was to bring out her "natural" submission to authority and innate maternal instincts. Young ladies were trained to have no opinions lest they seem too formed and too definite for a young man's taste, and thereby unmarketable as a com- modity. Ruskin's vision of girls as flowers to be plucked is the norm, and Mill's marriage between intellectual and emotional equals the aberra- tion. Needless to say, many a flower was plucked who knew nothing about sex except perhaps those superstitions surrounding menstruation discussed by the Showalters. Marriage could often prove a sexual and emotional disaster for those trained to be affectionate, yet asexual and mentally blank. While Mrs. Ellis, a popular writer of etiquette books, counseled the unhappily married woman to remember that her "highest duty is so often to suffer and be still,"[2] many must have felt themselves the domestic slaves John Stuart Mill described.

No matter how pervasive the ideal of marital submission and passivity became, those marriages that were most successful in Victorian novels showed spirited, even sharp-tongued, women who deviated from the narrow definition of femininity endorsed by the etiquette books. There is ample evidence that one could be a happily married woman without subscribing to the demands of an ideal. Yet, even here, one is struck by how often the happy marriages are between persons who have known each other since childhood, when presumably codes of behavior were more natural. Mary Garth and Mary Thorne, to use two examples, were true to themselves in the face of society's disapproval (though one should not forget that Mary Thorne thought it unwomanly not to give up her entire inheritance to Frank Gresham, even when the law made it possible for her to control part of it). And for every spirited Mary there

Introduction

was a Rosamond Vincy imitating Femininity to perfection, or a Dorothea wondering why she could not find fulfillment through social action.

Indeed, the clearest characteristic of the mid-Victorian period was how few women of character fit the ideal lady. Disfunctional and idle, those who did fit, such as Rosamond, engaged in flirtation and temptation within the confines of the home. The more outspoken, such as Charlotte Brontë's Shirley Keeldar longed for a richer life; if they could not follow St. Theresa, at the very least they could pursue a useful occupation:

> "Caroline," demanded Miss Keeldar abruptly, "don't you wish you had a profession — a trade?"
> "I wish it fifty times a day. As it is, I often wonder what I came into the world for. I long to have something absorbing and compulsory to fill my head and hands, and to occupy my thoughts."
> "Can labour alone make a human being happy?"
> "No; but it can give varieties of pain, and prevent us from breaking our hearts with a single tyrant master-torture. Besides, successful labour has its recompense; a vacant, weary, lonely, hopeless life has none."

When Mrs. Jameson, an early feminist, showed this passage to two men, one said the girl should emigrate, the other that she should marry.[3] Easy flirtations scarcely appealed to the passionate, yet with family affection the only legitimate outlet, many young women suffered the pangs of unrequited or false love, as described by Caroline.

The most popular alternative to vacuity for the middle classes was charity. Trained to be loving and emotional, without sexuality, young ladies threw themselves into church work, or perhaps with less uniform ardor, the serving of the family. As Professor Cominos points out, religious fervor was often an unconscious form of sexual sublimation, whereby the most enthusiastic religious women found a suitable outlet for their passions. Yet even here, the scope of actual *work* permitted women was very narrow. The making of useless objects for the local church, anti-Corn Law bazaar or missionary table could not satisfy the most ardent. A few took to philanthropy, but Octavia Hill complained about the curse of amateurism; to pay a woman to do charitable work meant that she ceased to be a lady, and that the work itself was no longer done for the highest moral reasons. While women were encouraged to "do good," they were positively prevented from effecting real change. Women were expected to dabble in charity and to remain free from excessive zeal or commitment. Indeed, some identified the absurdity of the more impractical philanthropic schemes with the relinquishment of traditional female "duties," as did Dickens in his portraits of Mrs. Pardiggle and Mrs. Jellyby. (Even Dickens' relationship with Angela Burdett-Coutts was that of an advisor who prevented a woman's enthusiasms from leading to too indiscriminate giving). Ideally in a Dickens novel one's good works extended no further than one's family and friends. The truly charitable were Esther Summerson and Little Dorrit.

If marriage often proved a disappointment, what of those who failed to marry? The unmarried woman was an important source of humor in music halls and in operettas. Society trained women for one function, marriage, and then mocked those who sought this idyllic state after having reached maturity. No longer innocent and ignorant, it was obscene and comic in performances that a middle-aged woman should still want marriage — or that any man would want her. The *Saturday Review,* violently anti-feminist throughout the century, passed judgment on women in one article, declaring that they could not be offered an alternative lest they never marry. Furthermore, the woman who proved herself unsuccessful in capturing a husband or who had the misfortune to lose him after marriage was dismissed with the comment, "she has failed in business, and no social reform can prevent such failures."[4] In an age of laissez-faire capitalism there could be no greater failure than this. The more charitable, however, argued that the training to become a wife and mother gave a lady all that was necessary in moral precepts and, after all, she would surely become a helpful aunt in a brother's home. Unfortunately, the problem was not moral but economic. Everywhere there was evidence that not all women could find places at their brothers' hearthsides. Elderly distressed women, impoverished seamstresses, and the poor governesses discussed by Dr. Peterson, all sought work because they had no alternatives — and few survived at the same social level they had been born to. The ultimate debasement, should moral precepts give way to economic necessity, was prostitution, which even the respectable might be forced into. Only the exceptionally fortunate and courageous might succeed through emigration, but societies offering assisted passage for women of good character were small and ineffectual. All social forces combined to leave the spinster emotionally and financially bankrupt.

The power of a dominant stereotype can often be measured by its hold in areas totally inappropriate to the objective conditions. Economic and social circumstances made it impossible for the working-class woman to attain the ideal of the perfect lady. Nevertheless, this ideal was admired by many members of the working class. Young women could not be as innocent and as ignorant as a middle-class girl. They lived in cramped houses, went to work early and everywhere saw the ravaged lives of those overcome by poverty, alcoholism and prostitution. But the better-off embraced premarital chastity and the family even more ardently than their superiors. They knew the dangers beneath them — one false step and a family's reputation was lost. For the respectable a "bad" sister could mean the loss of work for other members of the family, so moral purity had an added economic edge, somewhat different from the market value of virginity in the middle class. The family hearthside was an island of purity and peace under constant threat in a society undergoing such rapid change as nineteenth-century England. Knowledge without experience and a marriage centered in the home became the twin ideals portrayed by respectable working-class writers.[5]

Middle-class writers who were popular amongst the working class wrote about the moral purity of the reputable working class and the deserving poor. Dickens' little Em'ly insisted in the face of Rosa Dartle's contempt that she came from "folks who are as honourable as you," and that she "had been brought up as virtuous as you or any lady."[6] Dickens' sympathy was on the side of Em'ly and of her family against the false snobbishness of Rosa Dartle, who refused to believe that the lower classes could have the same moral and emotional standards as she. He, like Mrs. Gaskell and George Eliot, portrayed the sanctity of the working-class home in the face of the moral carelessness of upper-class men who thought they could freely dally with women beneath them. While the full opprobrium of society never fell upon gentlemen who considered poor women fair game, middle-class novelists presented a moral ideal which they hoped society would recognize — and to which many working-class families adhered.

As Professor Stearns documents, a rising standard of living in the petty bourgeoisie and labor aristocracy after 1870 led to rising social aspirations. From the time of the Ten Hours Movement women working outside the home had been condemned, primarily because they neglected their family duties, but not less because they undercut men's wages. The goal which some working-class men could reach by the end of the century was an income sufficient to support the entire family. Certainly it was difficult enough for a working-class woman with children to do everything necessary for her family without adding outside work to her responsibilities. On the other hand, the benefits of staying at home were ambiguous. A woman's expectations for any life outside the home were narrowed, and the ambitions of the young who did work and were independent were curtailed. Moreover, men perpetually degraded women because of their low earning power. The family economy in which the working wife participated was replaced by the single wage earner and the family based wife. The perfect lady under these conditions became the woman who kept to her family, centering all her life on keeping the house clean, the children well disciplined and her daughters chaste.

The relatively simple enforcement of the model of the perfect lady was the work of many elements in society. Women were educated to believe that they were, on the one hand, morally superior to men in their lack of sexual drive and, on the other hand, inferior because of their weaker natures. The chaste woman was seen as exerting an all-pervasive moral influence within the home (a rather narrow sphere, one would think, for so large an influence). The woman who broke the family circle, be she prostitute, adulterer or divorcée, threatened society's very fabric. The most unforgivable sin, as Roberts explains, was the married woman who committed adultery. If society condoned such action, its very life was imperiled, though seemingly heaven and the colonies could welcome *some* fallen women. Women themselves were the greatest enforcers of standards of moral behavior (defined in purely sexual terms); as Professor Cominos shows, Grundyism was a powerful force in the service of duty over passion and obedience over independence. Often the fierce condemnation of the fallen woman must have come from unconscious sexual fears and semiconscious fears of the attraction of an illicit relationship over connubial bliss. Those who did not live up to the expected standard were usually sufficiently socialized to feel pangs of guilt, if not the overwhelming remorse of little Em'ly. Only the very bottom of society was immune to so pervasive a model of womanhood.

How then could a Victorian woman break away from imitation — or guilty aberration — of the model of the perfect lady? The full answer is surely subject to interpretation, and far more research is necessary, but the new woman was in part a product of changed social and economic conditions, and in part the result of the courageous efforts of individual women who suffered social ostracism for their beliefs. The suffrage movement, educational reform, the campaign against the Contagious Diseases Acts and the fight to distribute birth control information all contributed to the downfall of hypocrisy and rigidity. By the 1880's the perfect lady could no longer hold her own unchallenged. Women increasingly demanded and gained constructive and useful roles in society. Job opportunities were opening to every class, making it possible for women to achieve economic independence (though often at great psychological cost, as George Gissing's *The Odd Women* [1892] illustrates). Social attitudes were also changing. According to Professor

Stedman in the 1880's and 1890's Gilbert was far softer in his satire of middle-aged spinsters than his predecessors in the music halls and mime. In popular literature independent women became heroines for the first time. Sexual attitudes also changed; the most consistent tenet of the women's movement was the application of female sexual standards to all of society. Only a few advanced thinkers recognized that equality would not lead to male continence, but female indulgence. The women and men of the late nineteenth century were never so Victorian as when they insisted upon radical economic and social change within the context of stern Victorian sexual mores.

In opposition to the late Victorians, the twentieth-century feminist movement until recently has centered on sexual liberation at the expense of social and economic freedom. Women are still largely excluded from circles of power, authority and prestige; marriage is still held out as the prime goal of every young woman. The percentage of women in higher education and politics has decreased since emancipation. In fact, the old ideal of the Victorian lady has been replaced by new and equally potent models condemning women to a less than equal position in society. These chapters document the feminine stereotypes women struggled against a hundred years ago, but only partially defeated. They should serve as a reminder not only of the distance women have traveled, but of the miles yet to go.

Bloomington, 1971   MARTHA VICINUS

Suffer and Be Still

WOMEN IN THE VICTORIAN AGE

1: The Victorian Governess

Status Incongruence in Family and Society

━━━━━

M. Jeanne Peterson

THE GOVERNESS IS A FAMILIAR FIGURE TO THE READER OF VICTORIAN NOVELS. Immortalized in *Jane Eyre* and *Vanity Fair,* she has made frequent appearances as the heroine of many lesser-known novels. And innumerable governesses appear as little more than a standard furnishing in many a fictional Victorian home. While twentieth-century acquaintance with the governess may come purely from the novel, the Victorians themselves found her situation and prospects widely discussed, frivolously in *Punch,* and more seriously in many leading journals of the time, so often in fact that one author on the subject of female labor in Great Britain suggested that readers were "wearied . . . with the incessant repetition of the dreary story of spirit-broken governesses."[1] The governess's life is described in what seem today to be over-dramatized accounts of pauperized gentle-women, "drifted waifs and strays from 'the upper and middle classes,'" who find their way to the workhouse and insane asylum.[2] And there are condemnations of these accounts as "comic pathos" and "a perfectly preposterous quantity of nonsense."[3] Books on the subject of women as workers, published in growing numbers throughout the Victorian period, devote a large amount of space to the governess.

The Victorians' interest in the governess went beyond that of entertainment or economic analysis. She was the subject of charitable endeavors, and at least one appeal reveals the sense that the dilemma of the governess was a problem that was expected to touch donors personally: "There is probably no one who has not some relative or cherished friend either actually engaged in teaching, or having formerly been so engaged."[4] Lady Eastlake spoke of "the cause of governesses" and urged in 1848 their "earnest and judicious befriending."[5] In London the Governesses' Benevolent Institution and Queen's College were founded to provide several sorts of assistance.

In terms of numbers alone, this attention to the governess seems somewhat excessive. There were about 25,000 governesses in England in 1851, but there were over 750,000 female domestic servants, not to mention women employed in industry.[6] And when one moves from simple statistics to the conditions of employment of women in this period, the suffering of the governess seems pale and singularly undramatic when compared with that of women in factories and mines. Victorian interest in the governess could not have stemmed from her political importance, for she had none. As militant as women may have been by the turn of the century, there is no trace of militance in the ranks of mid-nineteenth-century governesses. Moreover, the governess had no social position worthy of attention. She was at best unenvied and at worst the object of mild scorn, and all she sought was survival in genteel obscurity.

Modern treatment of the Victorian governess, when it is not set in the framework of literary analysis, takes two forms: either it is a study of the occupation itself without reference to the larger social scene, or the role of the governess is considered within the context of the movement for women's education and women's rights.[7] In our interest in later historical developments, we tend to ignore the immediate social context of the governess's occupation and the ways in which the dilemmas and contradictions of her employment may have helped to drive women's education and women's employment out of the home. By examining the governess's situation within the Victorian family, we may approach a better understanding of how the family functioned and of the values, problems, and fears of the Victorian middle class.

In mid-nineteenth century usage, the term "governess" could refer to a woman who taught in a school, a woman who lived at home and travelled to her employer's house to teach (called a "daily governess"), or a woman who lived in her employer's home and who taught the children and served as a companion to them.[8] The subject of this study is the governess who lived with the family, sometimes referred to as the "private governess." In considering her intimate position within the family, we may see most clearly the problems of the governess's place in Victorian society.

The employment of a gentlewoman as a governess in a middle-class family served to reinforce and perpetuate certain Victorian values.

But inherent in the employment of a lady was a contradiction of the very values she was hired to fulfill. The result was a situation of conflict and incongruity for both the governess and the family, a conflict which called forth a variety of responses from governess, family, and society.

From at least Tudor times the governess had been part of the households of the upper classes. In the nineteenth century, increasing numbers of governesses were employed by the English middle classes. The governess was a testimony to the economic power of the Victorian middle-class father, as were servants, carriages, and the other "paraphernalia of gentility." Although the governess was often behind the scenes and not as conspicuous as other items of genteel equipage, there were ways in which the family could indicate her presence in the home and display her as a symbol of economic power, breeding, and station. Drawing room conversations about the governess served to bring her into public "view." If she was foreign, her exotic history might be discussed. Even complaining about a governess was a way of "showing her off."[9]

The governess was also an indicator of the extent to which a man's wife was truly a lady of leisure. The function of the mother had traditionally been, in addition to housewifely duties, that of educator of the children. Both boys and girls in the middle-class family began their education with their mother. Boys were later sent to school or a tutor was hired for them, but girls continued to learn their roles as women from their mothers. Unlike cooking, cleaning, and scrubbing, the education of children was hardly classifiable as manual labor. For this reason the employment of a governess was even more a symbol of the movement of wives and mothers from domestic to ornamental functions.

Victorian parents sought a woman who could teach their daughters the genteel accomplishments which were the aims of female education. More important, they sought a gentlewoman. But the new ethos of the ideal woman was that of a woman of leisure and, no matter how occupied a lady might have been at home, an outside career was another matter — in Frances Power Cobbe's words "a deplorable dereliction."[10] If work *in* the home was thought to "pervert women's sympathies, detract from their charms,"[11] work for pay brought down the judgment of society and testified to the inferior position of both the wage-earner and her family. Sophia Jex-Blake's father told her that if she accepted a salary she "would be considered mean and illiberal, . . . accepting wages that belonged to a class beneath you in social rank."[12] Others put it more strongly: "Society has thought fit to assert that the woman who works for herself loses her social position." The women of the middle classes were very consistent in their attitude toward being paid: "they would shrink from it as an insult."[13] The image of the lady as a creature of leisure, enclosed within a private circle of family and friends and completely supported by father or husband, was reinforced by the ban on paid employment — a ban so strong that many who wrote for publication, even though writing at home, did so under pseudonyms, or signed their work simply "By a Lady."

The availability of "ladies" to teach the children of the middle classes depended on the one exception to the rule that a well-bred woman did not earn her own living — if a woman of birth and education found herself in financial distress, and had no relatives who could support her or give her a home, she was justified in seeking the only employment that would not cause her to lose her status. She could find work as a governess.[14]

The position of governess seems to have been appropriate because, while it was paid employment, it was within the home. The governess was doing something she might have done as a wife under better circumstances. She avoided the immodest and unladylike position of public occupation.[15] The literature of the 1840's suggests that there was a sudden increase in the number of gentlewomen without financial support in the years following the Napoleonic wars. Middle-class writers attributed the flood of distressed gentlewomen to "the accidents of commercial and professional life" to which the middle classes were subject.[16] From the research of twentieth-century historians it is clear that the number of single middle-class women in need of employment was a product not only of the unstable conditions of business in those years but also arose out of the emigration of single men from England to the colonies, from the differential mortality rate which favored women, and from the tendency for men in the middle classes to marry later.[17] But the Victorians' belief that economic distress had led to the declining position of these women suggests that problems of social and economic uncertainty were of more immediate concern to them. The Victorian stereotype of the governess, which explained why a lady sought employment, was of a woman who was born and bred in comfort and gentility and who, through the death of her father or his subjection to financial ruin, was robbed of the support of her family and was driven to earn her own living.[18]

A word should perhaps be included here about the possibility of upward social mobility through occupation as a governess. There are a few suggestions in the literature of the period that such attempts at social climbing were in fact taking place. Harriet Martineau, in an *Edinburgh Review* article in 1859, noted the practice of "tradesmen and farmers who educate their daughters for governesses" in the hope of raising their station in society.[19] There is no way of assessing the extent to which this took place, but it is clear that the Victorian middle class regarded such mobility as undesirable.[20] In the fiction of the period the governesses who were figures of evil or immorality were women of humble origins. Thackeray's Becky Sharp, for example, was the daughter of a poor artist and a French "opera-girl" who, in order to find employment, claimed origins in the French nobility. The wicked Miss Gwilt, in Wilkie Collins' *Armadale,* was an abandoned child whose origins were unknown and who was reared by a "quack" doctor and his wife. As will become clear later in this essay, the possibility of real upward mobility was a chimera. Indeed, employment as a governess was only of very limited use even in maintaining gentle status. It is sufficient here to note that however educated a girl from the "lower ranks" might be, she was still "ill-bred" in the eyes of those who made themselves judges of governesses. Conversely, however destitute a lady might be, she continued to be a lady.[21]

We have been looking at the governess from the point of view of the family that employed her. Her own viewpoint was very different, of course. Once it was clear that she had to seek a post as governess, the task of finding a situation was taken up through a variety of channels. The first source of aid was the help of relatives and friends who might know of a family seeking a governess. If such help was not available or effective, a woman was forced to turn to public agencies — newspaper advertisements or a placement service. Newspaper advertising was disliked, partly because of its public nature and partly because reputable employers were unlikely to utilize such a source. Experience with the falsification of letters of reference among servants obtained through newspapers had brought public advertising under suspicion.[22] The Governesses' Benevolent Institution, established in 1843, provided a registry for governesses seeking employment, and many seem to have used the service.[23]

Pay was notoriously low. Governesses were, of course, housed and fed, but they were expected to pay for such expenses as laundry, travel, and medical care. They had to dress appropriately, and it was wise for them to make their own provisions for unemployment and old age. A governess often tried to support a parent or a dependent sister or brother as well. According to some estimates, pay ranged from £15 to £100 a year. The larger sum would only be applicable to the "highly educated lady" who could find a position in a very well-to-do family. The average salary probably fell between £20 and £45 a year. To give some meaning to these figures it will be useful to compare them with typical salaries of other groups. The fairest comparison is probably with that of other domestic employees since they were also paid partly by maintenance:

	Banks, 1848-52	Martineau, 1859
Housekeeper	no data	£40-£50
Cook	£15-£16	£12-£18
Housemaid	£11-£11/13	£10-£14
Nursemaid	£11-£12	£5-£30

Mrs. Sewell, writing in 1865, equated the salary of nursery governess with that of lady's maid, that of an informed but not accomplished governess with that of footman, and that of a highly educated governess with that of a coachman or butler.[24] If board was worth £30 per year, then governesses were earning £50 to £95 a year (not including the cost of housing). A minimum income for a genteel style of life may be estimated at £150-£200 for a single person.[25] It would seem that, under the best of circumstances, a governess's income left her on the very edge of gentility, with no margin for illness or unemployment. Many governesses, between jobs, ill, or too old to work, turned to the "temporary assistance . . . afforded privately and delicately" through the Governesses' Benevolent Institution.[26]

The duties of a governess in a household were as varied as the salary she was paid. In some families, like those of Frances Power Cobbe and Edmund Gosse, the governess had set hours for lessons and her remaining time was free.[27] The Thackerays' governess acted as a chaperone, accompanying her pupil to French class.[28] Often governesses of adolescent girls would accompany them shopping, read aloud to them while they did fancy sewing, or simply sit in the background to watch over their social activities. Constant supervision of pupils seems to have been a common duty of governesses, and would have kept them busy all day, leaving little time for a life of their own. The constant supervision of children and young women resulted from the belief of many parents that indolence and lack of supervision might lead to "immorality."[29]

The difficulties which governesses had with their young charges were a well-known occupational hazard. A frequent theme of novels is the mistreatment and disrespect directed toward the governess by children, and her lack of authority over them and the failure of the mother to cooperate in discipline. Evidence about the problems of non-fictional governesses, though sparse, suggests that the novelistic theme was not unrealistic. In the Stanley family's correspondence, for example, there is a casual reference to the scratches and bruises which one of the children inflicted on the governess and the nurse.[30]

Occupational problems did not end with finding a position and coming to terms with the duties and the children. A governess always faced the danger of unemployment, either because her work with the children was finished or because her employers were dissatisfied with her. Inadequate preparation for teaching and faulty placement practices were often to blame for the frequent hiring and firing of governesses.[31] The aristocratic practice of continuing to support domestic servants who had outlived their usefulness after long service was not often extended to aged governesses in middle-class families. Long service was much less the rule, and paternalism was expensive. In the event of illness or old age and inability to work, the governess faced the prospect of charity, such as that provided by the Governesses' Benevolent Institution in the form of small annuities for retired governesses. The number was limited, however, and reports of governesses in workhouses or asylums were not uncommon.[32]

In many ways the situation of a domestic servant in the nineteenth century differed very little from that of a governess. But there were no crusades for nursemaids or domestic servants. And in spite of similar work situations, the stereotype of the down-trodden, pathetic governess stands in sharp distinction to that of the warm, jolly nanny who won the affection of her charges and often the sincere regard of her employers.

Occupational conditions seem not to have been the fundamental source of anxiety for the governess and her middle-class employers. The difficulty seems to have been rooted in her special social position rather than in the material facts. An examination of the social circumstances of a governess's life and the way that life fitted into the middle-class social structure and system of values reveals a tension that cannot be explained in terms of hours or wages.

One sensitive observer of the Victorian social scene made the following assessment of a governess's situation: "the real discomfort of a governess's position in a private family arises from the fact that it is undefined. She is not a relation, not a guest, not a mistress, not a servant — but something made up of all. No one knows exactly how to treat her."[33]

The observation is an acute one because it defines the problem as one of status and role. But one can go further and suggest that the real discomfort arose not from lack of definition but from the existence of contradictory definitions of the governess's place in society. In every aspect of the governess's occupational situation these contradictions in her social status are apparent.

As we have seen, the *sine qua non* of a governess's employment in the Victorian family was her social status as a lady. To quote Elizabeth Eastlake:

the real definition of a governess, in the English sense, is a being who is our equal in birth, manners, and education, but our inferior in worldly wealth. Take a lady, in every meaning of the word, born and bred, and let her father pass through the gazette [bankruptcy], and she wants nothing more to suit our highest *beau idéal* of a guide and instructress to our children.[34]

The governess is described here as an exception to the rule that ladies did not work for a living and, in spite of her loss of financial resources (and leisure), she retains a "lady's" status. But paid employment *did* bring a "lady" down in the world.

The Victorian "leisured classes" were, in part, defined in opposition to the "working classes," not because of the work or leisure of the men — for almost all of them worked — but by the leisure of the women. As one fictional uncle said (in Wilkie Collins' *No Name*) about his two well-bred, genteel, but technically illegitimate nieces, as he robbed them of their inheritance: "Let them, as becomes their birth, gain their bread in situations." And, as Mrs. Ellis put it: "It is scarcely necessary in the present state of society to point out . . . the loss of character and influence occasioned by living below our station."[35] Victorians continued to insist that the work of governess was an exception to the "theory of civilised life in this and all other countries . . . that the women of the upper and middle classes are supported by their male relatives: daughters by their fathers, wives by their husbands. If a lady has to work for her livelihood, it is universally considered to be a misfortune, an exception to the ordinary rule."[36] But their own definitions were too potent, and too important to them.

In the paragraph quoted earlier Elizabeth Eastlake says that the truly important components of a woman's social status are those related to birth and education and that the question of wealth is only minor. But in the same article she seems to reverse her position when she says: "There is no other class which so cruelly requires its members to be, in birth, mind, and manners, above their station, in order to fit them for their station." And, later, Lady Eastlake reverts to her earlier position and states emphatically that the governess is "a needy *lady*."[37] This contradiction, stated, or implied, is very evident in mid-century writing about the governess's social position. Mrs. Sewell, for example, quotes a governess who says, "My friends think I am lowered in social position and they are correct." But Mrs. Sewell continues to call the governesses "ladies" and to discuss their gentility and social position in terms that suggest no loss of status.[38] Sociologists call this conflict in the assessment of a person's social characteristics "status incongruence." The status incongruence of the Victorian governess was more than a matter of conflicting notions about the propriety of paid employment for a "lady." It reached into the operations of everyday life.

Earlier it was suggested that the home was the ideal place for a gentlewoman to be employed because she remained in her proper environment — but such employment was, in fact, an aggravation of her incongruent status. While employment in a middle-class home was intended to provide a second home for the governess, her presence there was evidence of the failure of her own middle-class family to provide the protection and support she needed. The structure of the household, too, pointed to the governess's anomalous position. She was a lady, and therefore not a servant, but she was an employee, and therefore not of equal status with the wife and daughters of the house. The purposes of her employment contributed further to the incongruence of her position. She was hired to provide the children, and particularly the young women of the family, with an education to prepare them for leisured gentility. But she had been educated in the same way, and for the same purpose, and her employment became a prostitution of her education, of the values underlying it, and of her family's intentions in providing it. Her function as a status symbol of middle-class gentility also perverted her own upbringing. She was educated to be a "nosegay" to adorn her "papa's drawing room," and as a governess she had sold herself as an ornament to display her employer's prestige.[39]

An individual's social position is intimately related to patterns of action — to the way others behave toward him and the behavior expected of him — what social scientists call "roles." Incongruent social status results in confused and often contradictory behavior, both from the individual and his or her associates. As Mrs. Sewell said of the governess, "No one knows exactly how to treat her." If we look at the behavior of the members of the family toward the governess from the perspective of her incongruent position, it becomes comprehensible as a statement-in-action of the contradictions they sensed.

The parents' treatment of the governess was characterized by great variability from family to family, and from day to day within a single family. In one breath, the mistress of the house might invite her to participate in some social event, and in the next would order her to work. Some families, like the senior Ruskins, included the governess in their circle when they entertained. Others required that she eat with the children unless it served their convenience to have her present at the dinner table.[40] John Ruskin scolded his readers for their behavior toward their governesses:

> what reverence do you show to the teachers you have chosen? Is a girl likely to think her own conduct, or her own intellect, of much importance, when you trust the entire formation of her character, moral and intellectual, to a person whom you let your servants treat with less respect than they do your housekeeper (as if the soul of your child were a less charge than jams and groceries), and whom you yourself think you confer an honour upon by letting her sometimes sit in the drawing-room in the evening?[41]

It is hardly surprising that "According to general report, the position of an upper servant in England . . . is infinitely preferable to that of a governess."[42] The servant had the advantage of an unambiguous position, and there was apparently no small comfort in "knowing one's place."

The behavior of the children tended to reveal and reflect the attitude of their parents. There was sometimes respect and affection, but more often there was disobedience, snobbery, and sometimes physical cruelty. A frequent theme of governess-novels was the triangle of governess, parents, and children, in which the unruly children pitted mother against governess and escaped the discipline due them. It is hazardous to assess from novelists' descriptions alone the extent to which these "trials of the governess" were a real problem, but the frequency with which articles and books dealt with the matter of how a governess should be treated, and urged parents to support her authority, suggests that the domestic dramas of the Victorian era had a firm foundation in English social life.[43]

As Ruskin says, servants, no less than parents and children, responded to the incongruity of a lady-employee in the house. Lady

Eastlake observed that "The servants invariably detest her, for she is a dependant like themselves, and yet, for all that, as much their superior in other respects as the family they both serve."[44] The governess usually had little power over the servants, and yet she was to be served by them. They resented her for acting like a lady, but would have criticized her for any other manner.

Her relationships with the world outside the family are a further extension of the conflicts within the family. She could expect to lose touch with the friends of her leisured days, because she no longer had either the money or the time for them. Her relations with men and women alike were strained by her position:

She is a bore to almost any gentleman, as a tabooed woman, to whom he is interdicted from granting the usual privileges of the sex, and yet who is perpetually crossing his path. She is a bore to most ladies by the same rule, and a reproach too — for her dull, fagging, bread-and-water life is perpetually putting their pampered listlessness to shame.[45]

Particularly revealing here is the conflict between the gentleman's conduct toward ladies and toward governesses. There was no easy courtesy, attraction, or flirtation between a gentleman and a governess, because she was not his social equal. The pattern of relations between gentlemen and their female domestics was not fitting either, because the governess was not entirely an inferior.[46]

Reared and educated with the same values as her employers and their guests, the governess was the first to be aware of the incongruities of her social position. She tended to judge herself by prevailing social standards and was often uncertain about how she should behave. Two modes of response stand out. One was self-pity, what Frances Power Cobbe calls the "I-have-seen-better-days airs," and an appeal for the pity of those around her. The other was for the governess to present herself to the world with an over-supply of pride, to compensate for the fear of slight or rebuff which she felt. If a governess sought pity, she was a bore; if she was proud, she was criticized for a "morbid worldliness" which made her over-sensitive to neglect and disrespect.[47] Given the inconsistent behavior of others toward her and her own confused self-estimate, it would not be surprising if Harriet Martineau was correct when she said that the governesses formed one of the largest single occupational groups to be found in insane asylums.[48]

What look like normal occupational hazards embellished with a Victorian taste for melodrama turn out to be products of conflict within a more complex social structure. The governess was caught in the cross-fire of conflicting social definitions and roles. She and her employers alike sought, in a variety of ways, to solve the dilemma that faced them.

One way of escaping the contradiction of the "employed gentle-woman" was to deny, or at least minimize, the fact of employment. The governess often viewed her position this way. The central features of advertisements in the London *Times,* for example, were not the occupational dimensions of the work sought — qualifications, pay and the like — but the personal position involved. In the words of one advertisement, it was "a comfortable home, the first consideration" (1 January, 1847). The loss of a governess's home, where she should have had not only maintenance, but protection, led her to seek a surrogate home in her employer's house. For both governess and employer this constituted what can be called a retreat to a traditional mode of relationship. The governess entered the economic market-place, but the employer tried, in his home, to preserve her gentlewoman's position, traditionally defined in terms of personal and familial relationships and not in the contractual terms of modern employment. In the situation of incongruence, rejecting the realities of the modern role was a means, artificial perhaps, of reducing the dissonance of family and employee. Mrs. Sewell captured this attitude when she wrote: "A situation is offered them: a home, in which they are to be quite happy. 'They will be so well treated, and made entirely one of the family.'" In endorsing the attitude of friendliness and respect for governesses by employers, she warned that the alternative was that the governess would become a disinterested paid employee.[49]

The denial of a governess's womanliness — her sexuality — was another mode of reducing conflict. The sexual dimension of the relationship of governesses and men in the household is so rarely mentioned in Victorian literature that it is worthwhile quoting a lengthy and rather circuitous description of it from *Governess Life.* In the passage from which this excerpt is taken the author has been discussing a variety of serious breaches of conduct on the part of the governess:

Frightful instances have been discovered in which she, to whom the care of the young has been entrusted, instead of guarding their minds in innocence and purity, has become their corrupter — she has been the first to lead and to initiate into sin, to suggest and carry on intrigues, and finally to be the instrument of destroying the peace of families. . . .

These are the grosser forms of sin which have been generally concealed from public notice . . . but none of the cases are imaginary ones, and they are but too well known in the circles amongst which they occurred. In some instances again, the love of admiration has led the governess to try and make herself necessary to the comfort of the father of the family in which she resided, and by delicate and unnoticed flattery gradually to gain her point, to the disparagement of the mother, and the destruction of mutual happiness. When the latter was homely, or occupied with domestic cares, opportunity was found to bring forward attractive accomplishments, or by sedulous attentions to supply her lack of them; or the sons were in some instances objects of notice and flirtation, or when occasion offered, visitors at the house.

This kind of conduct has led to the inquiry which is frequently made before engaging an instructress, "Is she handsome or attractive?" If so, it is conclusive against her [i.e., she is not employed].   (Pp. 14-15, see my note 20.)

Thus one of the stereotypes of the ideal governess came to be a homely, severe, unfeminine type of woman, and this is the image often conveyed in *Punch*. The trustworthy Miss Garth, in Wilkie Collins' *No Name*, had a hard-featured face, a lean, angular physique, and was known for her "masculine readiness and decision of movement." By contrast, Becky Sharp was an example of what havoc could be wrought by an attractive and unscrupulous governess in a family.[50]

These efforts at adjustment through denial of a governess's employment or her femininity were, in large measure, unsatisfactory. A better solution was to avoid the issue of status-assessment by employing a foreign governess. Part of the popularity of foreign governesses was, of course, due to the superior training they had had on the continent and the advantage all of them had in teaching a foreign language. But their foreign origins also avoided the incongruence which existed when an English gentlewoman was a paid employee in an English home. As Elizabeth Sewell said:

As a general rule, foreign governesses are much more agreeable inmates of a house than English ones. Something of this may be owing to the interest excited by difference of manner, dress, and tone; something, also to the imposing influence of a foreign tongue. . . . A good Parisian accent will always command a certain amount of respect. But most important, foreigners are less tenacious of their dignity . . . largely because of their ignorance of English customs.[51]

The difficulties of treating a governess both as a lady and as an employee were reduced by importing a woman who was less familiar with English manners and therefore less likely to recognize, and be offended at, a family's failure to treat her properly.

Another mode of coping with the dilemmas of incongruent status was, simply, escape. This might take the form of a governess's day-today isolation from the family circle, either by her choice or theirs, in order to avoid for the moment the stresses of conflicting roles. The more permanent way of escape for the governess was to leave the occupation entirely. But for a woman without means, the only way out was marriage. It is difficult to assess how frequently governesses married and succeeded in resolving permanently their status conflicts. Occasionally, Victorian memoirs refer to governesses marrying out of their occupation.[52] But these sources are, by virtue of being memoirs, likely to reflect the mores of a more stable group of upper-middle and upper-class Englishmen, who, although they might have considered it imprudent, would not have seen their status endangered by such a marriage. A more typical attitude is that described by Florence Nightingale and repeated frequently in writing of the time. "The governess is to have every one of God's gifts; she is to do that which the mother herself is incapable of doing; but our son must not degrade himself by marrying the governess. . . ."[53] Since one of the functions of marriage was to extend the connections of the family and to add, through the marriage settlement, additional income to the young family, the attractions of an orphaned, poverty-stricken girl would be very limited.

Just as foreign governesses in England served to reduce the problem of status incongruence for the Victorian employer, emigration of the English governess served to reduce conflict for her. She might choose to go to another part of England or, like the foreign governess who came to England, she might, if more adventurous or more desperate, go abroad. Lady Eastlake recognized the advantages of escaping the society and definitions which made a governess's life uncomfortable: "foreign life is far more favourable to a governess's happiness. In its less stringent domestic habits, the company of a *teacher*, for she is nothing more abroad, is no interruption — often an acquisition."[54] Such a move, however, would require that an Englishwoman admit the realities of her status as a paid employee and resign herself to the loss of her place in English society.

Between 1849 and 1862 several organizations were established which, among other activities, promoted the emigration of governesses to the colonies, where there were few women and better chances for employment. The organizations involved were the National Benevolent Emigration Society, the Society for the Employment of Women, and the Female Middle-Class Emigration Society. These agencies have been treated as part of the movement for improving the employment situation for all single women of the middle classes.[55] But it seems likely that two other motives were involved. The escape was to a place where status would be less ambiguous and less painful and where there was more chance of marriage and a permanent resolution to incongruence. The other purpose of the female emigration societies was to lure out of England the "half-educated daughters of poor professional men, and . . . the children of subordinate government officers, petty shopkeepers" — those daughters from the lower ranks of the middle class whose fathers had been educating them as governesses in order to raise their station in life — and failing emigration, they were urged to become shop assistants, telegraphists, and nurses.[56]

These attempts to resolve conflicts all involved an effort to maintain the traditional place of the woman in family and society. The middle of the nineteenth century saw the beginnings, ambiguous to be sure, of the shift toward professional, market-oriented women's employment. The first institutional symbol of this was the Governesses' Benevolent Institution, already mentioned, which was founded in 1843. Its purpose was to provide placement service, temporary housing for unemployed governesses, insurance, and annuities to aging governesses — services clearly oriented toward the market aspect of governesses' employment.[57] But the flavor, and often the substance, of the traditional view of the governess is apparent in the activities of the Institution which still spoke of "homes" for governesses, when referring to jobs. The G.B.I. did not agitate for the wider employment of gentlewomen and, in fact, attempted to narrow the profession by including only those women "with character." The institution further reinforced the differences between governesses and working women of lower status by giving governesses a separate source of charity in time of distress. In providing a home for ill and aged governesses, these charitable Englishmen believed they could keep at least a portion of them out of the workhouse which, bad as it was for the "lower orders," was supposed to cause even greater suffering to a woman of refinement and cultivation.[58] Such genteel charity went some way toward maintaining the fiction that members of the gentle classes were not sinking into the class beneath.

Queen's College, in London, was established in 1848 to provide education for governesses. The founders' purpose was to give governesses a training that would elevate their self-esteem, make them better teachers, and increase respect for them.[59] The school was also open to ladies who were not governesses, but there was no intention to overload an already crowded occupation. It was thought that "every lady is and must be a teacher — of some person or other, of children, sisters, the poor." And Queen's College was to prepare future wives and mothers for a better performance of their traditional role. The other reason for admitting them was related to that social and economic instability which was so often a topic of early and mid-Victorian discussion: "Those who had no dream of entering upon such work [i.e., governessing] this year, might be forced by some reverse of fortune to think of it next year."[60] The author of *Governess Life* saw another benefit arising from the improved education of lady-governesses at Queen's College: "The public will reap this great benefit from the improved mode of instruction, that the ignorant and unqualified will no longer be able to compete with the wise and good, and will therefore have to seek for other means of subsistence."[61] Along with the market orientation of professional training for teachers, the establishment of Queen's College was to widen the gap between those "true gentlewomen" who were driven downward into paid employment and the ill-bred, upwardly mobile daughters of tradesmen and clerks who were trying to rise through the governess's occupation.[62]

The mid-nineteenth century saw the beginnings of a movement to broaden opportunities for employment of women. Prominent women such as Harriet Martineau argued for increasing of such opportunities, and the *English Woman's Journal* began what amounted to a crusade for this kind of reform. But neither Miss Martineau's call for new jobs nor the *EWJ* campaign were intended simply to give new alternatives to unemployed, needy ladies. The need for more jobs for women, it was argued, arose from the fact that, in the closed market, many "incompetent" women were drawn into governess's work, resulting in "injury to the qualified governesses."[63] The *EWJ* was quite explicit in the matter: if other occupations were opened to women, "surely then the daughters of our flourishing tradesmen, our small merchants and manufacturers, who remain single for a few . . . years, may find some occupation more healthy, more exciting, and more profitable than the under ranks of governessing." Such girls might help their fathers and brothers in the shop or business, an alternative preferable to "rigidly confining themselves to what they deem the gentilities of private life, and selling themselves to a family but little above their own station for £25 a year."[64] Mrs. Sewell saw that if girls from cultivated, comfortable

Women in the Victorian Age

homes took up occupations without the pressure of poverty, it would help to break down "our English prejudices" against jobs other than governessing as suitable work for ladies.[65] But such change would not take place until the pressures of female militance, war, and the tensions inherent in the idea of woman as ornament, drove the middle classes to resign the leisured lady as a banner and bulwark of their gentility.

2: From Dame to Woman

W. S. Gilbert and Theatrical Transvestism

Jane W. Stedman

WHEN W. S. GILBERT AND ARTHUR SULLIVAN BEGAN THEIR COLLABORATION they resolved that "on artistic principles, no man should play a woman's part and no woman a man's."[1] This was a revolutionary intention, for transvestism was as much a staple of the Victorian stage as of the Elizabethan, although not as necessary, since, by the nineteenth century, audiences had long become accustomed to the presence of actresses in the playhouse. Victorian theatrical transvestism was obviously not the simple convention of boys playing serious feminine roles; in fact, this is the one sort of transvestism not found on the Victorian stage. Instead, young women played boys, male adolescents, young men, and even at times adult males; while middle-aged women were played broadly by male low comedians. Both sorts of transvestism had been inherited by the nineteenth century, but both were widely elaborated, particularly on the light musical stage where Nell Gwyn's and Peg Woffington's breeches roles were continued by such swaggerers as Madame Vestris and Mrs. Howard Paul, wearing the breeches of Captain Macheath. In Vestris's case, they were "the very tightest buckskins she could obtain to fit her shape."[2] Meanwhile, Robert Keeley as Sairy Gamp, Frederick Robson as Medea, and a long line of clowns followed and broadened the tradition in which Dicky Suett had played Moll Flagon in Burgoyne's comic opera *The Lord of the Manor*.

Men did not impersonate women seriously on the nineteenth century stage, although Robson came close to it; but women enacted non-comic male characters as well as semi- and fully-comic ones. Even classical actresses such as Charlotte Cushman and Ellen Tree readily wore decorous doublets or trousers and played such romantic young men as Romeo and Claude Melnotte, Miss Cushman even appearing as

Wolsey. Mrs. Keeley's greatest performance was her realistic Jack Sheppard in Buckstone's dramatization of Ainsworth's novel, for which she learned to box. In the 1870's Maggie Brennan undertook Pip in Gilbert's stage version of *Great Expectations,* but the *Theatre's* reviewer, after commending her brightness, intelligence, and freedom from offense, added "she cannot escape from the physical impossibility of the labour which she undertakes." Critics were more willing to accept transvestite performances of men about town, such as Miss Brennan's "Titeboy" in *Cyril's Success* by H. J. Byron, and the female impersonations of "swells" and "mashers" continued in the music halls with Vesta Tilley and Fanny Robina.

Young women regularly played little boys, a tradition surviving into motion pictures with Mary Pickford's Little Lord Fauntleroy. The transvestite's greatest opportunity, however, came in portraying delicate, pathetic, or witless adolescents, especially but not exclusively in dramatizations of Dickens' novels. These roles did not demand masculinity of face or broadness of shoulder, the audience's pity being intensified by the waif-fragility of Jennie Lee as Jo in *Bleak House* or of Mrs. Keeley as a white-faced, shivering Smike. Barnaby Rudge and Oliver Twist were also female roles, and Macready summed up the genre when he described the ideal Fool in *King Lear* (played in his production by teen-age Priscilla Horton) as a "fragile, hectic, beautiful-faced, half-idiot-looking boy."[3]

Women, of course, continued to play girls required by the plot to assume male disguise. Yet these characters were less frequent in Victorian than in Elizabethan drama, obviously because they were not played by boy actors, but also perhaps because a serious heroine's turning to male dress would suggest a certain indelicacy to audiences who associated ladylikeness with virtue. Or if the serious play had a contemporary setting, no visual excitement was to be gained from putting a well-shaped actress into muffling male garments. Fortunately, Shakespeare's hose-clad heroines were both picturesque and privileged for their author's sake. Male disguise appeared on the burlesque stage, but not as frequently as male impersonation. In Shirley Brooks's *Robin Hood and Little John* (1846) we have both: the title roles are both female, but Blondel is a girl who disguises herself as a minstrel boy to follow her lover, Little John, to the Holy Land. This plot device is reminiscent of folksong heroines who follow husbands or lovers to the wars in male attire, a motif which Gilbert later satirized in a Bab Ballad, "The Bumboat Woman's Story." Here an entire ship's crew consists of girls who have disguised themselves for love of Lieutenant Belaye. Poll Pineapple, the narrator, is now nearly seventy, "shrivelled with . . . work, and grief," her teeth "drawn by Time, the Thief." Her story itself deals with the days when she was barely sixty, soft-cheeked, sweet-eyed, and called "Little Buttercup" by Lieutenant Belaye. Poll's pet name and occupation anticipate those of Buttercup in *H. M. S. Pinafore*, but the later character is predicated on another transvestite tradition, that of the popular "dame" of burlesque and pantomime.

With the possible exception of Mrs. Keeley's wide range of male roles, it is to burlesques and their near cousins, the pantomimes and extravaganzas, that we must look for the basis of many Gilbertian characters and for the transvestite performances, both male and female, which played most frequently before the widest audiences. The feminine "principal boys" of these musical plays were a variety of soubrette, and their appeal was partly sexual as it was in Vestris's Macheath or Woffington's Wildair, and as it was not in the feminized Barnaby's and Smikes. Mythological and supernatural characters had always offered opportunities for the sort of physical display that Nelly Farren's silver tights provided when she played Mercury in Gilbert's *Thespis*. Mid-Victorians, irresistibly attracted to legs, watched the costume of the principal boys rise from near-knee-length in the 1860's to silken thighs in the 1870's. In Planché's fairytale extravaganzas and many of the later burlesques by the Broughs and Byron, the principal boy was jaunty and required an actress such as Priscilla Horton or Marie Wilton, cheeky, boyish, impudent — insouciant rather than provocative. Such roles are related in their innocent attractiveness to Shakespeare's Rosalind and to the tomboy, or "western" heroines of nineteenth-century American drama. Dickens described Miss Wilton's Pippo (*The Maid and the Magpie*) as "astonishingly impudent . . . stupendously like a boy. . . ."[4] Principal boys, like "dames", survived into twentieth-century pantomime, but the Horton-Wilton girl-boy is best preserved in revivals of *Peter Pan*, just as the descendant of the "dame" is best seen in *Charley's Aunt*.

Any character could be feminized for the Victorian musical stage (Oedipus, Chaucer, and Aramis were all played by women), but the male player of women's roles was much more restricted. He could hope only for low comedy, at best rising to grotesque characterization in non-musical farce, eccentric comedy, or melodrama. Just as Dickens' boys were played by girls, his comic women such as Mrs. Gamp and Tilly Slowboy were enacted by men. William Attwood even doubled the parts of Uriah Heep and Miss Mowcher in *Born with a Caul; or, The Personal Adventures of David Copperfield*, and Henry Widdicombe doubled Miss Mowcher and Mr. Micawber in *David Copperfield the Younger of Blunderstone Rookery*, both in 1850. Yet it is again in pantomime, burlesque and extravaganza that the Victorian "dame" was most typical. Often the dame appeared as a foil for, or comic partner of, a principal boy. Thus J. L. Toole was a ludicrous Zerlina to the Little Don Giovanni of Nelly Farren; and Paul Bedford a Norma "six foot two or three in her sandals" to the "killing Roman roué" of Mrs. Grattan.[5] Even the innocuous characters of Mother Shipton and Mother Bunch were male roles in pantomimes, as was Aladdin's knock-down, drag-out, slapstick, widowed mother.

The mid-Victorian dames had always two characteristics in common: they were at least middle-aged and they were at least very plain, if not positively hideous. Their make-up was caricature, their action slapstick even in as relatively restrained a character as F. C. Burnand's Sappho "got up to represent a very prim middle-aged lady", or his Minerva, "made up as a sort of Cornelia Blimber, spectacles and all."[6] They were, in short, animated comic valentines.

Other characteristics which the dame might possess include a hasty, even a cruel temper; shrewishness; an unrequited passion; an avid love of flattery; and a misplaced dependence on the disguising powers of cosmetics and false hair. Robert Brough's Medea, for instance, admits, "I fear I'm rather vicious" and "I sometimes bite."[7] Burnand's Sappho loves Phaon "with all the gushing ecstasy of a young girl of fifty, which she was if she was a day." But it is the question of appearance which preoccupies these characters most, and a stereotypic scene jeering at them and the camouflages they use appears in play after play, preserving a transvestite memory of the flyttings of heroic drama and of Lady Wishfort at her toilet table. These attacks, sometimes put into the mouth of the dame herself, varied in intensity. Minerva merely says that hers is "nature's face improved by art", but Queen Isabella admits that her hair has changed from golden to almost black in a few days:

> JOSE: By food?
> QUEEN: Well, rather by a course of *dye it*.[8]

More prolonged personal insult was the general rule, however, even in the earlier, elegant Planché, whose Baroness Grognon, although played by a woman, is referred to as a raven, a screech-owl, a vulture, a Gorgon, a horrid scarecrow. This is a far more imposing list of epithets than those addressed to Gilbert's Katisha, who is merely an "ill-omened owl".

In most scenes the dame is told to her face that she is repulsive, always with the puns typical of burlesque dialogue. In *Conrad and Medora*, William Brough's travesty of Lord Byron's *Corsair*, the reigning beauty, Gulnare, taunts a faded favourite, Zuliema:

ZULI. I blush for you.
GUL.   You can't your paint beneath —
ZULI. 'Tis false!
GUL.   Just so.
ZULI.   You say this to my teeth!
GUL. To teeth — to hair — to all the charge extending,
     That wig — the head and *front* of your offending.
ZULI. I'll have you bow-stringed![9]

Grognon and Zuliema were played by women, but the roles in no way differed from the predominant male dames of the 1860's.

False hair and false teeth appear in all forms of Victorian popular comedy, off-stage as well as on. They are staples of humorous verse and comic journalism, which often made them the object of satirical attack. Criticising the moral principles of cosmetics presumably palliated the supposed rudeness of making personal remarks. For example, *Judy's* "A Pretty Little Alphabet for Pretty Little Ladies" included references to:

D is the dye used to turn her curls red;
E is her ear which is wax as a dolly's;
F is the fashion, which prompts all these follies;
. . .
T the false teeth that she shows when she talks;
U's unreality — bane of the age;
V the vain feeling that makes it the rage; . . .[10]

It is obvious that under the guise of admonishing vanity, the comic journalist could be as abusive as he chose. On stage there was less attempt to justify jeering since the plot-function of the ugly woman made her unsympathetic anyway. She separated young lovers or, if she was a wicked stepmother, she harassed the heroine. Occasionally she was valued for her money in spite of her personal drawbacks, as when King Uxorious answers his daughter's objection to Grognon's three-score years with "She has three-score millions, yearly!"[11] The unattractive man married for his money in Victorian comedy was not so frequently nor so ridiculously depicted as the plain woman courted for hers. Unattractive men were more often pursued for their titles, and here the pursuing woman is as laughable as the pursued male. An amusing balance is struck, however, in Gilbert's *The Gondoliers*, where the Duchess of

Plaza-Toro says it was very difficult to love her husband, "but I said to myself, 'That man is a Duke, and I *will* love him.' Several of my relations bet me I couldn't, but I did — desperately!"[12] The old man in love with a young girl was treated more sympathetically than the middle-aged yearning spinster and, although male characters such as Lord Dundreary or Sir Harcourt Courtly were ridiculous for dyeing their hair or affecting boyishness, the laughter at age, ugliness, and their disguises was most often directed against women, not men.

In the entire range of dame roles, only one was played as seriously and pathetically by an actor as Smike was by an actress. This was Robson's performance of Medea, a combination of the tragic and the grotesque. The burlesque ends with Medea giving Creusa a poisoned veil, killing her children, and attacking Jason, whereupon her dagger is changed to a jester's wand by Orpheus. Robson's most dramatic effect was his depiction of Medea's bewilderment at the abrupt reversal to comedy. Later, Dan Leno achieved a proto-Chaplin wistfulness and a certain realism in portraying elderly working-class women, but the tragic scope of Robson's dame was unique, depending as it did on the temperament of an unusual actor rather than on the playwright's lines.

In assigning women characters to men there was no question of *physique du rôle,* for the slapstick was not beyond an actress's athletic powers. The dame roles in extravaganza, unlike the rougher pantomime, were scarcely violent, as demonstrated by the fact that actresses sometimes did play them. In fact, male burlesque roles written for Charlotte Saunders were as exertive as any dame's. Short, fat, but Herculean, Charlotte played the "most robustious" of Richard III's, and as Hercules she wore a black beard and enormous false muscles. The perpetuation of the dame, then, was not a physical necessity, but was in part owing to the conservatism of the English theatre audience, which resisted change in familiar stage ritual and which preferred type casting for its favorites. The tradition was strongly supported by the availability of an unusual number of good male comedians during most of the century, so that there was almost always a supply of excellent dames. The popularity of ugly women characters, whoever played them, was reinforced by the popularity of this type in Victorian comic journalism and in popular fiction,[13] as well as by more classic examples in the works of Fielding, Sheridan, and the Restoration dramatists.

A man playing a feminine role could safely go further than a woman beyond the undefined but recognized limits of good taste in gesture, intonation, and ad lib—although it must be admitted that surviving texts of most plays in which they appeared are scarcely *risqué*. Certainly the difference in sex between role and impersonator might permit both dames and principal boys to play verbally on their dual identities as Viola does when, disguised as Cesario, she longs for a beard — but not on her own chin. Yet these roles as written were comparatively free of *double entendre*, the laughter evidently arising from the audience's recognition of the impersonation rather than from a deliberate and overt exploitation of duality in the lines. In an unsophisticated, visual way, the dame's female "mask" over a male face presented the discrepancy between form and content which is the basis of comedy. And finally, the caricature dames no doubt afforded an audience relaxation from that idealization of Woman which was at least a public tenet of the age. Stepping from her pedestal in the grotesque shoes of the male comedian, woman thus showed herself as earthbound as man; the impersonation made it possible to laugh at "her" without feeling uncomfortable at a lapse in chivalry.[14]

This is not to say that burlesque transvestism of both sorts went without criticism. Reviewers, when they praised principal boys, had always felt compelled to add some variant of Dickens' phrase in regard to Marie Wilton: "perfectly free from offense." *Offense*, a favorite word, was never defined; it would seem, however, to mean behavior which deliberately called attention to the actress's womanhood and in some way explicitly degraded it, for Dickens had found Miss Wilton's boyishness inoffensive because it was "unlike a woman." Little objection was provoked by the minimal physical by-play between two women on stage. If reviewers called a burlesque indecent they were thinking of legs rather than lesbianism; disapproval of principal boys rose as costumes became more abbreviated.

By the end of the 'sixties, dame roles were frequently criticized by reforming reviewers, although audiences had not tired of them. "Q" of *The Athenaeum* dismissed the male queen of Burnand's *Elizabeth; or the Don, the Duck, the Drake, and the Invincible Armada* (1870) with "I do not object to a man being dressed as a woman[,] only I require the man in the assumed garb not to transgress the bounds of decorum we set for the personage represented."[15] He added that in this instance the audience disapproved too. The "Theatrical Lounger" of *The Illustrated Times* (possibly Gilbert himself) had already objected more strongly to Thomas Thorne's portrayal of Joan of Arc. In spite of Thorne's cleverness, the reviewer insisted that "no actor can be seen to advantage in women's clothes" and "Joan of Arc played by a coarse man is simply a disgusting sight."[16]

Before burlesques were refined out of popularity, however, Gilbert had time to write several transvestite roles for principal boys and to replace masculine dames firmly with actresses. In Gilbert's journeyman burlesques or extravaganzas (the terms were practically interchangeable by the 'sixties, except that the latter was less invidious than the former), light male roles played by women include Nemorino in *Dulcamara* (1866), Tonio and the "swell" trio: Earl of Margate, Marquis of Cranbourne Alley, and Sir Peckham Rye in *La Vivandière* (1867); Thaddeus and Florestein in *The Merry Zingara* (1868); Robert and Raimbault in *Robert the Devil* (1868); Pollio in *The Pretty Druidess* (1869); and Hilarion, Cyril, Florian, Arac, Guron, and Scynthius in *The Princess* (1870), as well as other, secondary characters. Actresses also appeared in breeches roles in Gilbert's non-burlesque musical plays of the early 'seventies. All these parts were in the sprightly Horton-Wilton tradition, their closest approach to slapstick being a very brief drunken scene for Florestein or recurrent boxing "business" for Peter in *Creatures of Impulse*, played by Maggie Brennan. Gilbert, like other burlesque writers, obviously found that lines which would sound silly when spoken by a man became piquant in the mouth of a girl, yet so little feminized is his dialogue that when he eventually turned *The Princess* into *Princess Ida*, he transferred unchanged many of the lines for Hilarion and his friends, even though the speakers were played by women in the burlesque and by men in the opera. Finally, in *The Gentleman in Black* (1870) and *Happy Arcadia* (1872), Gilbert evolved a kind of intellectual transvestism in which souls or personalities might shift bodies so that the identity and/or behavior of one sex might be temporarily imposed upon the physique of the other.[17] In *The Gentleman in Black* only male souls are interchanged, but since one of the men was played by a woman something of the same incongruity obtained.

All the broadly comic male roles in these plays were assigned to actors. When Charlotte Saunders appeared in *The Merry Zingara* it was as the Gypsy Queen, not as Devilshoof, and she played with "serio-comic earnestness." Most important, the dame roles were played by women with the very brief exceptions of the non-speaking part of Mary I in the waxworks scene in *Robert the Devil* and the small role of Gammer Grey in *Harlequin Cock-Robin and Jenny Wren*, Gilbert's only pantomime. Nor are there stereotypic dame roles in all his burlesques. Lady Blanche in *The Princess and the Gypsy Queen*, while comic, are not insulted by others or themselves, and ridicule of false hair and cosmetics is directed against younger women. Only in *La Vivandière* and *The Pretty Druidess* do conventionally developed dame characters appear. In *The Pretty Druidess*, Norma is not yet middle-aged, but her husband tells her, in a series of puns, that she is wrinkled, damaged, fat, and rouged. He is, however, reacting angrily to her furious discovery that he has left her for the younger Adalgisa. Norma herself addresses her Druidesses in a parody of Hamlet's advice to the players:

> Avoid all so-called "beautifying," dear.
> Oh, it offends me to the soul to hear,
> The things that men among themselves will say
> Of some *soi-disant* beauty of the day,
> Whose face, when with cosmetics she has cloyed it,
> Out-Rachel's Rachel! Pray you, girls, avoid it!
> . . .
> Oh, there be ladies whom I've seen hold stalls —
> Ladies of rank, my dears, to whom befalls
> Neither the accent nor the gait of ladies;
> So clumsily "made up" with Bloom of Cadiz,
> Powder, rouge, lip-salve — that I've fancied then
> They were the work of Nature's journeymen!
> Let her, whose hair is black with lustre mellow,
> Not dream of using dye to turn it yellow —
> She'll find it argues (when at length she loses it)
> A sad ambition in the fool that uses it![18]

In *La Vivandière*, the Marchioness of Birkenfelt was played by Harriet Everard, who later created the role of Little Buttercup. Before we meet the Marchioness, her long-lost husband remembers her as a scold whom he went to war to escape. At her first appearance, a stage direction describes her as having *"all the appearance of a faded Coquette, and her manner is characterized by an affectation of extreme juvenility"*;[19] later she *"coyly conceals her face"*. Although she is fifty and her daughter nineteen, she insists that she has just come of age. The susceptible Pumpernickel and the simple Sulpizio consider the Marchioness a fine woman, but Lord Margate ridicules her to her face. In this scene, Gilbert, working in conventional punning dialogue, turns the situation so that the dame more thoroughly insults herself by reporting the "absurd" things people say about her.

> MARCHS. Some people say and tell me as a duty,
>   My cheeks are much too ruddy for a beauty.
> LD. MAR. The wretch who said so is with falsehood tainted,
>   They're nothing like so ruddy — as they're painted!

MARCHS.	That I should use more powder!
LD. MAR.	Powder? *Puff!*
MARCHS.	And that my figure's padded!
LD. MAR.	Padded? *Stuff!*
MARCHS.	My hair a wig! that's rudeness pretty blunt!
LD. MAR.	Rudeness? I stimatize it as *affront.*
MARCHS.	That it's stained yellow — things which I denied first.
LD. MAR.	*You* stain your tresses yellow? You'd have *died* first.
MARCHS.	I've even heard it said that I'm too stout!
LD. MAR.	Oh you're mistaken there — they meant, no doubt
	Some of the many charms with which you're graced.
	As you've no use for them, have *run to waste.*

Reviewers did not object to Gilbert's substitution of women for men in the dame roles, nor to his principal boys; indeed, they described his burlesques as singularly free of vulgarity, sometimes even too slow for the audience. Moreover, they did not suggest that Gilbert's treatment of the Marchioness was unusually cruel or indicative of a personal dislike for middle-aged women. Perhaps the conventional burlesque format kept reviewers from associating the character with a real woman, but even had they done so, Gilbert was less brutal than many of his predecessors.

Nevertheless, when Gilbert in the 'eighties created Lady Jane (in *Patience*) and Katisha (in *The Mikado*), reviewers began to find him in bad taste, a criticism from which his reputation has never fully recovered. Although critics, including those in the twentieth century, have tended to lump together all the middle-aged feminine characters of the Gilbert and Sullivan operas, these characters differ markedly in their assimilation of elements of the dame.

The series begins with Diana in *Thespis:* "an elderly Goddess. . . . carefully wrapped up in Cloaks, Shawls, &c. A hood is over her head, a respirator in her mouth, and galoshes on her feet." Diana is merely one of the aged Olympian deities, and her comedy is no different than that of Apollo, "an elderly 'buck' with an air of assumed juvenility. . . ." What may be called cosmetic satire is distributed impartially: Mercury brings false teeth to Jupiter; false hair and hair dye to Apollo; and false hair, powder and rouge to Venus. In *Trial by Jury* a dame character is alluded to but not seen: the rich attorney's elderly, ugly daughter, who " 'may very well pass for forty-three/In the dusk, with a light behind her!' " She has been jilted by the Judge, but most of the dame characters in the following operas make successful marriages, sometimes to younger men. Nor are they necessarily ugly. Captain Corcoran amorously calls Buttercup "A plump and pleasing person!", while the Boatswain describes her as "the rosiest, the roundest, and the reddest beauty in all Spithead." The stage make-up for these roles, except Katisha's, has never been caricature; the costumes have always been attractive, often elegant. While the Fairy Queen (descended also from the Fairy Queens of pantomime as well as from Wagner's Brünnhilde) is stout "in moderation" and her lines about curling inside a buttercup and swinging on a cobweb are comic, she is not ridiculed. The Duchess of Plaza-Toro alludes to her own "threatening appearance" when she explains how she tamed the Duke's temper, but on stage she looks handsome. Even Lady Blanche, taken over from Gilbert's earlier burlesque, is merely pompous and pedantic in manner and, if she is more ill-mannered than the other Gilbert contraltos, she owes her jealousy as much to Tennyson's original as to her burlesque inheritance. Several of these roles were created, and all were played in early revivals, by Rosina Brandram, of whom Gilbert said that she could never contrive to look more than an attractive twenty-eight.[20]

There is a closer resemblance to the dame in the characters of Ruth, in *The Pirates of Penzance* (1879), and Dame Hannah, in *Ruddigore* (1887). Both take part in slapstick action, and Ruth's age is made the subject of laughter. After a first act in which she is simply an expository character, Hannah is kidnapped by old Adam, whose young master has instructed him to carry off a maiden. Hannah is not physically grotesque, but she is comic in supposing that Ruthven wants to "lay unholy hands" upon her and in her preparations to defend her honour (which, of course, is not threatened):

[DAME HANNAH, *who has taken a formidable dagger from one of the armed figures, throws her small dagger to* SIR RUTHVEN

HAN. Harkye, miscreant, you have secured me, and I am your poor prisoner; but if you think I cannot take care of myself you are very much mistaken. Now then, it's one to one, and let the best man win! [*Making for him.*]

The Pirates of Penzance is closer in time to the burlesques, and here the entire characterization suggests a toned-down dame part. Ruth, a hard-of-hearing nursery maid, apprenticed the child Frederic to a band of pirates. She has remained with them as a "piratical maid-of-all-work," the relationship between herself and the grown-up Frederic parodying that between Thaddeus and the grown-up Arline in *The Bohemian Girl*, which Gilbert had already burlesqued in *The Merry Zingara*. When Frederic decides to leave the pirates, he and the Pirate King hand Ruth back and forth, each unwilling to rob the other of this "treasure." Frederic promises to marry Ruth if she is really as fine a woman as he has been led to believe. Hers is a sweet face, but he has not seen another woman since he was eight years old. When Frederic remarks that "A lad of twenty-one usually looks for a wife of seventeen", Ruth replies that he will find her "a wife of a thousand!"[21] Frederic answers, "No, but I shall find you a wife of forty-seven, and that is quite enough." In these lines only Ruth's age is considered; she is not represented as physically gross or repulsive, and she herself candidly thinks she is a fine woman. The only unpleasant references to her person occur in the duet after Frederic has seen the genuine, youthful beauty of Major-General Stanley's daughters. Furious at what he considers Ruth's deception, he tells her, "you're plain and old. . . . Your face is lined, your hair is grey." From this point on, allusions to Ruth's looks disappear. She joins in the final decorously slapstick battle between pirates and police, and in Gilbert's stage-picture at the finale pairs off with the Sergeant. Indeed, a photograph from the 1900 revival of *Pirates* shows a slender, attractive Rosina Brandram as Ruth, ogled by a flirtatious Walter Passmore as Sergeant.[22]

Reviewers of Gilbert and Sullivan operas raised little objection to most of these roles. The *World* (9 January 1884) said that Miss Brandram had in *Princess Ida* "the ungrateful task to look a horrid old maid, and conscientiously does it"; but the *Standard* (2 January 1884) merely described her Lady Blanche as "stern and sedate." Photographs of Miss Brandram in this role do not justify the *World's* adjectives. The question of taste arose for a few reviewers in the Fairy Queen's lines referring to her own size, especially since the actress (Alice Barnett) was tall and sturdy, but no reviewer called her undignified. When the first performance of *Ruddigore* was booed, a letter to the editor of the *St. James Gazette* listed among the causes the "jarring effect" of Dame Hannah's "mock heroics,"[23] yet the *Morning Post* commended the actress's "true melodramatic style." It was only to Lady Jane (played by Miss Barnett) and Katisha (played by Miss Brandram) that marked exception was taken, and these are the two roles in which elements of the dame, though sublimated, are most evident.

Lady Jane is the only plain member of the train of Rapturous Maidens who adore and follow the poet Bunthorne. When they transfer their affections to the poet Grosvenor, she remains true to Bunthorne and follows him in a train of one. She represents the ultimate absurdity of the Aesthetic craze, being simultaneously the physical antithesis of a Burne-Jones figure and its most enthusiastic imitator: "I droop despairingly; I am soulfully intense; I am limp and I cling!" Lady Jane is not directly insulted except briefly by Bunthorne when he is angry. Instead, the comments on her looks are made by herself; she realizes the nature of her own appearance and even asserts it. "A pretty damozel *you* are!" Bunthorne exclaims. "No, not pretty. Massive," answers Jane. In soliloquy she cautions Bunthorne, "do not dally too long, Reginald, for my charms are ripe, Reginald, and already they are decaying. Better secure me ere I have gone too far!" After a recitative ending on the pun "To 'make up' for lost time" and containing allusions to false hair, rouge, and powder, Jane sings alone on stage:

> Silvered is the raven hair,
> Spreading is the parting straight,
> Mottled the complexion fair,
> Halting is the youthful gait,
> Hollow is the laughter free,
> Spectacled the limpid eye —
> Little will be left of me
> In the coming by and by!
>
> Fading is the taper waist,
> Shapeless grows the shapely limb,
> And although severely laced,
> Spreading is the figure trim!
> Stouter than I used to be,
> Still more corpulent grow I —
> There will be too much of me
> In the coming by and by![24]

The details of this song seem invented to substantiate the paradox formed by the juxtaposition of the last two lines of each stanza. The effect of the song is both wistful and funny; it suggests self-knowledge and wry self-acceptance, and it is in effect totally unlike the traditional abuse of the dame. Both audiences and reviewers found Miss Barnett's performance very amusing, but the latter seized upon her proportions (described as Brobdignagian by an earlier reviewer) and took Gilbert to task for questionable taste in what the *Telegraph* called "a part written up ostentatiously to her wealth of physical development." In thus demonstrating Gilbert's lack of delicacy, his critics had no hesitation in themselves publishing personal comments on Miss Barnett's size. When she did not appear in the next opera, *Princess Ida*, the *Illustrated Sporting and Dramatic News* exclaimed, "where, oh where, is our old friend of Titan proportions, Miss Alice Barnett? Surely a Gilbertian opera is not complete without her?" (12 January 1884).

Even more than Buttercup and the Fairy Queen, who both marry men whom they adore, Lady Jane makes a markedly advantageous match by Victorian social standards. The Duke of Dunstable, "a great matrimonial fish," chooses her "in common fairness" since the other

Women in the Victorian Age

Rapturous Maidens possess in their personal appearance all that is requisite for happiness. Jane delightedly accepts, and the opera ends on the unusual note of tenor paired romantically with contralto.

In Katisha the sublimation of the dame is complete. Unlike Lady Jane and the rest, she is a huntress rampant, as suggested by her name and her slip of "my prey" for "my pupil." Other characters in *The Mikado* comment on her features, sometimes, although not always to her "caricature of a face," but none is so forthright as herself. When Pooh-Bah attempts to flatter her by calling her lovely, Katisha, like Lady Jane, replies, "That's not true." She revels in her ugliness and makes a distinction of it, behaving paradoxically like a great self-conscious beauty: "I am an acquired taste — only the educated palate can appreciate *me*." Katisha's "left shoulder-blade is a miracle of loveliness. People come miles to see it." Her right elbow "has a fascination that few can resist." Katisha's make-up is more exaggerated than that of the other Gilbert dames, partly because of the *japonnerie* of the opera, partly as a necessity to the comedy of such moments as Ko-Ko's wooing in which both characters behave like the juvenile leads to whom they bear so little physical resemblance. Katisha's transcendent sense of her own ugliness is, moreover, the satiric parallel of Yum-Yum's equally outspoken assertion of her own beauty: "Yes, I am indeed beautiful! Sometimes I sit and wonder, in my artless Japanese way, why it is that I am so much more attractive than anybody else in the whole world. Can this be vanity? No." While Katisha's behavior when Ko-Ko proposes is reminiscent of the grotesque coyness of the dame, it is also the behavior of a kittenish young girl. Here the comedy comes, not from an abuse of Katisha, but from the audience's perception of the discrepancy between her character and appearance on the one hand, and her behavior on the other, and from the surprise when Katisha suddenly reverts to character while keeping in the ostensible young-girl framework. Her sentence is pure Dora Spenlow except for its key word, which is pure Katisha: "And you won't hate me because I'm just a little teeny weeny wee bit blood-thirsty, will you?"

Reviewers again found that Gilbert had offended against good taste in creating Katisha, presumably for the same reason that they had objected to Lady Jane: Katisha admits that she is tough, unattractive, and "sufficiently decayed." Their reaction suggests that they were really in agreement with what they took to be Gilbert's position but that they thought it ungallant of him to say so. In short, they did not believe Katisha's very sensible speech: "You hold that I am not beautiful because my face is plain. But you know nothing; you are still unenlightened. Learn, then, that it is not in the face alone that beauty is to be sought." Had Katisha continued in a moral vein to point out that real beauty is found in the mind or heart, reviewers might have found her in better taste. But Gilbert refused to take any cliché seriously, and moved her beauty to her shoulder-blade. Nevertheless, audiences were delighted with Katisha, and critics praised Miss Brandram's performance.

Although Gilbert's comic women preserve memories of their burlesque antecedents, there are certain important differences to be noted. Cosmetic comedy is at a minimum; obviously uncomplimentary remarks are rarely made in the presence of the plain women, while unfavorable comments to or about them are to some extent palliated by the tense situations in which they occur — for example: Frederic's anger at being deceived, Bunthorne's disappointment, Ko-Ko's horror at having to marry or be boiled in oil. Even Katisha is at first described merely as "an elderly lady", and Bunthorne gratefully tells Jane, "After all, there is no denying it, you're a fine figure of a woman!" Nor are any of these characters ultimately left alone or rejected. As we have seen, Jane makes the most successful marriage, in a worldly sense, of any woman in *Patience*, and Katisha has "a very good bargain" in Ko-Ko, as Ko-Ko himself tells her. Lady Sangazure weds Sir Marmaduke Pointdextre, the Fairy Queen marries Private Willis, and Dame Hannah marries Sir Roderic. Dame Carruthers secures Sergeant Meryll's hand if not his heart. The Duchess of Plaza-Toro is already married. "Tough old" Baroness von Krakenfeldt is loved by miserly Grand Duke Rudolph for her compatible stinginess, and their marriage is prevented only by Rudolph's betrothal in infancy to the Princess of Monte Carlo.

Gilbert also allows many of these characters lyrics or lines which arouse genuine, if necessarily temporary, sympathy. Ruth admits that her hair gradually grew gray, and Katisha has three solos which are comic only in contrast to their singer and which are sung "straight" on stage, unaccompanied by audience laughter. They are serious moments in which Katisha assumes a more recognizably human emotional status than any other character in *The Mikado*. Her solos are "Oh fool, that fleest/My hallowed joys!"; "The hour of gladness/Is dead and gone"; and "Hearts do not break," all of which deal seriously with the loss of love.

Finally, and most important, Gilbert used the characters of Ruth, Lady Jane, and Katisha not merely to satirize middle-aged spinsterhood, but also to satirize the premium which his contemporaries placed on youthful beauty. Each has lines which clearly indicate that youth and beauty are not the only qualities advantageous in a marriage. Here Gilbert obliquely recurs to the familiar Victorian theme of "masks and

　　　　　　　　　　　　　　　　Women in the Victorian Age

faces" with its admonition against judging by surfaces, as Ruth and Jane assert that they have more love to give than the "affection raw and green" of young girls, and Katisha condemns "Pink cheek, that rulest/Where wisdom serves!" While Victorians were perfectly prepared to admire Dora Spenlow and Yum-Yum for being young and triumphing in their loveliness, they were unprepared for a Jane or a Katisha who triumphs in her age and ugliness. Even Sullivan shared this refusal to see a middle-aged woman as capable of romantic love. During the writing of their penultimate opera, he objected to the character of Lady Sophy "to me . . . unsympathetic and distasteful . . . . it is necessary that she should be very old, ugly, raddled, and perhaps grotesque, and still more is it necessary that she should be seething with love and passion (requited or unrequited) and other feelings not usually associated with old age."[25] This sentence of Sullivan's shows us how deeply rooted was the assumption that intense love was limited to the young, and his description is more appropriate to Fielding's Mrs. Slipslop than to a Gilbertian dame. Gilbert replied that Lady Sophy need be no more unattractive than the actress who played her (Miss Brandram again), that she was in love with King Paramount as a dignified woman of forty-five might be with a man of fifty, and that her passion was not as gross as Sullivan evidently imagined. In fact, this king and governess constitute the main romantic interest of *Utopia Limited* since the juvenile leads have already fallen in love and declared themselves to each other before the opera begins. Lady Sophy, in her refusal to marry anyone but a blameless king, foreshadows the much younger Gwendolyn Fairfax's equally idealistic determination "to love someone of the name of Ernest." Gilbert's middle-aged couple fulfill each other's ideals of purity (which are very Victorian) and, although as a governess Lady Sophy suggests Dickens' Mrs. General, Paramount is passionately devoted to his "prudish paragon," who represents the final transformation of transvestite dame into middle-aged attractiveness.

In contrast, Scaphio, the elderly wise-man of Utopia, who, like Patience, has never loved till now, cherishes the ideal of "a semi-transparent Being, filled with an inorganic pink jelly," finally realized in Princess Zara. Scaphio's fellow wise-man, Phantis, a mere fifty-five, also loves the princess and supposes "that she does not regard me with absolute indifference, for she could never look at me without having to go to bed with a sick headache."

In spite of what we have seen, Victorian criticism of Gilbert's taste in presenting his remodelled dames was negligible compared to that of the twentieth century. Victorian gallantry was perhaps shocked when it realized it had laughed at women rather than at men pretending to be women, once the protective coloration of burlesque was removed; but Victorian critics knew other writers more invidious than Gilbert. Audiences enjoyed the dame in whatever dress, and Shaw, who objected to making fun of stout, mature ladies, admitted that in creating such characters Gilbert had perfectly understood his public.[26]

Nevertheless, as the tradition of transvestite dames attenuated and the Savoy libretti outlived their own comic milieu, they began to be taken as *sui generis*,[27] and critics untroubled by Congreve's Lady Wishfort accepted as an article of faith Gilbert's "loathing" of Katisha. Sir Arthur Quiller-Couch announced that Gilbert's cruelty in exposing middle-aged women to public derision was "so thoroughly caddish that no critic can ignore or . . . extenuate it." Gilbert, he said, insisted "on the physical odiousness of any woman growing old. . . . Gilbert shouts it, mocks it, apes with it, spits upon it. He opens with this dirty trump card in *Trial by Jury*. . . ."[28] Louis Kronenberger also found Gilbert notoriously sadistic toward unattractive women, his worst jibes seeming "not only what the Victorians would have called caddish, but what later generations might suspect of being faintly pathological."[29] Isaac Goldberg was magisterial: "The shade of Sir William has not yet fully atoned for his cruel treatment of aging woman-kind."[30] Hesketh Pearson decided that Gilbert created his aging females out of a dislike for his mother (p. 94). Even Edmund Wilson has pronounced these characters "a tiresome betrayal of all that was worst in Gilbert: a streak of vulgar cruelty and a tendency to rely on formula."[31] As a matter of fact, the dame roles have as much variety as any of Gilbert's character groups and distinctly more than his nominal heroines. Perhaps Gilbert's "sadistic" treatment of ageing women would not have become such an article of faith had he retained a lyric cut out of *The Gondoliers* before production. It is sung by Tessa to Don Alhambra:

> . . . you're old and wrinkled —
> It's rather blunt, but it's the truth —
> With wintry snow your hair is sprinkled:
> What *can* you know of Love and Youth?
> Indeed I wish to speak politely;
> But, pray forgive me, truth is truth:
> You're old and — pardon me — unsightly,
> What can you know of Love and Youth!
>
> You are too aged to remember
> That withered bosom's earliest glow;
> Dead is the old romantic ember
> That warmed your life-blood years ago.
> If from our sweethearts we are parted
> (Old men know nothing of such pain)

> Two maidens will be broken-hearted
> And quite heart-broken lovers twain!
> Now pray, for goodness' sake, consider
> I've no desire to be uncouth;
> But we are June & you're December —
> What *can* you know of Love & Youth![32]

Tessa is more polite than the usual insulter because Don Alhambra is the Grand Inquisitor, a personage far superior to her in class and power. The closest equivalent situation involving a dame would be Pitti-Sing's teasing of Katisha, but generally Gilbert's dames are not cheeked by their inferiors.

Fortunately, the myth of Gilbert's "cruelty," though widespread, is by no means universal and rests largely on elements extraneous to the texts of his plays and their stage history. It has, however, attracted both the gossipy dilettante who also likes to speculate on Shakespeare's second-best bed, and the Freudian critic to whom Victorian figures seem particularly vulnerable. In looking for psychological implications, however, one may more profitably ask whether Katisha's self-exaggeration is evidence of Gilbert's antipathy to, or of his identification with his creation. For like Katisha he understood that observers impose a mask whose exaggerations are often in the eye of the beholder rather than in the lineaments of the face. Gilbert accepted the mask of ferocity and cynicism which he admitted was his public label, and he played with his public caricature for comic effect. Around his scowling figure, drawn by his own hand, he once wrote: "I loathe everybody" — "I love to bully" — "Everybody is an Ass" — "I am an overbearing beast" — "I hate my fellowman"—"confound everything"—"I like pinching little babies" — "I am an ill-tempered pig, & I glory in it — W. S. Gilbert."[33] Yet in his private correspondence he told a forty-year-old friend that she had "been in the pride and glow of lovely life for the last twenty years, and you will be delightful to look at and talk to twenty years hence."[34]

Perhaps the extension of the "elderly, ugly" myth in an era which has freed itself otherwise from claims of the genteel suggests that twentieth-century attitudes toward middle-aged women have not changed radically from late Victorian attitudes, even though protectiveness is no longer a practical mode of asserting male domination. Perhaps the myth may be taken as evidence that Gilbert did create from the transvestite dames feminine characters with sufficient identity to seem women in their own right. Certainly, in his hands the middle-aged comic spinster took on an energy and independence which dramatists before and after him gave only to the high-spirited heroines.

3: Victorian Women and Menstruation

Elaine and English Showalter

> And if a woman have an issue, and her issue
> in her flesh be blood, she shall be put apart
> seven days (*Leviticus*, XV, 19).

FEW TABOOS EVOKE AS FORCEFUL AND AS UNIVERSAL A RESPONSE AS THOSE surrounding menstruation. Even the redoubtable Marquis De Sade, who took prurient delight in moldy feces and decapitated dogs, appears to have regarded menstruation with faint distaste. In *The 120 Days of Sodom*, the bawd Duclos speaks of a menstrual fetishist on the seventh day, but she says: "I shall lay little emphasis upon the following passion, for I realize that there are not many in your midst, Messieurs, who are its votaries; however, you have commanded me to tell everything and I obey."[1] And the lechers, in this case and against their custom, feel no urge to experience what they have just heard about.

Small wonder, then, that even Victorians as open-minded as Florence Nightingale or John Stuart Mill maintain an almost complete silence on the subject. O. R. McGregor, surveying the bibliography on women in Victorian England, remarked in 1955 that research on sex was almost impossible; "the Victorian bedroom door is firmly shut in the investigator's face,"[2] as he puts it, and to no subject does this apply more certainly than to menstruation. Unlike sexual activities, moreover, menstruation has no literary reflection, true or false. Since 1955 scholars have managed at least to peek through the bedroom door, and by combining these revelations with the scientific writings on the subject, one can arrive at some tentative conclusions.

It is hard to comprehend how little even scientists and doctors knew about human reproduction in the nineteenth century. In the first half of the century it was generally believed that the menstrual flow came from an excess of nutrient in the female; eggs were thought to descend from the ovaries only as a consequence of intercourse. However inaccurate that might be, it would appear rational enough to dispel the mystical taboos, but such was not the case. An early authority, John Elliotson, wrote in 1840: "To regard women during menstruation as unclean is certainly very useful . . ." and he noted without comment: "In this country, it is firmly believed by many that meat will not take salt if the process is conducted by a menstruating woman."[3]

In 1845 Dr. Adam Raciborski discovered that the eggs were ejected spontaneously.[4] The new theory which was based on this finding can scarcely be called progress. George R. Drysdale represented a progressive point of view, as an active campaigner for birth control and social reform. His *Elements of Social Science*, first published in 1854, had many editions and sold tens of thousands of copies; the edition from which we quote was the twenty-fifth, published in 1886. Drysdale explained: "Menstruation in woman corresponds exactly with the period of heat in female animals, and differs only in the unessential particular, that in woman there is an external sanguineous discharge" (p. 66).

Charles Knowlton was another progressive; his *Fruits of Philosophy*, first appearing in 1832, also had many editions and sold tens of thousands of copies. In the 1870's Charles Bradlaugh and Annie Besant reissued the work with footnotes by Drysdale, which were meant to bring the physiology up to date. Like Sir William Acton, whose quasi-medical endorsement of female sexual anesthesia has been discussed by Steven Marcus, Knowlton credits many sexual superstitions, for instance that nocturnal emissions are a disease and that onanism leads to insanity. Drysdale does not correct Knowlton on these points. Knowlton is equally unreliable regarding menstruation: "During its continuance, the woman is said to be unwell, or out of order. Various unpleasant feelings are liable to attend it; but when it is attended with severe pain, as it not infrequently is, it becomes a disease, and the woman is not likely to conceive until it be cured. During the existence of the 'turns' or 'monthlies,' as they are often called, indigestible food, dancing in warm rooms, sudden exposure to cold or wet, and mental agitations should be avoided as much as possible."[5] Logically enough, both Knowlton and Drysdale conclude: "it is believed that although conception may occur at other times, it is much more likely to happen from intercourse a few days before or after the menstrual periods" (p. 39), an opinion amply fortified by references to other authorities.[6]

The belief that women were unusually susceptible to shocks during menstruation was by no means new — Sade regarded it as the best time for plunging girls into vats of icewater or telling them their fiancés were dead — but according to Mary Jacobi, an American physician who launched the first serious attack on the idea in 1877, the discovery of spontaneous ovulation had given it a semblance of scientific validity. She wrote: "The entire succession of processes seemed the more surprising because more recently demonstrated, and to cause a greater perturbation of the economy, because occurring at intervals. For the first time the periodicity of menstruation began to be considered as a morbid circumstance."[7] Whether the discovery of spontaneous ovulation is responsible or not may be questioned, but there is no doubt that menstruation came more and more to be regarded as incapacitating. Dr. Jacobi quotes numerous texts, for example: "We could hardly allow to a female physician convicted of criminal abortion, the plea that the act was committed during the temporary insanity of her menstruation; and yet at such times a woman is undoubtedly more prone than men to commit any unusual or outrageous act"; "women are unfit to bear the physical fatigues and mental anxieties of obstetrical practice, at menstrual periods, during pregnancy and puerperality . . ."[8]

Clearly, scientific fact and scientific theory were being influenced by the prevailing social or ethical doctrine of woman's inferiority, so that even relatively progressive investigators like Knowlton and Drysdale were governed by prejudices rather than scientific truth. The same arguments, grotesquely exaggerated, were put into service by ardent antifeminists like James MacGrigor Allan, who, addressing the Anthropological Society of London in 1869, said:

Although the duration of the menstrual period differs greatly according to race, temperament, and health, it will be within the mark to state that women are unwell, from this cause, on the average two days in the month, or say one month in the year. At such times, women are unfit for any great mental or physical labour. They suffer under a languor and depression which disqualify them for thought or action, and render it extremely doubtful how far they can be considered responsible beings while the crisis lasts. Much of the inconsequent conduct of women, their petulance, caprice, and irritability, may be traced directly to this cause. It is not improbable that instances of feminine cruelty (which startle us as so inconsistent with the normal gentleness of the sex) are attributable to mental excitement caused by this periodical illness. . . . Michelet defines woman as an invalid. Such she emphatically is, as compared with man. . . . In intellectual labour, man has surpassed, does now, and always will surpass woman, for the obvious reason that nature does not periodically interrupt his thought and application.[9]

The violent revulsion from feminine physiology which informed this attack did not prevent its respectful reception by the Society, whose members responded with some criticism, but not with derision.

A similar revulsion seems to have been felt by our other major informants regarding Victorian sexual mores — the pornographers. Steven Marcus observes that on the rare occasions when menstruation is mentioned in relation to sexual activities, "it almost invariably brings those activities to a temporary halt."[10] Moreover, these accounts are very vague and have little documentary value, but a few relevant details may be pieced together from *My Secret Life*. The author tells us that he learned about menstruation (which he usually calls "the monthlies" or "poorliness") from his first mistress, a maid named Charlotte, when he was sixteen. "Ah, that menstruation was a wonder to me, it was marvellous,"[11] he recalls; but he offers no direct account of the causes and the management of menstruation thereafter. He does say that he did not like having intercourse with menstruating women (III, p. 587), although he managed to overcome his distaste on several occasions. At least one of his girls had her first menstruation shortly after intercourse with him, and had not been told anything about it by her mother (III, p. 488). In the early volumes of his narrative, he reports that women did not ordinarily wear drawers, but menstruating women usually wore a napkin or clout. At no point, significantly, does he mention working-class women or prostitutes, the classes with which he had most sexual contact, being incapacitated by menstruation. Maids seem not to have excused themselves from any part of their arduous routine.

Some American works, written in or about the nineteenth century, cast light on the hygiene of menstruation, and it seems reasonable to suppose that English customs would have been similar, if not identical. In Victoria Lincoln's study of the Lizzie Borden murder case, there is a description of the menstrual napkin of the 1890's, made of birdseye, and slightly smaller than a baby diaper.[12] These were rinsed in the water-closet, and put to soak in copper washtubs. *Eve's Daughters*, a manual by Marion Harland published in New York in 1882, recommends a common-sense approach to adolescent menstrual discomforts: for abdominal cramps, hot ginger tea, hot water bottles applied to the feet, and gin and water as a last resort. For backaches, the author recommends an Allcock's porous plaster. None of these remedies, she points out, should be necessary for more than two days, and the use of opium, laudanum, or paregoric is strictly forbidden (ch. XII).

An American controversy over co-education in colleges and universities was the occasion for the fullest and most revealing discussion of menstruation in the Victorian journals. In 1873 Dr. Edward Clarke of Harvard College published a small volume called *Sex in Education*, in which he argued that higher education was destroying the reproductive functions of American women, by overworking them at a critical time in their physiological development. Clarke's book appalled American feminists — Marion Harland's manual was one reply to it. Another educator, M. Carey Thomas, the first president of Bryn Mawr, recalled in 1908 that "we did not know when we began whether women's health could stand the strain of college education. We were haunted in those days by the clanging chains of that gloomy little specter, Dr. Edward H. Clarke's *Sex in Education*. With trepidation of spirit I made my mother read it, and was much cheered by her remark that, as neither she nor any of the women she knew, had ever seen girls or women of the kind described in Dr. Clarke's book, we might as well act as if they did not exist."[13]

In England, Clarke's book sparked debate in several leading journals. The *Westminster Review*, in an article entitled "American Women: Their Health and Education," disputed Clarke's argument that menstruation was debilitating, and required abstinence from physical and mental labor for one week out of every four. The author argued that it was "well known to physiologists, physicians, and women, that the periodic function of really robust and healthy women is performed with regularity and without pain or constitutional disturbance, and hence their ordinary work or occupation is neither interrupted nor even interfered with meanwhile" (102 [1874], 490).

In the *Fortnightly Review*, Henry Maudsley used Clarke's book and his arguments as the basis for an attack on the educational and professional aspirations of women. The menstrual myth gave him a scientific justification for his anti-feminism. If it could be demonstrated that education caused a constitutional degeneration in women, they could be denied education on apparently humane grounds. Maudsley made menstruation the major evidence of his argument that "women are marked out by nature for very different offices in life from those of men, and that the healthy performance of her special functions renders it improbable she will succeed, and unwise for her to persevere, in running over the same course at the same pace with him."[14] The difference held even if women never married or never had children. Women could not afford to risk any menstrual disorder, since irregularity or suppression was associated with other diseases. Maudsley concluded that women could never hope to equal masculine accomplishments, because their physiology acted as a handicap, body and mind being "for one quarter of each month during the best years of life . . . more or less sick and unfit for hard work" (p. 480).

The next number of the *Fortnightly* contained a sharp rebuttal of Maudsley by a woman physician, Elizabeth Garrett Anderson. She began by rebuking him for discussing such a subject in the first place: "We cannot but suggest that there is grave reason for doubting whether such a subject can be fully and with propriety discussed except in a professional journal" (p. 582). Nevertheless, the damage had been done, and Dr. Anderson forced herself to take up the unpleasant subject in order to answer Maudsley's arguments. She answered them, in fact, fully and frankly, speaking presumably from professional and personal experience, and her reply suggests that the extent of female invalidism was much exaggerated by male doctors. She pointed out first, that most adult women completely disregard menstruation in relation to their normal activities; it is worth noting that no woman discussing the subject indicated a necessity to remain in bed for the duration of the period. Among the working classes in particular, work went on "without intermission, and, as a rule, without ill effects." Her statement that domestic servants did not request, and were not given, any dispensation during menstruation, agrees with the incidents related in *My Secret Life.* On the other hand, Dr. Anderson believed that adolescence was a critical period for women, and that teachers ought to allow for weakness in girl students. Any kind of fatigue might be dangerous, whether it resulted from long walks, riding, dancing, or lifting heavy weights.

Clarke and Maudsley were not presenting new ideas; they merely publicized the new scientific evidence for prejudices which had existed throughout the century. The menstrual myth underlies much of the literature devoted to the woman question in Victorian journals, but without the Clarke controversy, we would not be able to identify it so surely. There can be no question, however, that George Henry Lewes had menstruation in mind when he explained, in 1852, why women were unlikely to become great writers: "For twenty of the best years of their lives — those very years in which men either rear the grand fabric or lay the solid foundations of their fame and fortune — women are mainly occupied by the cares, the duties, the enjoyments, and the sufferings of maternity. During large parts of these years, too, their bodily health is generally so broken and precarious as to incapacitate them for any strenuous exertion."[15] Since he was talking about unmarried women writers like Jane Austen and Charlotte Brontë, he did not really mean maternity. Similarly, Anne Mozley in 1869 objected to John Stuart Mill's *The Subjection of Woman* on the grounds that the average woman was constitutionally unfit for university education.[16]

The Victorians' ideas about menstruation furnish a remarkable example of the way in which scientific knowledge reflects, rather than determines, the moral biases of an era. More remarkable still is the almost total disappearance, outside of scientific literature, of any explicit allusion to this large area of human experience, whose importance was in fact exaggerated by the prevailing superstitions, prejudices, misinformation, and medical opinion. Because the taboos so effectively prevented any frank discussions of a woman's normal experience, it is difficult if not impossible to estimate the real impact of menstruation on women's lives or on their society. Yet we should not fall into the error of believing that because it was not named, it was not there. Among the phenomena related to menstruation in the terms of Victorian science are: general beliefs of the age, such as women's inferiority and weakness; certain well attested social facts, such as widespread invalidism among women; and various literary commonplaces, such as illness resulting from emotional shock. It seems highly probable that their plausibility to the Victorians depended on the unspoken understanding that "the monthlies" were to blame.

4: Marriage, Redundancy or Sin

The Painter's View of Women in the First Twenty-Five Years of Victoria's Reign

Helene E. Roberts

ARTISTS HAVE LONG USED WOMAN'S BODY AS AN OBJECT. THEY HAVE REDUCED her image, nude or clothed, to volumes, textures and surface tones. Like peaches and pears, a woman's body allowed the attractive play of light and shade on a pleasing composition of curves, spheres and smooth surfaces. It not only titillated the erotic in man, but was in its very geometry aesthetically pleasing. The woman's body fitted much better than the man's into Hogarth's theory that curves were more beautiful than straight lines and into Winckelmann's theory that beauty consisted of continuity and smoothness. The male body might express character, as Winckelmann had put it, but only the female could achieve beauty.

This celebration of physical beauty might be fine for the pagan Greeks or the popish Venetians, but to the pious Victorians it suggested a too free indulgence of the senses. The Victorians shied away from the voluptuous flesh tones of the nude and even from the sensuous gleam of satins and jewels. There were some notable exceptions, as in the paintings of the nude by William Etty and William Frost, the spiritual but fleshy "stunners" of Dante Gabriel Rossetti, and the society portraits of A. E. Chalon, Charles Baxter, and Frank Stone. All of these painters emphasized the sensuous qualities of their subjects. Charles Baxter, in his painting, *The Sisters* (Plate 1), for example, typifies a Victorian pink and plump ideal of beauty.[1] The sister on the left is rather innocent and demure, but the other sister, with her loose gown slipping off her shoulder and her coquettish glance aimed at the viewer, is quite sensuously provocative. The lighting heightens the curves of her face, shoulder and partially exposed breast, and the disarray of their hair and the near embrace of the two figures adds further erotic overtones. The "Keepsake" annuals and gift books heavily exploited this sensuous vein in Victorian art, though they attempted to camouflage it with romantic and historical trappings. The sensual never totally disappeared, even from the walls of the Royal Academy, but it did give way, during the first twenty-five years of Victoria's reign, to the more elevated refinements of sentiment. Indeed, the painters' use of women to stimulate the viewers' sentiments rather than their senses formed a major characteristic of early Victorian art.

This appeal to sentiment required that the painter renounce the tactile surface qualities of womanly beauty and emphasize the actions and the qualities of character which would awaken emotional interest in the viewer. Instead of merely showing a pretty girl in some mildly provocative pose, as Charles Baxter was doing, the artist who aimed to evoke sentiment must tell enough about the heroine's character to prove her worthy of regard. The artist must also involve the heroine in a situation in which her responses will win the viewer's sympathy. In other words, the artist must tell a story.

The problem of how to translate an event occurring in time to the spatial dimension of painting is a notoriously difficult one. Painters of scenes from history and literature have long grappled with it. The artist can only show one moment in time, his characters can only make one gesture or express one emotion, yet he must suggest a continuity of action. Little daunted by what might be thought impossible, Victorian painters became adroit at exploiting visual signs and contriving associative stimuli. They suggested the past and anticipated the future, they revealed well-hidden secrets and predicted impending doom. They led viewers through complex relationships and moral dilemmas commonly thought to be the province of the novelist. Painters relied heavily on the fact that the Victorian art public belonged to a literate society. Their middle- and upper-class audience at the annual exhibitions of the Royal Academy had read the same novels and poems. They easily recognized character stereotypes from minimal indications and eagerly filled in backgrounds to the actions represented. Often a familar image was all that was needed to release a flood of sentimental associations; at other times the painter provided such a maze of meaning-laden clues that he lost most of his audience. Review articles in the periodicals sometimes read more like a puzzle solution than a critical evaluation of a work of art. The amount of visual information in these narrative paintings required realism of style and high finish. The viewer must be able actually to read the title of the sheet music on the piano for it might hold the key to the whole message of the painting. Or the black border of the

PLATE 1

CHARLES BAXTER

The Sisters

[47

crumpled letter might be the necessary detail to bring a tear to the viewer's eye.

I WOMAN'S MISSION

Sentiment's favorite domain in Victorian times was near the warm cozy hearth of the home where the wife, sweet, passive and long-suffering, waited patiently for the return of her husband. Writers such as Mrs. Ellis had already clearly defined the woman's role: "The love of woman appears to have been created solely to minister; that of man, to be ministered unto. . . . As it is the natural characteristic of woman's love in its most refined, as well as its most practical development, to be perpetually doing something for the good or the happiness of the object of her affections, it is but reasonable that man's personal comfort should be studiously attended to."[2] Painters, too, depicted women busy ministering to their loved ones. George Elgar Hicks, in his *Woman's Mission: Companion of Manhood* (Plate 2), exhibited at the Royal Academy in 1863, shows the loving wife in her subordinate role of consoler to her grief-stricken husband.[3] The husband holds in his left hand the letter with the revealing black border. The crumpled envelope on the floor suggests the hurried anxiety with which he has torn open the letter. He covers his face with his hand to conceal his emotion. Perhaps the recently dead relative is represented in one of the pictures on the mantel where he rests his elbow. His wife, clinging to his arm, her upturned face full of loving concern, tries to comfort him. Even in his grief the husband neither turns to his wife nor leans on her; he is still the oak, she the vine. It is only in Sir John Everett Millais' *The Order of Release, 1746* (London, Tate Gallery), exhibited in 1853, that the wife shows her strength and the husband his dependency on her. But here Millais makes the woman of the lower class and sets the scene in another country and century. Perhaps most significantly of all, he chose Effie Ruskin for the model in this scene of most unnatural dependency. *The Order of Release, 1746* was painted a year before the annulment of Effie's marriage to Ruskin and two years before her marriage to Millais.

Hicks uses other details to show that the wife's concern for her husband's welfare is constant. On the table his mail is carefully arranged, a gleaming coffeepot and dishes have been readied for his return, a bouquet of flowers has been placed on the mantelpiece. The wife is no Baxter coy seductress, but a rather plain woman, her hair done simply and neatly, her dress a modest one befitting a dedicated wife

PLATE 2 GEORGE ELGAR HICKS

Woman's Mission: Companion of Manhood

and homemaker. The plain dark color of her dress reflects the light, but not in a fashion inviting to the touch, or revealing of a sensuous body underneath.

The qualities distinguishing this new Victorian heroine were different from those epitomizing the womanly ideal in paintings of the past. She lacked the spiritual intensity of a medieval martyred saint, the sexual directness of a Titian Venus, and the earthy solidity of a Rubens goddess. Neither did she display the playful eroticism of a Boucher coquette or the aristocratic elegance of a Lawrence portrait, but she did represent a sweetness, a gentleness, an earnestness and a definite domesticity of her own. "The women's pictures by Titian, Raphael, Rembrandt, Van Dyke, and Velasquez are magnificent as works of Art," said Millais, in many ways the most Victorian of painters, but he added, "who would care to kiss such women?" Few great masters of the past, he continued, had known "how to do justice to woman and to reflect her sweetness."[4] It was the sweet, passive, obedient wife, busy within her domestic setting, showing her concern and appreciation for her masculine protector, apprehensive for his comfort and safety, ever watchful of his reputation, that brought a throb of emotion to the manly breast of Millais and his Victorian contemporaries, and brought a new kind of painting to the walls of the Royal Academy. J. L. Tupper, writing on "The Subject in Art" for the *Germ*, expressed this new interest in domestic subjects when he asked "Why to worship a martyred St. Agatha, and not a sick woman attending the sick? . . . . Why to love a *Ladie in bower* and not a wife's fireside?"[5] The fireside, of course, did not eliminate the battlefield as a subject for the painter, nor did the contemporary wife in her suburban villa totally supplant the heroine from literature and history.

The major artistic event of the year, the annual exhibition of the Royal Academy, included well over a thousand works of art, most of them paintings. The more traditional subjects of landscape, portraits, history, religious painting and literary scenes continued to dominate the cluttered walls, but the domestic scenes of painters like Thomas Webster, Thomas Faed, George Smith, C. W. Cope, Frederick Goodall, and Hicks, chronicling the daily activities of women within the home, gained steadily in popularity. The *Spectator* in 1852 added the category "Domestic Pictures" in its review columns to cope with the increasing numbers.

"We English are unquestionably a domestic people, everything that partakes of home comforts and enjoyments is dear to us," writes a reviewer in the *Art Journal* of Winterhalter's *The Royal Family* in 1850.[6]

Even royalty shows a relaxed casualness within the family circle. Domestic scenes were set in the royal mansion and the humble rural cottage as well as in the suburban villa and the modest town house. The variety of activities is even greater. The early Victorians visiting the Royal Academy exhibitions could view the family at prayers, at interminable meals, on holiday at the sea, on picnics in the country, at birthday and wedding celebrations or just enjoying the domestic hearth. The return of the man from work, from war, from the sea or from a journey was a very popular theme. Sometimes the point of view will shift. When the artist takes the man's role we see the warmth and coziness of the home and the joyful welcome emphasized; but when he assumes the woman's, we see the anxiety and worry underlying her patient waiting. The woman has anxious moments, too, at the bedside of her sick child, but more often it is the pleasant activities which are chosen for paintings: the mother reading to her children, watching them play, dressing them, walking with them and instructing them in the ways of charity to the poor. Victorian paintings dealt with woman's role as guardian of social and cultural values less often than with her domestic role, but occasionally they did picture her reading to herself or to her children, playing the piano, singing or attending the opera.

The early Victorian artists were enthusiastic in their testimonials to domestic life. They infused family life with a healthy vigor and a pleasurable companionship, and made marriage a much more attractive prospect than did Mrs. Ellis with her tone of dutiful sacrifice. Children are enjoyed, played with, even spoiled, rather than repressed or disciplined. Despite the sentimentality of these paintings there is about them a strong sense of reality. They have a life and spontaneity that could only be achieved by those who believed in the existence of these domestic values. The sentimentality in the countless paintings of middle-class family life was no figment of the painter's imagination; it existed within many Victorian families. It was an ideal that was, in part, attained. Many Victorian memoirs tell of a happy childhood and a close family life that supports the reality suggested by these domestic paintings.

The seamy side of family life was avoided. The early Victorians, aided by the august and uplifting Royal Academy, found it better to ignore shameful shadows on their family ideal. There were no scenes at the annual exhibition of brutal husbands beating their wives, no seductions of housemaids by the master of the house, and hardly a hint of the oppressive restrictions on the life of a married woman. R. B. Martineau, to be sure, depicted the drinking and gambling husband, Augustus Egg reproved the erring wife, and C. W. Cope showed a neglectful mother reading a French novel. But these are very rare exceptions, and they do not probe the depths of vice and sin. Few paintings suggested that marriage could be anything other than unrelieved bliss. There was no indictment of marriage during this early period — nothing like Sir William Quiller Orchardson's sophisticated paintings of the 1880's, *The First Cloud* and *Marriage de Convenance.*[7] Perhaps Thomas Faed's *Faults on Both Sides,* exhibited in 1861, with its man and woman seated side by side in grim-lipped silence, suggests an occasional tension in marriage, but what Faed portrays is obviously only a lover's quarrel and one that will soon be made up, perhaps with the help of the dog anxiously watching them.[8] A slight difference of opinion, a slight quarrel — one in which the wife could perceive the greater wisdom of her husband and submit to his judgment — could easily be embraced within the orthodox view of family life. Less orthodox was J. L. Brodie's heroine of *The Last Resource* of 1853, who says, in effect, "I do not wish to marry," a heretical position for a Victorian woman. True the man she is refusing is a "stiff and formal looking gentleman, past the prime of life," and the extreme consternation of her parents at her refusal puts the painting in a comic vein, but this is her last resort, and she chooses to turn it down for the alternative of a single life.[9]

Few painters adopted the theme of the rejected suitor. The Victorian faith in marriage was too universal and too deep to question. Far more appealing to the painters was the suspense which the anticipation of a successful match could arouse, the pathos that could be coaxed from the theme of unrequited love, and the grief evoked by the bereavement of a widow. William Powell Frith of *Derby Day* fame, for example, painted at least two different compositions of *The Proposal,* while both Arthur Hughes and Frank Stone painted versions of *The Tryst.*[10] Many other painters depicted the course of courtship from first meeting to happy marriage. Even more touching were the scenes of postponed marriages and broken engagements. Arthur Hughes in *The Long Engagement* shows a curate, too poor to marry, clasping his fiancée's hands under a tree.[11] He is looking heavenward, perhaps attempting to console his impatient sweetheart with the recitation of the quotation which accompanied the painting:

> For how myght ever sweetness be known
> To hym that never tastyd bitterness?

Her sad eyes gaze reproachfully at her name "Amy" years ago carved so hopefully in the tree trunk and now, perhaps like her love, fading and becoming effaced by the encroaching ivy. The contrast of the lushness of the forest setting, the spreading ferns, the blossoming flowers, would make her extended maidenly existence seem even more unnatural to the Victorians so sure that being a wife was the beginning of a woman's life and that motherhood was its culmination.

One of the simplest and most poignant paintings of the theme of unrequited love is Millais' *The Wedding Card — Jilted* (Plate 3) of 1854.[12] It is the portrait of a girl who has just opened the telltale announcement of the title. Her eyes are clouding with tears at the realization of her loss. The subject, of course, could have been painted with the excessive sentimentality characteristic of some of his later paintings of children, but Millais has used restraint. The tears are only suggested, the emphasis is on the control the girl exercises over her emotions. The portrait is a realistic one: the girl, though far from ugly, has a firm chin and intelligent eyes suggestive of courage and will rather than the superficial beauty of the vain and frivolous. She is very different in conception from the sisters in the Baxter painting. Her anxious gaze suggests her loss is too great to express in a flood of tears.

Not all domestic paintings that advocated married life were equally discriminating. Some were a just and proportionate reflection of the pleasures of family life and evoked a true sentiment, while others overstated the case with a cloying sentimentality. The relationship of mother and child, for example, is one that is capable of engendering great warmth, affection and love. A true portrayal of this relationship has an appeal few can ignore. But the same sentiment, exaggerated, or inflated to a pretentiously high moral plane, can undermine the sense of truth and reality that was the aim of these domestic paintings. Take the attitudes shown by the reviewer toward Charles Robert Leslie's *Mother and Child* in the *Athenaeum* (No. 967, p. 480), 2 May 1846:

Here is, indeed, the exulting bounding joy of nature, as it exists today, — as it must have been whenever the mother's heart leapt at the contemplation of the round limbs and dreamy guileless face of her infant offspring. What an observer of life is Mr. Leslie! How sweetly the little hand is suffered to be nestled in the neck of the mother! What is *mere* Art where the holder of the brush is the wielder of an influence over the deeper seated moral feelings of our nature?

It is such expressions of exaggerated sentimentality that lay the Victorians open to charges of hypocrisy, for the same society whose "deeper seated moral feelings" could be so moved by the mere representation of a mother and child also permitted, through neglect and callousness, wretched slums where nearly half of those "dreamy guileless faces" died before they reached maturity.

PLATE 3   SIR JOHN EVERETT MILLAIS

The Wedding Card — Jilted

54]

Some Victorians could not endure the flood of paintings on court-ship, marriage and family life. Occasionally there is a hint that domestic scenes are trivial and empty, at least as subjects for paintings. The art critic of the *Saturday Review* (III, 475), 23 May 1857, questioned the justification of scenes like Cope's *Breakfast Time — Morning Games*. He also explained why he thought Cope and other artists continued to paint them in such large numbers: "His canvases are addressed to the *materfamilias*, and they gain the applause he is not ashamed to aim at. ... Was such an incident worth telling except, of course, on the chances (doubtless very considerable) of selling it? What aims at fifty thousand married ladies is sure to attract one bidder." He might also have said that what supported and protected the patriarchal family and made attractive the traditional woman's role within it, pleased the prosperous middle-class male patron as well.

II THE REDUNDANT WOMAN

Painters could represent the middle-class woman's life with a minimum of hypocrisy because, at its best, it could approximate the Victorian ideal. But who could idealize the miserable life of a slum woman and make it both acceptable to fastidious tastes and still recognizable? Rural poverty could be made to pass if doctored with large dollops of sentimentality. The early Victorian artist was quite willing to adapt the eighteenth-century picturesque rural scenes of cottage life to the nineteenth-century taste for romantic escapism. At the very time that England's newspapers were using the Royal Commission reports on children in agriculture and select committee reports on the Poor Law to reveal the dismal hovels, meager diets, the wide unemployment and the utter ignorance of the rural poor, the painters pictured rustic country-women happy in their cozy warm cottages or pastoral landscapes. To the Londoner, beset by smoke, crowded omnibuses and a hectic pace of life, the picture of a woman tending a cottage evoked a pleasing nostalgia of a happier England. The Victorians bought such paintings in droves. "These cottage firesides are coming in legion upon us," complained the *Art Journal* (n.s. IV, 167) in 1852, "a cottage-interior mania seems to have set in." The Victorians chose to ignore the facts of industrial England for an idyllic reverie of a bucolic cottage with a rosy-cheeked cheerful mother beaming over her tattered but happy children. It is one of the enigmas of Victorian character that a people so capable of sym-pathy, so benevolent, so earnest to do good, could so easily dissipate their energies in a sentimental tear over a patently false representation of contemporary life.

That the Victorians chose to ignore or to misrepresent unpleasant facts is no doubt partially due to their inability to resolve the ideals of political economy with the realities of both urban and rural poverty, but they had also inherited the idea from the eighteenth century and from Reynold's *Discourses* that art should represent nature as it should be, not as it is: the ideal and the general, not the real and the particular. The best of middle-class life exemplified their ideal and could be represented realistically; poverty and moral depravity were a different matter. Sordid tales were not thought to be the stuff of which high art was made. One must go to book and periodical illustrations by the Cruikshanks, John Leech, and "Phiz" to see the poor and the corrupt. The depiction of wretchedness and misery were not sufficiently ennobling for the walls of the Royal Academy. Social ills, though of course regrettable, were of transient interest; art was permanent. The purity of womanhood was one of nature's most blessed creations and it should not be sullied in paint. The artist, unlike the journalist or the novelist, did not grovel in filth. "Though we have our Newgate literature," pontificated the *Athenaeum* (No. 655, p. 401), 16 May 1840, "we are still happily, in Art, far from that state which, in the search after strong effects, permits the seeker to riot among all that is physically and morally monstrous, hideous and distorted." Nor did the newly affluent middle-class families who in large numbers made up the artist's new patrons wish to be reminded of the human misery upon which their prosperity flourished. "It is not the office of Art to present to us truths of an offensive kind," cautioned a reviewer in the *Art Journal* (n.s. IV, 173) in 1852, "these are abundant in every-day life and it is in Art that we seek refuge from them."

Only a few artists chose to present truths offensive to their potential patrons. Mrs. Hurlston, for example, in *The Women of England in the Nineteenth Century* exhibited at the Society of British Artists in 1852, pointed directly to the great inequalities in Victorian society by contrasting two views: one of rich, lavishly dressed, bejeweled women in an opera box, the other of a poor starving seamstress.[13] George Frederic Watts, George Smith, and Millais also represented distressed women, but none of these works hung at the Royal Academy. It required considerable resourcefulness to cast the representation of the social ills of women in a form acceptable to the official guardians of high art.

Richard Redgrave was the first and the most persistent in exercising this resourcefulness. Now better remembered as the co-author with his brother of *A Century of Painters of the English School* (1866), he was a frequent exhibitor between 1825 and 1883 and an important official in the government art schools. Redgrave painted numerous paintings of the social grievances of women, all of which were hung at the Royal Academy. They were even, on occasion, honored by being hung on the line. He succeeded because he emphasized the pathetic, not the squalid, quality of distressed women. His heroines, from the genteel poor or the impoverished middle classes, were clean, neat and pretty, his style was delicate and soft — the Mrs. Opie of painting, as one reviewer described him. He told pathetic stories about unfortunate women, but his paintings rarely express strong emotion or deep suffering. He asked for greater compassion and kindness for his heroines, but it is doutbful whether his paintings would evoke great feelings of guilt in the observer. More likely they produced an attitude of patronizing condescension, or at best a slight pang of remorse easily purged by a few tears and a soon-to-be-forgotten resolution to be kinder in the future.

Redgrave exhibited at the Royal Academy between 1840 and 1847 a series of paintings showing the plight of what the social critic W. R. Greg called the "redundant woman" — women not fortunate enough to marry, "who in place of completing, sweetening and embellishing the existence of others are compelled to lead an independent and incomplete existence of their own."[14] Due primarily to the emigration of men to America and the Commonwealth, an unusual number of women in England had no chance of entering that blessed state of matrimony so vividly depicted by Victorian painters. Greg quotes the population statistics of 1851 to show that of every 100 women over twenty, 57 were married, 12 were widows and 30 were spinsters. He also estimates there must be 1,248,000 women in England and Wales "unnaturally" single. What these women should do with their lives, especially when they needed some means of support, was a problem much discussed in books, periodicals and newspapers. A working-class girl could go into domestic service, find employment in a factory or shop or become a seamstress. In all of these the work was hard and tedious, the hours painfully long, the pay pitifully low, the treatment frequently harsh. Many took their chances with life on the streets. Even fewer alternatives were open to the educated middle-class girl. She could be a governess and not much else. Though the governess might be immune from physical maltreatment, her position had its own kind of degradation.

Redgrave's first painting on the theme of the redundant woman, *The Reduced Gentleman's Daughter,* was exhibited at the Royal Academy in 1840.[15] It depicted the embarrassment suffered by an impoverished gentlewoman applying for a position and being cruelly ignored and taunted. He selected his subject from an article in the *Rambler,* and dressed his characters in period costume, but the contemporary relevance was obvious.

In 1843 he exhibited *Going to Service,* in which a young girl leaves her home in a wagon for the unknown future of life as a servant; *The Fortune Hunter,* in which a young man forsakes his poor girl friend for a rich girl; and *The Poor Teacher* (Plate 4), his most famous painting.[16] In this picture the teacher or governess sits in her schoolroom sadly gazing at the floor. In her lap she holds the black-bordered letter she has been reading, and on the piano the piece of music she has been playing, "Home, Sweet Home," tells of where her thoughts are. There is a melancholy and tired repose to the beautiful young teacher, making her loneliness more poignant in contrast to the bustle and activity of the domestic scenes exhibited around her. The viewers probably brought with them a full background of what the life of a governess was like from the many novels in which she figured as a stock figure of pathos. Or like Redgrave himself, they may have had personal experience to draw from. His sister, Jane, had known the loneliness and misery that was the governess' lot. While a governess she had contracted typhoid fever, and had come home to die, still a young woman. In true melodramatic fashion a mysterious gentleman provided a bed of flowers for her coffin's final resting place. Redgrave painted four versions of this painting. In the one reproduced here (now at the Victoria and Albert Museum), he has painted in three young charges, considerably lightening the tone and mood. He did this at the request of his patron, John Sheepshanks, who was too tenderhearted to bear contemplating the homesick teacher alone in her classroom.

Redgrave next turned to championing the cause of the distressed needlewoman with *The Sempstress* of 1844, illustrating Thomas Hood's popular and affecting poem, *The Song of the Shirt,* and then with *Fashion's Slaves* of 1847 (location unknown). In the latter a lady of fashion lounging on a sofa, severely reprimands an exhausted and meek-looking young needlewoman who has arrived too late with the garment on which she has worked day and night. The woman of fashion points angrily to the clock, her scent bottle in her hand, her novel at her side, while the maid scowls at the unfortunate seamstress — "Pain waiting on the breath of exacting caprice" as one critic described it.[17] Redgrave is saying more than just "be kind to the poor seamstress." His use of the plural in the title implies the lady is also a slave, a victim of the false values of fashion and vanity. He might also have been critical, as

PLATE 4   RICHARD REDGRAVE

The Poor Teacher

were others, of the system whereby a seamstress would work twenty hours a day to provide the ball dresses for the fashionable season, and then would be without work and without food during the "off season."

Although sometimes praised for his moral intentions, Redgrave suffered criticism for his choice of subjects. These criticisms varied from accusations of "theatrical," "commonplace" and "trite" by the *Spectator* (XVI, 451), 13 May 1843, to the smug assessment of the *Athenaeum* (No. 1021, p. 552), 22 May 1847: "Praiseworthy as may be the motive which makes the language of his Art picture . . . injustice . . . , the taste for dwelling on such matters is, yet, not a sound one. Mr. Redgrave has employed himself on these for some years, but we doubt the policy of doing so for the reputation of his pencil. The end of Art is pleasure; and to dwell habitually on the dark side of humanity is to miss that end." Ironically, a decade later, when Redgrave had turned to landscape painting, critics showed a greater appreciation for his moral message. J. Dafforne, writing in the *Art Journal* (n.s. V, 205) in 1859, praised Redgrave for his "social teachings" and declared that "One of the highest aims of artists ought to be to make Art a teacher of moral, of social or of religious truths: it should offer 'line upon line, and precept upon precept' to guide mankind into the right way of living, of acting and of thinking."

Redgrave, though he noted improvements, was much affected by the misery and brutality of life seen on the London streets. He declared that his avowed purpose in painting *The Sempstress, The Poor Teacher, Fashion's Slaves* and other pictures was a moral one: "It is one of my most gratifying feelings, that many of my best efforts in art have aimed at calling attention to the trials and struggles of the poor and oppressed. . . . I have had in view the 'helping them to right that suffer wrong' at the hands of their fellow men."[18] Whether his art actually had some effect is debatable. Certainly any significant improvement of conditions for seamstresses or of governesses occurred only much later and represented the interaction of many forces. His contemporaries, at any rate, accorded him credit for helping to affect the shift in public opinion which, in large part, underlaid social change. The *Art Journal* claimed he was more effective in creating sympathy for the unfortunate than "a host of pamphleteers."[19] *The Sempstress* won a charming tribute from P. F. Poole, a fellow member of the Royal Academy. Poole wrote Redgrave upon seeing the painting: "Believe me, I think it is the most powerful for truth and touching from its pathos of any picture I have ever seen. Who can help exclaiming, 'Poor soul: God help her?' If any circumstances could make me wage war against the present social arrangements, and

PLATE 5   GEORGE FREDERIC WATTS

The Seamstress

make us go down shirtless to our graves, it is the contemplation of this truthful and wonderful picture."[20]

Ironically Poole's sacrifice of his shirts would have left the seamstress worse off than before. What she needed was to be paid a living wage for a standard day's work. The grinding necessity to work from twelve to twenty hours every day for earnings that would not provide adequate food nor comfortable lodgings was what made her life so hopeless. G. F. Watts in his painting, *The Seamstress* (Plate 5), painted about 1850, emphasized, more than Redgrave, this hopelessness and despair. Watts' seamstress is seated alone in a bleak and dingy room dimly lit by a single candle. The furniture consists of a bare wooden table and chair. A shirt lies in her lap. Her head rests in her hand, her hollow eyes stare blankly ahead of her. Her thin body is clad in a plain, shabby dark-colored dress. Watts touchingly suggests how debilitating and depressing is her hopeless situation. She evokes the same sympathy as did Thomas Hood's poem, *The Song of the Shirt*, which had inspired both Redgrave and Watts.

> With fingers weary and worn,
> With eyelids heavy and red,
>
> . . . .
>
> In poverty, hunger, and dirt
>
> Sewing at once, with a double thread,
> A shroud as well as a shirt.

Watts' painting goes beyond the pathetic. It depicts a suffering that can only be degrading, never ennobling. His emaciated woman resembles in feeling some of the starving elongated figures of Picasso's blue period. Watts is not merely telling a sad story with the help of a series of visual clues, nor is he depending on literary associations to provide a background of pathetic circumstances. He manages to impart, directly, a deep despair.

Watts painted two other pictures of distressed women at about the same time, *Under a Dry Arch,* which shows an old dying woman huddled in the only shelter an unfeeling world affords her, and *Found Drowned,* which shows a young suicide found near Waterloo Bridge (Compton, Watts Gallery). Both pictures reminded Victorians of that grim and harsh reality which was often the only alternative for many Victorian women to the ideal of domesticity. With these paintings Watts, like Redgrave, had hope of "arousing pity for human refuse."[21] Watts and Redgrave were the exceptions, however; most painters had trouble selling enough of their work to keep themselves and their families from a similar abject poverty. They could not paint pictures that their prospective patrons would not want hanging in their dining rooms. Middle-class Victorians could ruthlessly exploit the working woman but they did not want to be reminded of that exploitation.

III   THE FALLEN WOMAN

The appalling conditions of female employment pushed many young girls into still another grim harsh world, the world of prostitutes, mistresses and unwed mothers. The double standard and the stern unforgiving attitudes toward unwed motherhood frequently left no other choice to a woman than to sell herself on the street. Using the census figure of 42,000 illegitimate children born in the year 1851, William Acton estimated that one-twelfth of the unmarried women in England and Wales must have "strayed from the path of virtue." Police files in 1850 listed 8,000 known prostitutes in London and more than 50,000 in England and Wales.[22] The fallen woman, as Victorians liked to call the victim of seduction, though she represented a large and functionally important segment of Victorian womanhood, was hardly deemed an appropriate subject for art. The prudery and escapism that objected to depicting "the dark side of humanity" represented by *The Poor Teacher* would hardly condone representations of the sordid life of a woman of the streets, or even the luxurious sin of a kept woman. Redgrave was again the first one to exhibit a painting on this theme at the Royal Academy with his diploma painting of 1851, *The Outcast* (Plate 6), presented to the Royal Academy upon his election as full Academician.[23] *The Outcast*, a very melodramatic work, shows the stern and unforgiving father pointing to the open door as the daughter, hugging her illegitimate child to her breast, prepares to go out into the cold and snow outside. Her brother hides his head in his hands, one sister pleads with the father for mercy, another in despair clenches her fists against the wall. The letter on the floor doubtless has played its part in exposing the daughter's sin and determining her ruin. It is not obvious, as in other of Redgrave's paintings, that he means the young woman, beautiful and innocent appearing though she is, to gain the viewer's total sympathy. The picture may also serve as a moral warning to young ladies to avoid this path to disaster. Frederick Walker's mother and child wandering through the deep snow in *The Lost Path* of 1863 suggests a similar message.[24]

William Holman Hunt in *The Awakening Conscience*, exhibited in 1854, treated the subject of the fallen woman with much greater in-

The Outcast

genuity.[25] Given the Victorian context, the conception of this painting was brilliant. First he chose a theme familiar in Victorian art and dear to the Victorian moral sensibility — that of the sinner resolved to repent (the awakened conscience) — and applied it to a new subject, the fallen woman. Frequenters of Academy exhibitions would have remembered the theme. In 1849 Redgrave had exhibited an *Awakened Conscience,* showing a man who, upon the intercession of an angel, turns with horror from the cup of alcohol or of poison from which he had been about to drink. In 1853, the year before Hunt's painting was exhibited, the Royal Academy exhibition included an *Awakened Conscience* by Thomas Brooks showing a band of tramps reduced to remorse by the sight of a praying child. Spencer Stanhope's prostitute in *Thoughts of the Past,* exhibited in 1852, had shown signs of remorse, but not with the same symbolic complexity or religious intensity that characterized Hunt's *Awakening Conscience.* His repentant sinner, a kept mistress, starts up from her lover's lap with a sudden and deep pang of conscience. They have been sitting in front of the piano singing and playing "Oft in the Stilly Night" (*The Light of Other Days,* by Thomas Moore). The music is resting on the piano, its title prominently displayed. Hunt relied on the fact that the lyrics would be familiar to Victorian viewers and that they would link her remorse to a memory of a more innocent love in her past as suggested by the words of the song:

> Oft in the stilly night,
>   Ere slumber's chain has bound me,
> Fond memory brings the light
>   Of other days around me;
>   The smiles, the tears,
>   Of boyhood's years,
> The words of love then spoken;
>   The eyes that shone,
>   Now dimm'd and gone,
> The cheerful hearts now broken.

The music for Tennyson's song, "Tears, Idle Tears," from *The Princess,* lies on the floor further confirming the woman's troubled conscience and her nostalgia for the past.

> Tears, idle tears, I know not what they mean,
> Tears from the depth of some divine despair
> Rise in the heart, and gather to the eyes,
> In looking on the happy autumn-fields,
> And thinking of the days that are no more.

Motivated by these memories of her past, she experiences a revelation and resolves to escape. The large mirror reflects the fresh innocent greenery of nature; the bright sun invites her to flee away from her sinful existence into the clean healthy air. A cat under the table toys with its prize of a bird captured from the outside, as the "tigerish" man (as one commentator called him) has toyed with the soul of his once innocent mistress. The very wallpaper speaks in allegory — the corn and grapes of the design are being eaten by birds as the guardian Cupid slumbers. Even the painting's frame, with its marigolds and ringing bells symbolic of sorrow and warning, adds to the theme. The confusing motto, from Proverbs 25:20, becomes clear, once the state of mind of the heroine is understood: "As he that taketh away a garment in cold weather, so is he that singeth songs to a heavy heart."

The moral and religious message was further strengthened by the fact that Hunt exhibited this picture as a companion to the *Light of the World,* his famous painting of Christ with a lantern knocking at the firmly shut door, representing the soul of a recalcitrant sinner. He thus suggests spiritual communication as the source of his sinner's conversion, in addition to the emotional association suggested by "Oft in the Stilly Night." Hunt makes the girl's lover the unconscious transmitter of a divine message through his idle playing of a popular song. "My desire," said Hunt, "was to show how the still small voice speaks to a human soul in the turmoil of life."[26]

Hunt abandoned the sentimental pathos of Redgrave for the melodramatic depiction of the Victorian religious experience. His painting introduced a stronger moral and religious message. The viewer should no longer respond to the woman's plight with condescending pity but with righteous awe that a sinner has been punished, or with jubilation at the prospect of a sinning soul saved by repentance. The idea that redemption was possible for a woman who had fallen into the ignorant error of seduction or, worse, into the vile depths of prostitution, was in accord with the abstract preaching of the Evangelical, High Church, and Nonconformist doctrines. In the concrete, however, it proved a very difficult idea to accept. Mrs. Gaskell's novel, *Ruth* (1853), based on just such a theme, found a hostile reception. Gladstone accosted prostitutes in the street and brought them home to his wife for reclamation, but not without severe criticism. Even Hunt's painting of the stirrings of conscience in a guilty soul was thought eccentric and in bad taste. Some viewers were just confused; others, too impatient to read the complex symbolism of the painting, assumed it to represent a quarrel between brother and sister. Ruskin soon set them straight with his letter to *The Times* which praised the painting, analyzed the symbolism, and read its moral meaning into every detail.

Even to the mere spectator a strange interest exalts the accessories of a scene in which he bears witness to human sorrow. There is not a single object in all that room, common, modern, vulgar . . . but it becomes tragical, if rightly read. That furniture, so carefully painted, even to the last vein of the rosewood — is there nothing to be learnt from that terrible lustre of it, from its fatal newness; nothing there that has the old thoughts of home upon it, or that is ever to become a part of home . . . ? Nay, the very hem of the girl's dress, which the painter has laboured so closely, thread by thread, has a story in it, if we think how soon its pure whiteness may be soiled with the dust and rain, her outcast feet failing in the street.[27]

The critical reaction to *The Awakening Conscience* meant less to Hunt than his great disappointment when Annie Miller, the young model for the woman, failed so totally to comprehend the depth of its moral message. Annie, a very beautiful but unrestrained and uneducated young girl whom Hunt had rescued from the London slums, was to have turned art into life. Hunt made her his protégée, arranged for her to have lessons in elocution, dancing and deportment, and to be cared for and watched over during his two-year absence in the Near East. Upon his return he expected to find a changed Annie, metamorphosed by her lessons in decorum and the example of the *Awakening Conscience* into a prim, proper and submissive lady whom he would take as his wife. But Annie had too much spirit for that. In defiance of Hunt's instructions she kept company with a notorious rake and a fashionable prostitute, and she sat for Rossetti and Boyce, painters not approved by Hunt. Disappointed and angry at his inability to control Annie, Hunt finally admitted his failure: "If she cannot be preached to from the texts of her own bitter experience then she cannot be awakened at all."[28] The final irony is that it is not Annie Miller's face that stares out of the present painting. The original face had been too discomforting for the purchaser, Thomas Fairbairn, who requested that Hunt retouch it. Hunt did so with such excessive zeal that he completely obliterated Annie's face and repainted it with another's.

Though he failed in real life, in his painting Hunt had made a giant step. He had taken the fallen woman, the symbol for the Victorians of what was physically and morally monstrous, a creature unworthy to be represented in art, and elevated her into a religious, an almost saintly symbol — the woman taken in adultery, the Magdalene. She is the sinner whom Christ did not forget, the damned soul whom He helps to redemption.

At about the same time Rossetti tried to paint a similar moral theme from contemporary life in his *Found* (Plate 7).[29] Perhaps influenced by his friend William Bell Scott's poem, *Rosabell*, he chose to depict a drover bringing a calf to market in London and there, in the

PLATE 7   DANTE GABRIEL ROSSETTI

Found

early morning light, finding his former loved one. She is now a prostitute slumped in despair against an unyielding brick wall. The man attempts to lift her up, but she turns from him, averting her head, too full of shame to look into his face. Superficially this looks like a very Victorian moral tale, the sentiment of which any churchman would approve. True, it might not be in good taste to represent the subject at all, especially to show the prostitute in her bedraggled silks, fringe and feathers. But her obvious sense of shame should allow her ample motivation for repentance. However, there is something wrong with the picture. Rossetti could never finish it despite several firm commissions and intermittent attempts. His own attitudes toward women, even so-called fallen women, as seen in his personal life and in his poem, *Jenny*, were far more sympathetic than the smug reprimand to erring women that *Found* suggests. Furthermore, the composition does not work. There is good dramatic tension between the two main figures, their hands pulling against each other, her body straining, her head stubbornly turned, but the calf obtrudes, distracting the eye from the two main figures. If the calf is covered up, the composition has much greater strength and coherence. Why is the calf there anyway? Is it only to tell us that the man is a drover? His clothing suggests a rough country life; the calf could have been pushed into the background.

When Rossetti first began this picture he wrote his mother and specifically asking that they look for a brick wall and a calf, "a white heifer calf," for him to use as models. So apparently the calf was to be important, perhaps as a symbol for the prostitutes being brought to market to be bought and sold. But this reason is too obvious, too simple, too unimaginative, as a complete explanation. Could not Rossetti have given the calf such prominence in order to say something more about the prostitute? The poor struggling calf is in a cart, kept from moving by a halter on her head and a weblike net covering her whole body, a clear representation of entanglement and restraint. Could not the net and halter suggest the restrictions, the shackles, which the drover would impose on a wife to force her compliance and submission? It is a speculation, of course, but one not a variance with the look of harsh respectability of the drover. He looks very severe, in his high leggings closely buttoned up the sides of his legs and his smock primly adorned with tight regular rows of stitching. At the time Rossetti was working on this picture, Hunt was involved in his attempt to make Annie Miller conform to his mold of a proper young wife, but she preferred to choose a more casual and less restricted life that included a proscribed relationship with Rossetti. Was not Rossetti, in *Found,* commenting on that restricted

PLATE 8 AUGUSTUS EGG

Past and Present No. 1

PLATE 9   AUGUSTUS EGG

Past and Present No. 3

quality of married life that drove young girls into the freer, more exciting life of adultery or prostitution? Perhaps Rossetti was never able to finish *Found* because he could not make his message clear nor integrate it into his composition with the ingenuity Hunt had managed in his *Awakening Conscience.*

In 1858 Augustus Egg's clear condemnation of the adulterous woman proved a more congenial demonstration of the righteous morality of the orthodox. He did not allow the sinner sympathy or redemption; his was a stern moral lesson depicting the inevitable wages of sin. Like Hogarth whose moral tales were greatly admired for their message, if not for the candor with which they depicted sin, Egg chose to present his cautionary sermon in a series of paintings. Though now called *Past and Present No. 1* (Plate 8), *No. 2,* and *No. 3* (Plate 9), the paintings were originally exhibited at the Royal Academy with only a quotation, "August the 4th — have just heard that B—— has been dead more than a fortnight, so his poor children have now lost both parents. I hear she was seen on Friday last near the Strand, evidently without a place to lay her head. What a fall hers has been!"[30] The first painting (in point of time) pictures the scene of discovery of the wife's infidelity. The husband sits amazed and shattered by the secret that has just been revealed by the fatal letter he holds in his hand. The wife lies prostrate at his feet, her hands clenched above her head. Various symbols in the painting reflect the collapse of this ill-fated family. Their two little girls glance up from the house of cards they have been building, which now, in symbolic imitation of their real household, tumbles to the ground. An apple, cut in half, reveals a wormy core. On one side of the cold unlighted hearth, a portrait miniature of the wife hangs beneath a painting of the Fall, and on the other side the husband's miniature hangs beneath *The Abandoned,* the painting of a shipwreck exhibited by Clarkson Stanfield two years earlier at the Royal Academy.

The two other paintings in Egg's series occur at the same time, a fact which Egg cleverly communicates by the use in each scene of an identical moon and an identical wisp of cloud. In one of them, the two children, now grown to adolescence, lonely and despairing at the loss of both their parents, whose miniatures hang on *their* wall, gaze out their window at the cold impersonal moon. In the last painting, the wife huddles under one of the arches of the Adelphi, the pale thin legs of her illegitimate child protruding from under her shawl. She too looks up at the moon, no doubt full of anguish and remorse. But Egg allows no hope of repentance for the sinner this time. The wages of sin is death. The Adelphi arches under the Waterloo Bridge had become the symbol of

Women in the Victorian Age

last resort for the destitute and homeless before they cast themselves into the Thames. It is the same scene as that in Watts' *Found Drowned*. And Thomas Hood's well-known poem, *The Bridge of Sighs*, is also set under Waterloo Bridge, where

> The bleak wind of March
> Made her tremble and shiver;
> But not the dark arch,
> Or the black flowing river:
> Mad from life's history,
> Glad to death's mystery,
> Swift to be hurl'd — ·
> Anywhere, anywhere,
> Out of the world!

The viewer's eye is led out from the huddled figure under the arch straight along a path formed by pilings to the cold moonlit Thames lapping at the dark pier. Just as the viewer's eye irresistibly follows this moonlit path, so must the woman's despair force her down to a watery grave. This final journey to oblivion is ironically commented upon by the torn posters advertising "Pleasure Excursions to Paris — Return" and the tone of bitter humor is intensified by another poster advertising two plays with the titles, "Victims" and "A Cure for Love."

Egg's parable is cast in a tone of moral righteousness. There is little sympathy in the painting for the wife. One does not know what circumstances surrounded her adultery, but one does not need to know; such a monstrous act against the family could not possibly allow, whatever the circumstances, for much sympathy. Furthermore, her guilt is multiplied by the implication that she caused the death of her husband and the abandonment of her children to an unknown and doubtless cruel fate. An innocent girl seduced and led into a life of sin, like the woman in Hunt's *The Awakening Conscience,* might find forgiveness, but a wife and mother was a different matter. There is no thought that she deserves mercy or that the husband could have forgiven her and welcomed her back into his arms, thereby avoiding the multiple tragedy. A double standard which preached forgiveness for an erring husband would not tolerate such charity for a wife.

The sowing of wild oats by the unmarried man, or even the adulterous relationships of a married man, though not approved by Victorian moral standards, was in large part condoned by society. Ford Madox Brown, in a painting unfortunately never finished, was one of the very few Victorian painters to question the burdening of the woman with the greater share of guilt. In *Take Your Son, Sir* (Plate 10), the woman thrusts forward her naked child, demanding that responsibility

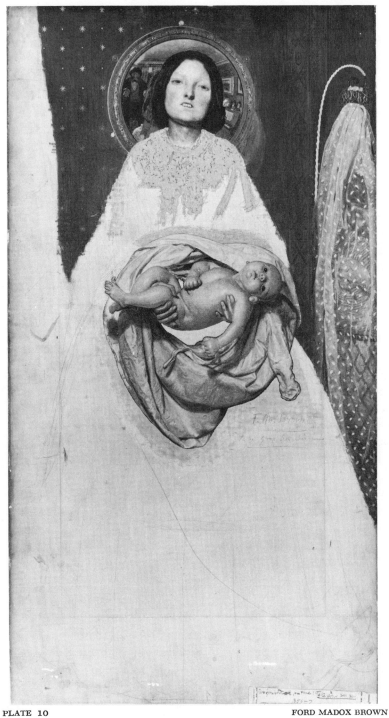

PLATE 10   FORD MADOX BROWN

Take Your Son, Sir

74]

for the conception of the child be shared.[31] The child, too, already a being who makes his own demands, gazes accusingly out from the picture, his unblinking glance claiming his paternity. The use of the traditional Madonna and Child composition for this unorthodox purpose is clever and brave. The mantle-like dress of the woman further suggests the Madonna; even the mirror reflecting the man she is confronting, doubles as a halo. The drapery encircling the child and the force of his movement toward the viewer makes it seem as if the child has been newly plucked from his mother's womb. This is one of the few paintings that directly confronts the audience with its moral charge. It allows no sentimental out, no smug cliché. What a pity it was never finished, exhibited or reviewed.

If the paintings of contemporary life which hung on the walls of the Royal Academy during the first twenty-five years of Victoria's reign provided the only extant evidence of what women's lives were like during that period, we should have to believe that nearly all women were contentedly involved in ministering to the comforts of their husbands and children. They might spare a few brief moments from their busy life for books or music, but basically their myriad domestic duties and pleasures were all-encompassing and deeply satisfying. In the painter's view the middle classes exemplified the domestic values best, the rural poor were the happiest of all classes, and the industrial working classes existed not at all. The few women not married were either eagerly anticipating that blessed state or were deploring the pathetic circumstances in which life without a male protector had left them.

This view had a very rough correspondence to reality, but it left out a great deal. Some of the fondest memories of Victorians, no doubt, centered on family life, but Victorians became blind to how restricting a role this could be to women and how harsh were the alternatives to it. The Royal Academy accepted few paintings that threatened the precarious logic of laissez-faire or the carefully cultivated myth that dominance was the natural right of the male.

The Victorians seemed to have a compulsive necessity for seeing the world as they wished it to be. They preferred to view the comfortable refuge they had created in their middle-class homes rather than that coarse and brutal working-class life that many had so recently climbed out of. They preferred to see their happy and contented wives in their setting of affluent materialism rather than the miserable seamstresses and victims of the harsher workings of political economy. Most of all, they preferred to see the sweet and innocent wife who evoked their strongest moral sentiments rather than the wicked women of the Battersea pleasure gardens who led even proper Victorians into sinful transgressions.

A few painters tried to break the pattern, to present a different view of what it was like to be a woman in early Victorian England, but their paintings did not win high favor at the Royal Academy and all of them turned to other subjects. Redgrave left the championing of the redundant woman and painted pleasant landscapes peopled with happy laborers or pious worshippers on their way to church. Watts retained some of his social consciousness but expressed it in allegorical terms, while Brown turned to history painting and other themes in contemporary life. Hunt found it easier to preach his moral sermons in Biblical settings, and Rossetti expressed himself with much greater eloquence and compassion in his poem, *Jenny,* than in *Found.* Nevertheless, the paintings of these men, while few in number, did constitute a more serious and moral view of women than the orthodox domestic role admitted.

The Victorian artist may have emancipated his heroine from being a sensuous object, the role woman had played throughout much of art history, but he firmly chained her to the hearth in a role even more restricting. He made the role as attractive as possible, and he pictured the alternatives as grimly as the fastidious sensibilities of the Royal Academy would allow. The message was clear:

> Man for the field and woman for the hearth:
> Man for the sword and for the needle she:
> Man with the head and woman with the heart:
> Man to command and woman to obey;
> All else confusion.
>
> Tennyson, *The Princess.*

5: A Study of Victorian Prostitution and Venereal Disease

E. M. Sigsworth and T. J. Wyke

TO READ MOST HISTORIES OF BRITAIN IN THE NINETEENTH CENTURY, EVEN those which purport to be written by social historians, is to gain the impression that the Victorians procreated by some form of remote control.[1] One would rarely imagine that they were sexual animals or that their sexuality expressed itself, both in and out of marriage, with an abundance and catholicity of taste which causes one to wonder how they acquired a reputation for respectability and rectitude. That in their literature they were sedulous propagators of their own mythology; that the Victorian novel, for example, rarely has anything explicitly to do with sex;[2] that euphemisms concealed reality so that prostitution was "The Social Evil" and gonorrhea and syphilis were "The Contagious Diseases" or "The Social Diseases," all help to explain the perpetuation of that reputation. What is less clear is why historians should until recently have failed to take into account the abundant evidence to the contrary. Prostitution and venereal disease were the subject of repeated Parliamentary inquiry. Those who wished to repeal the Contagious Diseases Acts of 1864, 1866 and 1869 published at least 520 books and pamphlets on these topics, while those seeking to maintain and extend them generated a comparable flow.[3] Between 1870 and 1885, 17,367 petitions against the Acts bearing 2,606,429 signatures were presented to the House of Commons, and during the same period more than 900 public meetings were held by supporters of the repeal campaign, matched again by meetings held by their opponents.[4] Since these meetings were often very fully reported in the press, an additional flow of information was readily available for an even wider public. While the quantity of evidence may not be matched for the years preceding and following those when the Contagious Diseases Acts were at the center of public controversy, prostitution and its causes and particularly those effects which resulted in venereal disease were frequently dealt with in works which though primarily medical were by no means confined to a medical audience. Of these the best known is, of course, by William Acton.[5] Earlier works include Ryan, Tait, Talbot, and the important article in the *Westminster Review* in 1850.[6] Very important and reviewed extensively was *De la Prostitution dans la Ville de Paris* by A. J. B. Parent-Duchâtelet, designated as the "Newton of Harlotry."[7] The first edition in 1836, however, dealt only with Parisian prostitution, the section on "La Prostitution en Angleterre" being added by Gustave-Antoine Richelot in 1857. At a more popular level, there was, a little later in 1861, the well-known section by Bracebridge Hemynge on London prostitution in volume IV of Mayhew's *London Labour and the London Poor*. In addition, the amount of material directed at doctors through their professional journals far exceeded that published for a wider audience.

I

Trying, as did contemporaries, to measure the number of prostitutes in nineteenth-century Britain is an exercise comparable in futility with attempts by theologians to estimate the number of angels who could be accommodated on the head of a pin. Reliable estimates are impeded by the nature of the profession. Firstly, the problem of "clandestine" prostitution (emphasized by all contemporaries) is, by definition, statistically intractable. Secondly, it was widely acknowledged that the numbers of prostitutes fluctuated inversely with the state of trade and employment. Thirdly, within these longer-term fluctuations, there were also seasonal variations in the numbers of prostitutes.[8] Most observers deal only with London, acknowledged to be the place to study "la prostitution anglaise. C'est la son centre naturel."[9] Occasionally estimates were made of provincial prostitution, which was found almost overwhelmingly in urban centers. Colquhoun in 1797 estimated that there were 50,000 London prostitutes.[10] Talbot, Ryan and the Bishop of Oxford all place the figure at 80,000 in the late 1830's and early 1840's.[11] Whitehorne, in 1858, opined that one sixth of unmarried women between the ages of 15 and 50 were prostitutes — an alarming figure of 83,000.[12] These figures, however, are little more than guesses repeated by one writer borrowing from another as though repetition would establish credibility. As for the country as a whole, the *Westminster Review* on different occasions placed the numbers at 50,000 and 368,000.[13] The latter figure, were it valid, would have made prostitution the fourth largest female occupational group.[14] Apparently more conservative were the police estimates:

Police Estimates of Known Prostitutes[15]

	London	England & Wales
1839	6,371	—
1841	9,409	—
1857	8,600	—
1858	7,194	27,113
1859	6,649	28,743
1860	6,940	28,927
1861	7,124	29,572
1862	5,795	28,449
1863	5,581	27,411
1864	5,689	26,802
1865	5,911	26,213
1866	5,554	24,717
1867	5,628	24,299
1868	5,678	24,311

These, however, relate only to prostitutes known to the police and, as Hemynge commented of the 1857 Metropolitan figure, "this is far from being even an approximate return of the loose women in the Metropolis. It scarcely does more than record the circulating harlotry of the Haymarket and Regent Street."[16]

Attempts to measure provincial prostitution provide for Edinburgh various repeated estimates. Knox in 1857, repeating Tait's estimate of 1840, suggested that there were 800 "open" and 1,160 "secret" prostitutes (p. 231). Logan in 1871 repeats exactly the same figures.[17] Robinson, however, with an apparent display of independence, put the total at 1,700, of whom 600 were either "sly" or "occasional."[18] For various other northern towns, Logan suggested that in Leeds in 1840 there were 700 "harlots" (p. 32), while in Manchester there were about 1,500 (p. 35). In Bradford in 1851 there were 130 prostitutes known to the police and 2,249 in Liverpool in 1869.[19] The impressionistic picture conveyed by these estimates emphasizes that prostitution was predominantly a London trade though paradoxically at first sight, legislation sought to deal neither with London nor the other large towns for which contemporaries obtained estimates.

Given the unreliability of the statistics, one cannot say whether the incidence of prostitution was increasing or decreasing during the nineteenth century or compare that century with other periods. It nevertheless seems clear that Victorians in the 1840's and 1850's thought that *both* prostitution and venereal disease were increasing. This opinion arose partly from concern at the increasingly visible evidence of prostitution in London streets, which was frequently the subject of complaint in *The Times*.[20] Albert Smith, writing in *Household Words* (XVI, 264), 12 September 1857, depicted vividly the nightly saturnalia in the Haymarket and Piccadilly. The Gardens at Cremorne and Vauxhall, the Argyll Rooms and various dancing rooms were notorious haunts for prostitutes.[21] Acton, after his "pilgrimage" to the Ratcliffe Highway complained of the "modern plan of these public-house amusements enabling the mechanic, his wife and his daughters, to rationally spend the evening," but, alas, to be exposed to witnessing "the vicious and profligate sisterhood flaunting it gaily ... accepting all the attentions of men, freely plied with liquor, sitting in the best places, dressed far above their station, with plenty of money to spend and denying themselves no amusement or enjoyment, encumbered with no domestic ties, and burdened with no children ... this actual superiority of a loose life could not have escaped the attention of the quick-witted sex" (1870, pp. 23-24). Elsewhere, "between Spitalfields and Bethnal Green ... a market for the hire of children is held on Mondays and Thursdays between 6 and 7 A.M. ... A father or mother brings her child to the market! They cry them like common merchandise ... they deliver them ... to the dissolute equally as to the master of regular habits" (Knox, p. 29). The additional and international implications of this sector of the market were later revealed in dramatic detail.[22] On the Ladies' Mile of Rotten Row, possibly less esoteric tastes were titillated by the high-class whores who in brougham or on horseback were scandalizing polite society.[23] Acton asked, "Is society growing more virtuous? Is it not quite the reverse, and patent to everyone that there is a change passing over it, and that not in the right direction?" (1870, p. 299.)

Contemporary impressions in themselves prove little about the real incidence of prostitution. There were, however, added reasons why the mid-Victorians thought that prostitution was actually increasing. Ever conscious of the material precepts of political economy, they tended to look at the question as a market situation in which forces operated on the sides of supply and demand.

As to supply, contemporaries pointed to certain expanding classes of female employment — women in the needle trades, shop-girls, domestic servants, women employed in factories or in agricultural gangs. Their common characteristic was to work long hours for low pay. The low wages were themselves the reflection of the lack of opportunity for female employment which sharpened the competitive forces while depressing rates of pay. Low earnings, even when employed, it was argued, presented a compelling temptation to supplement income with the receipts from prostitution. As a widowed slop-worker related to Mayhew in his investigations among needlewomen, "One of my boys was alive at this time and we really could not live upon the money. I applied to the Parish and they wanted me to go into the house; but I knew if I did so, they'd take my boy from me, and I'd suffer anything first. At times I was so badly off, me and my boy, that I was forced to resort to prostitution to keep us from starving."[24] When employment was not available, the compulsion was more acute: "During seasons of prosperity, debauchery is merely the trade of prostitutes by profession . . . but in times of distress . . . necessity alone has driven them to the streets" (Knox, p. 122). An unemployed fifteen-year-old girl related to the anonymous author of *My Secret Life:*

She said, "I buy things to eat; I can't eat what mother gives us. She is poor, and works very hard; she'd give us more, but she can't; so I buy foods, and give the others what mother gives me; they don't know no better, — if mother's there, I eat some; sometimes we have only gruel and salt; if we have a fire we toast the bread, but I can't eat it if I'm not dreadfully hungry." "What do you like?" "Pies and sausage-rolls," said the girl, smacking her lips and laughing. "Oh! my eye, ain't they prime, — oh!" "That's what you went gay for?" "I'm not gay," said she sulkily. "Well, what do you let men fuck you for? Sausage-rolls?" "Yes, meat-pies and pastry too" (Marcus, p. 107).

Apart from poverty itself, a further potent factor helping to swell supply was the environment of the urban poor who so often lived, loved, slept and died together in the overcrowded slums, devoid of sanitary amenities, with families living in squalid and packed houses in which children acquired from an early age intimate knowledge of the facts of life. In such an environment virginity was fleeting, fragile and cheap. As Mayhew commented, "The philanthropist may exert himself on their behalf, the moralist may inculcate even the worldly advantages of a better course of life, and the minister of religion may warn them of eternal penalties which they are incurring, but there is an instructor in mischief, of which they must get rid ere they make any real progress in their laudable efforts and that is THE SINGLE BEDCHAMBER IN THE TWO-ROOM COTTAGE."[25]

Should the girl have avoided, or emerged intact from, such influences there remained other dangers of exposure to corrupting forces at her eventual place of work. The young servant girl who came to London or to another large city from the countryside was regarded as being especially vulnerable, removed from her family and exposed perhaps to the attentions of male members of the household, with whom her bargaining position was obviously weak.[26] The factory girl, employed for long hours in hot and crowded conditions in circumstances which Victorian moralists commonly deplored, was exposed to different but also malign influences.[27]

It was not only the equation of poverty with prostitution which was stressed, but the "love of vanity" was sternly denounced: "If I seek to number the operative courses other than passion of the woman, I am met on the very threshold of the task by vanity, vanity, and then vanity — for what but this are love of dress and admiration and what sacrifices will not tens of thousands of the uneducated make to gain these?" (Acton, 1857, p. 21.) The theme was echoed by a Plymouth doctor: "As a medical man, I will give my opinion as to what encourages prostitution; idleness and the love of finery. Some girls won't work if they can help it; they will take the easiest way of obtaining money and they will have their dress; they must have their false hair . . . and their long trains to their dresses like their mistresses."[28]

Immediately below the overtones of moral censure lies the recognition of the extension of economic motivation — a choice between the limitations of available and socially sanctioned occupations and the attractions, short run though it might be, of prostitution. What may have begun as the satisfaction of the basic need for food could after all generate the idea that the other and less basic desire for fancy clothing could equally be obtained by hiring out one's body, especially when its price is a function of its attractiveness.

As to whether, having hired it out, the female body provided a bonus of sexual pleasure, opinions varied. The *Westminster Review* (1850, pp. 456-457) was clear about women being sexually inert:

Women's desires scarcely ever lead to their fall for the desire scarcely exists in a definite and conscious form, till they have fallen. In this point there is a radical and essential difference between the sexes: the arrangements of nature and the customs of society would be even more unequal than they are were it not so. In men in general the sexual desire is inherent and spontaneous and belongs to the condition of puberty. In the other sex, the desire is dormant, if not non-existent, till excited by actual intercourse. . . . If the passions of women were ready, strong and spontaneous in a degree even remotely approaching the form they assume in the coarser sex, there can be little doubt that sexual irregularities would reach a height, at which, at present, we have happily no conception.

Later, Acton echoed: "I should say that the majority of women (happily for them) are not very much troubled with sexual feeling of any kind," and, allowing for aberrant exceptions ("nymphomania, a form of insanity"), had no doubt, "that sexual feeling in the female is in the majority of cases in abeyance . . . and even if roused (which in many instances it never can be) is very moderate compared with that of the male."[29]

Quite apart from subsequent revisions of the nature of women's sexual responses and appetites which indicate an entirely contrary point of view,[30] several important qualifications need to be made. Firstly, not all contemporaries were agreed about the essentially passive sexual role of women. Thus, a correspondent in *The Times*, 4 November 1847, wrote, "One would really think, to listen to some sentimentalists, that man alone derived any sensual gratification from these indulgences, and that there were no animal passions in woman to tempt her in the same direction. Women yield, not to the solicitation of men, but to the solicitations of their own impure desire; they are, and must be, perfectly well aware of the consequences of a want of chastity, but in the pursuit of pleasure they choose to shut their eyes to them." Secondly, there appears to be a good deal of confusion about the categories of women to whom a lack of sexuality is attributed. It is thus not clear whether passivity is simply inherent or is shed after experience of sexual intercourse. On the other hand, prostitutes and mistresses are placed in a quite different category compared with married women:

Many of the best mothers, wives and managers of households, know little of or are careless about sexual indulgences. Love of home, children, and of domestic duties are the only passions they feel.

As a general rule, a modest woman seldom desires any sexual gratification for herself. She submits to her husband's embraces, but principally to gratify him; and, were it not for the desire of maternity, would far rather be relieved from his attentions . . . the married woman has no wish to be placed on the footing of a mistress (Acton, 1865, p. 113).

If one follows Marcus' interpretation of Acton (pp. 29-32), then another dimension of confusion would be introduced, since he suggests that Acton may be distinguishing between the degree of sexuality of "working-class females" as opposed to women drawn from other social classes. The justification for this view, however, seems to be fragile and its satisfactory demonstration would require far more evidence than he adduces.

Victorian opinion on the innate sexuality of women was cloudy and divided so that its contribution to the causes of prostitution must remain doubtful, but one also encounters divided opinions about the role of seduction as a cause of prostitution. It was, however, generally held that women were particularly vulnerable in certain types of employment, such as domestic service. Consistent with his belief in the sexual passivity of the female, Acton was clear that the act of seduction was essentially initiated by the male (1857, p. 173). Seduction, generally considered to be a male act, was at times seen as the first step which led the victim to the streets: "In London there are now hundreds of such women in every phase of degradation, whose history is comprised in these words: seduction — desertion — prostitution."[31] The prevalence of this viewpoint led both to an attack on the unbridled exercise of male lust and to calls for reinforcing existing legislation against it.[32] "She falls! And for man's mere passing pleasure is irretrievably ruined! Surely there must be something grossly, radically wicked in the ethics of society which permits the vice — too often the villainy — of man to pass unnoticed and unpunished, and allows his triumph over weakness to depress his victim into an abyss of misery. The hard-hearted cruelty of the world's sentence is transparent to the eye of equal justice. The gratification of his animal passions — the natural passions implanted in him — alone is man's excuse; and can such a plea for crime be listened to? What sin is there which may not find a justification on such terms as these?"[33] In spite of such rhetoric, other writers insisted that seduction was rarely the cause of prostitution. Robinson, in 1866, assigned it an inferior causal role,[34] while a later article in the *Lancet* (II, 535), 30 September 1882, was even more definite: "A great deal of arrant nonsense is talked and written about 'seduction' and the 'betrayal of women.' Practically, not a tithe of the young women alleged to be led astray *are* so conducted into the paths of vice."

Needless to say, contemporaries found a variety of other contributory causes.[35] Following the work of Marcus, it is hardly surprising to find that a readily available supply of pornographic books and — a side effect of technological advance — of photographs and pictures receives its share of blame: "The traffic in obscene pictures and books in England is no less remarkable. Commercial houses . . . are exclusively devoted to this kind of merchandise. . . . Numerous hawkers spread these pictures and books all over the kingdom. Boarding schools for girls and boys were infested with them. . . . Now, thanks to associations for the suppression of vice, the traffic is not carried on so openly but it still subsists, through the windows of a great number of shops, principally tobacco shops in populous quarters, the most licentious and exciting pictures are exposed to view. . . ."[36] It was also argued that deliberate efforts to augment the supply of prostitutes were made by brothel keepers and others. "White slavery" in reverse procured a supply for the "first-class houses" and, "as if it were a legitimate commerce, the masters of these houses contract with country carriers for the girls they bring to town at so much per head" (Knox, pp. 86-87). Such testimony followed repeated attempts to introduce legislation to diminish the practice of procurement culminating in "An Act to Protect Women from Fraudulent Practices for Procuring Their Defilement," which prescribed a maximum sentence of two years with hard labor, but which seems to have been ineffective.[37] There was in fact no complete agreement about the primacy of any single cause, and it is difficult to see how there could have been, given the impossibility of assigning any form of quantitative measurement. Prostitution was a social phenomenon of which the causes were numerous and varied, complex and sometimes interdependent. It is true that on occasion one finds a writer stressing the primacy of one cause or another, but no mono-causal explanation was then offered.

II

On the demand side of the market, no doubts surrounded the existence of the male sexual appetite comparable to those which questioned the sexuality of women. The essence of the problem was how to gratify those appetites in situations in which either because of social or institutional pressures marriage was deferred or, after marriage, if the wife proved — as so much contemporary opinion declared to be the case — sexually inadequate and unsatisfying to her husband.

For middle-class men, there is a repeated body of opinion that the deferment of marriage was increasing and this increasing gap between the onset of puberty and morally sanctioned sex in marriage, given the undoubted sexual appetite of the male, was causing an increase in the demand for female prostitutes. The *Lancet* (I, 137), 5 February 1853, analyzed the problem in the following terms:

> There is more celibacy . . . the more luxuriously civilised a state becomes, the stronger is engendered in its individual members the feeling of the "necessity of keeping up appearances." The more luxuriously civilised that state, the more numerous and diverse are the circumstances which constitute such "appearances." Now, from the difficulties and expenses attendant upon the procurance of them, and the odium attached to a fall off from their exhibition, or loss of caste, the single man finds quite enough to do to procure them, and "keep up appearances" for himself, and dreads the embargo of a wife and family, increasing as they would not only the "appearances," but the odium he would suffer if unable to maintain them.[38]

The consequences of this extended celibacy were, argued the *Lancet*, either a resort to prostitution or "another evil resulting in the abomination of prematurely exhausted powers."[39] This view, aimed at a medical audience, was subsequently given wider publicity, though without reference to the alternative of masturbation, in an often quoted letter to *The Times*, 9 May 1857, by "Theophrastus."[40] A clear and vigorous view of the implications of socially enforced celibacy was stated by J. C. Whitehorne (p. 20):

We forbid a wife except to very few gentlemen, and to the very many gentlemen, the harlot has taken her place. Thousands of legal and medical students and the junior members in both professions are living in sin more or less systematic. To a great extent it is they and their fellows in other professions and trades who, I firmly believe, pay and keep going the harlotry that meets us in the streets of London, flaunting and defiant. Our harlots exist in the numbers they do in London because young gentlemen and young ladies cannot and dare not marry without ceasing to be gentlemen and ladies. . . .

Aside from the alleged growth in demand from the unmarried males of the middle classes, the *Lancet* (I, 137) 5 February 1853, also recognized that there existed another important source of demand — the army and the navy — for whom legislation rather than social pressure dictated celibacy. "If prostitution does and will exist in civil life amongst *celibats*, to hope or believe that soldiers and sailors, healthy, vigorous men, will refrain from promiscuous sexual intercourse (for the majority are not allowed the chances of any other) would be a dream of Utopia."

The demands of married men for the services of prostitutes receive relatively much less attention in contemporary literature than those arising from the plight of the enforced celibate. Yet it would seem likely that they too formed an important element in the demand for prostitutes. For the relatively wealthy classes, the common phenomenon of dynastically or economically arranged marriages would be likely to lead to situations of mutual sexual dissatisfaction, especially if, as contemporary mythology had it (Whitehorne, p. 7), "the woman regarded her sexual role as one of duty rather than of pleasure." Further, during the previous period of "enforced celibacy" the husband might well have become a client of prostitutes who, if their power for sexual gratification was indeed superior to that of the wife, would very likely continue to exercise an attraction after marriage. It must also be remembered that marriage, whether sexually harmonious or otherwise, was, once contracted, difficult to end by divorce. The divorce rate, though rising after 1857, still remained very low.[41] A vivid light is shed on extramarital accommodation by the following report:

In a recent examination of a man named D——, before the Court of Bankruptcy, Birmingham, the bankrupt stated (and had entered the expenses in his schedule), that he was constantly in the habit of visiting brothels . . . and that, among numerous items of a most extravagant nature, there appeared one of £2,000 a year for a kept mistress. Mr. Smith, the solicitor for the bankrupt, stated publicly that "if the examination be pursued, parties now living in happiness with their families may be brought before this court for examination, and disclosures made which must inevitably ruin their domestic peace. Some men in this town, respectable in their stations, must have their names brought before the world as visitors of a brothel. . . . The persons I refer to are holding important positions in the town and, as I am anxious to avoid such disclosures, I would rather throw up the case . . . than proceed."[42]

It is interesting also that contemporary literature deals mainly with the demands of middle-class men, with the important exception of the armed services. That a working-class demand also existed cannot be doubted, given the frequency with which prostitution is associated with drinking, and especially with the beer-houses which after 1830 catered to the thirst of the working man. (Henriques, III, 11-44, 146-173) Nevertheless, prostitution may have been less commercialized insofar as the environmental factors which were said to foster sexual immorality may well have meant that working-class men had less need to purchase what was freely available. It is difficult to resist the impression that prostitution resolved itself into a physical expression of the class structure of Victorian society. While all the available evidence points to a supply of prostitutes drawn from the working classes, the demand upon which contemporary opinion concentrated came from the wealthier classes of society. Working-class men contributed to demand, but middle- or upper-class women hardly contributed to supply! The class bias of the market was recognized by Acton:

It cannot be denied by anyone acquainted with rural life that seduction of girls is a sport and a habit with vast numbers of men, married . . . and single, placed above the ranks of labour . . . Many such rustics of the middle class and men of parallel grades in country towns employ a portion of their spare time in the coarse, deliberate villainy of making prostitutes. . . . Men who themselves employ female labour, or direct it for others, have always ample opportunities of choice, compulsion, secrecy and subsequent intimidation, should exposure be probable and disagreeable . . . With these and with the gentlemen whose *délassement* is the contamination of town servants and *ouvrières*, the first grand engine is, of course, vanity . . . (1875, p. 175).

Prostitution not only satisfied the sexual appetites of the middle-class male, it also performed the important social function within the context of the Victorian family of preserving the virgins of the wealthier classes and shielding their married women from the grosser passions of their husbands, though of course at a considerable risk of infection with venereal diseases.[43]

The toleration of prostitution is reflected in the absence of any serious legislative attack on the problem until the Contagious Diseases Acts of 1865-1869 which, with the aim of curtailing venereal disease among the armed forces, attacked the problem by arresting and if necessary detaining in hospital infected prostitutes. The existing laws did not recognize the act of prostitution itself as a crime but only solicitation and the creation of a public nuisance, whether the latter was by the prostitute or the brothel keeper.[44] Further, attempts to enforce the law with any rigor were inhibited by the numerical inadequacy and on occasion corruption of the police (*The Times*, 24 June 1841), to say nothing of the unwillingness of the offended party to take legal action which might impugn his sexual morality. At times, of course, a public outcry against the openness of prostitution brought a burst of police action.[45] Attempts to alter the legislative status quo were largely unsuccessful, foundering upon the opposition to legislation against prostitution either because it would entail state recognition of a vice, or because the effects of prostitution provided a divinely sanctioned punishment for sexual sin far more terrible than the law could provide. Thus, in introducing the second reading of "A Bill for the More Effectual Suppression of Brothels and of Trading in Seduction and Prostitution," the Bishop of Exeter was very explicit:

There was nothing in the Bill that had any relation whatever to the suppression of prostitution. In saying this, it would not be imagined that he looked on prostitution as a light evil, but this he could say, he did not think it was a matter for legislation — the punishment of prostitution he held to be a thing impossible, and why was it impossible? He had no notion that the wisdom of man could devise a punishment that should inflict so much of suffering and degradation as prostitution itself. . . . He held prostitution to be an awful punishment in itself, which the God of Mercy had designed in order to terrify innocent females from falling into these tremendous evils which were appointed as a punishment for the violation of chastity (Hansard, 3S, LXXV, c.878, 14 June 1844).

The only occasion on which the law attempted to affect the demand by men for the services of women dealt, in fact, with the act of procuring rather than the rescue of the prostitute (Whitehorne, p. 58).

Rather than legislative action contemporaries favored other remedies of a general moral kind to curb demand for prostitutes:

We differ completely, it will be seen, from those who call upon the Government to attempt by any special acts to regulate or repress prostitution. . . .

The grand battle, however, with prostitution must, we are convinced, be fought in the heart of man himself; there alone can the labour of regeneration be worked out. Instruct the young better to regulate their passions. Bring men to a true knowledge of what the thing called prostitution really is. Learn them to judge it as a crime and to shun it as a dishonour.[46]

General moral exhortation, however, was to be supplemented by the provision of morally preferable alternatives to which men could turn: "Public libraries, debating classes, chess clubs and educational institutions are the battlefields whereon these men should be taught, and indeed are being taught to fight against the flesh . . . gymnastic exercises, too, must not be forgotten."[47] Beginning with a general call for moral regeneration, women as well as men were included. For women, there was an added practical remedy, the provision of "Homes of Refuge" or "Female Penitentiaries" and "Redemption Societies," which sought to reintegrate the repentant prostitute into society by the application of a regime of frugal living and high thinking stimulated by a constant stream of religious instruction.[48] They were, however, small and financially weak. Those prostitutes with whom they succeeded were usually placed in domestic service, returning them to a way of life which the analysts of the causes of prostitution recognized as dangerous. Although well meant, such schemes did nothing to attack the causes of prostitution, and it is difficult to disagree with Acton's judgment that they were "but paltry, peddling scratches on the surface of evil."[49]

Having dealt with the general factors affecting the market for female prostitutes, it is important now to turn to a special aspect of the problem of prostitution in which the action and attitudes of authority helped to increase at once both demand and supply. It has already been pointed out that sailors and soldiers provided an important part of the demand side of the market because of their celibacy. The problem, however, was more complex than this suggests and was bound up with the nature of service life. In the army, barrack conditions were appalling. The evidence before the 1857 Army Sanitary Commission and the subsequent investigations revealed a mortality rate of soldiers double that of a comparable group in civilian life.[50] For this a large portion of the blame rested on barrack conditions — overcrowding, lack of ventilation and defective sanitary facilities. For troops living in barracks, for example, only 618 enjoyed correct and efficient ventilation, 32,540 men were exposed to deficient and defective ventilation and 42,589 resided in barracks in which no means of ventilation were provided at all (Barracks and Hospitals Sanitary Commission *Report,* 1861, XVI, 38). It is understandable that the troops were not attracted to stay in their barracks and sought alternatives. Quite apart from their physical defects, there was little to do in the barracks to dispel the ennui of long leisure hours.[51] In such circumstances the attractions of drink and women must have been singularly compelling: "Such is the character of the undercurrent of the camp, so far as the men are concerned, and their mode of spending their leisure time; and such is the character of the places to which they are in the constant habit of resorting. No system could be better imagined, or more successfully carried out, if the object were to sap gradually the health of the soldiers, to induce early debility and to hasten a premature death."[52]

Enforced celibacy was not required of all men. Though with regimental variations, the general rule was that six out of every hundred men were allowed to marry and to bring their wives to live in the barrack rooms. The soldier granted the privilege of marriage, however, received no extra allowance, and until 1857 no separate accommodation was provided for man and wife: "the evidence is, that they are provided for in different ways in different regiments; in some they are lodged in the rooms with the unmarried men, with no means of separation from them except a curtain suspended round the bed; in other regiments the married people are placed in barrack rooms apart from the unmarried men, but with several couples in the same room."[53] In such an environment, strongly reminiscent of the conditions of the civilian poor, the indiscriminate mixing of the sexes can hardly have raised the tone of sexual morality.

But what, it might be asked, of those troops unable officially to marry? The evidence is that they often did so unofficially. Their wives were necessarily lodged outside the barracks in accommodations which, again in the absence of an allowance, had somehow to be paid for. Exactly how doubtless varied, but in a situation in which large numbers of troops were, as argued above, forced into the streets in search of diversion, it would not be surprising to find these soldiers' wives augmenting the local supply of prostitutes or "camp followers" and becoming part of the general scene of licentiousness and depravity which characterized towns and villages in the neighborhood of barracks and camps publicized in *All The Year Round* in 1864: "there is, as I have shown, around every barrack and camp an outlying circle of misery and sin, a haunting spectre which holds up its withered hands in mockery of all the tinsel. It has never been otherwise; for wherever large bodies of men congregate, these elements of wretched creatures will be found whose life is a long sin and unceasing misery."[54] What was true of such army towns applied also, though for rather different reasons, to naval towns.[55]

Whereas little was done legislatively to attack effectively the problem of prostitution, its inevitable result, venereal disease, was the subject of a growing campaign for legislation. The *Westminster Review* (1850, p. 493) drew the distinction clearly, "Prostitution per se is a sin against taste, morals, and religion; but it is one of those vices, like bad temper, hatred, malice, and covetousness, which however noxious, it is not a part of the duty of government actively to repress or punish: the propagation of syphilis is an overt act of public mischief, a crime committed against society, which it clearly falls within their province to prevent." That this legislation sought to attack the problem only in selected army and naval towns, rather than in the large cities — especially in London — where prostitution was also rife, is partly explained by the special circumstances arising from service life and the high rates of venereal infection among a readily identifiable sector of society. Legislation was intended to reduce these rates of infection, but it was through the agency of the prostitute that it sought to operate.

III

The high venereal disease rates among soldiers and sailors were a matter for concern especially to the medical profession. Partly perhaps because of the inadequacy of known specifics in the attempted treatment of venereal diseases,[56] the medical profession began increasingly to turn its attention to the possibilities of diminishing the rates of contraction of the diseases by some form of legislated control. In the absence of any form of intervention by the government, the treatment of venereal disease had been left entirely to the doctors, hospitals, chemists and quacks, and in England and Wales there was only one hospital, in London, solely devoted to this end.[57] This contrasted strongly with the active role of some continental governments, especially in Belgium and France, where venereal diseases were controlled by a legislated system of police-supervised inspection of prostitutes coupled with a licensing system.[58]

The possibility of introducing comparable systems of control was first mentioned in the *Lancet*, in 1843, in a review of a book by Dr. H. Prater.[59] Three years later the *Lancet*, in a series of editorials, explored the question in detail. In the first two of these, the Belgian and French systems of regulation were examined and the point made that although, "There can be no doubt that they are arbitrary, so much so, indeed, that were they not directed, through motives of the purest benevolence, to the suppression of a severe and fatal disease, they would nowhere be tolerated for a moment. We, however, agree entirely with those who think that, in this case at least, the end to be obtained justifies the means" (21 March 1846, I, 339). Following Acton's paper on venereal diseases which drew attention to the statistics of venereal infection in the services and the civil population,[60] the *Lancet* (7 November 1846, II, 511) re-inforced its advocacy of government action without specifying its pre-cise form and with some pessimism:

We must no longer confine our attention to the drains and sewers; we wish to eradi-cate syphilis, and must not let it lurk in the dark corners. It is useless to brand it with infamy; it will only spread the more. It must be met like other evils; it must be investigated by scientific men; its consequences must be pointed out, and the best means of prevention tried. . . . It was a long time before the public became convinced how interested they were in improving the sewerage of towns; it will, we feel assured, be some considerable period before Government will even deign to investigate the consequences of syphilis. There is a *prestige* in favour of other sanitary measures which syphilis is far from obtaining.

In 1850 the cry for state action on continental lines was outlined more specifically in the *Westminster Review* (1850, p. 502), which recommended the appointment of a special department connected with the Board of Health to deal specifically with venereal disease. Its sug-gested activities would be "the establishment by authority of a sufficient number of Lock Hospitals, and the subjecting all prostitutes . . . to a periodical medical inspection, with the prompt sequestration or removal to the hospital of all who were found diseased. This measure might in time be followed up by extending the power of these special offices to the arrest and imprisonment of all prostitutes who should be found practising their occupation without certificate that they had undergone such medical inspection within a given time." Thus, fourteen years be-fore the government enacted the first Contagious Diseases Act, a clear call had been made for detailed regulations which were, at least in part, included in the Act. In the intervening period the government had con-fined its direct activity solely to the establishment of lock wards at Portsmouth costing £1,800 initial outlay and an annual grant of £500.[61] That legislative action failed to emerge earlier is explicable in terms of the lack of complete agreement as to its necessity or morality, and it is therefore important to consider the arguments of both sides — arguments which were to rage with increasing fierceness after the 1864 Act was passed.

In favor of intervention it was argued that the diseases were particularly insidious since they were spread by the guilty to the inno-cent: "Were the diseases merely to afflict those persons who have ex-posed themselves to contagion in the haunts of vice, it might be con-sidered merely a just punishment for moral depravity. But such is not the fact. The innocent victims of syphilis are infinitely more numerous than the guilty; for it is a disease which follows vice and crime down to 'the third and fourth' generations; syphilis in the parents being, it is generally considered, one of the chief causes of scrofula, pulmonary consumption and other fatal distressing diseases in their children."[62] This was the first point made by the *Lancet* in the opening of its campaign for action in 1846, and it was to be reiterated regularly in the following decades: ". . . it blights the infant in the womb, and contaminates the milk drawn by the child from its mother's breasts. It respects neither virtue, nor purity, nor innocence, which are alike defenceless against its indiscriminating and corrupting influence" (*WR*, 1869, p. 202).

A natural mixture of horror, disgust and pity for the innocent was therefore important in motivating those who sought state action. There were, however, more specific and mundane arguments for control which though having a general implication were directed particularly at the armed services. Here it was argued was: "an exceptional body, a creature of state necessity. It has peculiar claims on the State . . . the government . . . is responsible for the health of the army and navy. What may be the causes of danger to that health is an irrelevant question, whether they are or are not connected with immorality; we must have our army, if we possibly can, healthy and not diseased" (*The Times*, 25 August 1863). It was thus the state's duty to intervene to protect the armed services against the ravages of venereal disease as a matter of public safety, for the defense of the country was involved, and as a matter of ensuring a proper return on the taxpayers' money from a fighting force undebilitated by preventable disease: "Of the health of the soldier and sailor, we are ever bound to be careful on the broad principles of humanity; but now, when their services are so much required, utilitarianism goes hand in hand with the higher reason" (*Lancet*, 21 January 1854, I, 77; see also 15 January 1853, I, 62). Using evidence on venereal diseases from the Army and Navy medical reports,[63] a *Times* editorial (19 August 1863) commented: "The calculations are enough to frighten any-one. They yield the result equivalent to the withdrawal of every single soldier in the army from the strength of the establishment of more than eight days. . . . Scrofula, paralysis, and consumption follow in the track of the original complaint, and hundreds of fine young men are discharged with broken constitutions before they have repaid the cost of their training by any service whatever. We think we must have made out a case for interference."[64] We have here an echo of the utilitarian reasoning which Edwin Chadwick had earlier advanced in favor of general public health legislation.

Although the arguments in favor of state regulation eventually, but temporarily, carried the day they did not do so in the absence of opposition. As with prostitution, there was the argument that venereal diseases were the natural and just retribution divinely ordained for the punishment of illicit intercourse and that to interfere in any way with its working would be morally wrong: "the miseries which prostitution spreads abroad amongst the sons and daughters of men are the legitimate results of the unholy traffic; the avenging finger of an offended Deity is plainly visible in them; to interfere between the evil and its consequences is to come between Eternal Justice and those who have outraged her laws; these sorrows must run their undisturbed course. . . ."[65] Further, legislation of the kind proposed with powers of inspection and detention would be an infringement of personal liberty — a statement of the classic laissez-faire point of view. Even worse, for the state to intervene would be to provide state recognition of a vice and thus to descend from the higher "moral" position which non-intervention was thought to represent. It was also feared that "the recognition of prostitution by the Government, quite independently of its immoral character, tends in some degree to encourage the very vice it would control" (*BFMR*, 1858, p. 406). The statistical evidence adduced from continental experience which was alleged by the supporters of intervention in England to demonstrate its efficacy was also challenged, and denied.[66]

The repeated publication in the Army and Navy *Reports* of the continuing high rates of venereal infection with accompanying appeals for state action to deal with the problem, which were taken up, published and debated in the medical press, were the basis for the increasing concern.[67] In this atmosphere, following a government inquiry in 1862, the attention of Parliament was focused on the subject in 1863 and again early in 1864 in the debates on the army and navy estimates (3S Hansard, CLXIX, c. 1334, 16 March 1863; CLXXIII, c. 1142, 25 February 1864; CLXXV, c. 35, 5 May 1864). While aware of the arguments against state intervention, the Government nevertheless introduced "A Bill for the Prevention of Contagious Diseases at certain Naval and Military Stations" on 20 June 1864. By 29 July it had received the royal assent. The circumstances attending its enactment were to be the target of severe subsequent criticism (Scott, p. 14).

The Act applied to Portsmouth, Plymouth, Woolwich, Chatham, Sheerness, Aldershot, Colchester, Shorncliffe, the Curragh, Cork, and Queenstown. It was to endure for an initial period of three years. Its provisions were to be implemented by a special body of plain-clothed policemen drawn from the Metropolitan force operating under the supervision of the Admiralty and the War Office and not under that of the local police. Should a member of this special force or a registered doctor believe that a woman was a common prostitute (a term left undefined), then he might lay such information before a Justice of the Peace who was then to summon the woman to a certified hospital established under the Act for medical examination. Should she refuse, then the magistrate could order her to be taken to hospital and there forcibly examined and if found, in either case, to be suffering from venereal disease, then she could be detained in hospital for a period of up to three months. Resistance to examination or refusal to obey the hospital rules could be visited with one month's imprisonment for the first offense and two months for any subsequent offense. They might, however, submit voluntarily to examination without a magistrate's order, but if infected became liable to detention (27 and 28 Victoria, c. 85).

The Act, after Parliamentary inquiry into its operation, was re-enacted in 1866, (29 and 30 Victoria, c. 35).[68] Its revised provisions were now extended to Chatham and Windsor, and the Admiralty and War Office were empowered to provide hospitals with visiting surgeons and inspectors or, as in the case of the Royal Albert Hospital in Devonport, to add lock wards to existing accommodation. Also in 1866, provided that the magistrate was satisfied on oath of the truth of the information laid against the woman, or where the woman voluntarily submitted, she would be ordered to be examined fortnightly for a year to discover whether or not she was infected and, if during that year she were found to be so, then could be detained in hospital for a period up to six months on medical recommendation. A clause was also inserted to provide moral and religious instruction for those detained in hospital. In 1869, the provisions of the Act were again amended, following a further Parliamentary inquiry, and extended to Canterbury, Dover, Gravesend, Maidstone, and Southampton and to within a radius of ten miles of all the named towns (32 and 33 Victoria, c. 96).[69] Should six months in hospital not be judged sufficient for her cure, then a further period of three months' detention in hospital could be ordered. If the woman were judged unfit for examination by the surgeon and if he also thought that she might be diseased, she could be detained in hospital for up to five days.[70] These provisions of the Acts were to remain in force until their suspension in 1883 and removal from the Statute Book in 1886.

Partly because their application was limited and local and partly due to public ignorance of the provisions, organized opposition to the Acts did not begin to gain momentum until late in 1869, when Mrs. Josephine Butler's attention was drawn to the Act of that year by Drs. Taylor and Worth of Nottingham.[71] A little earlier, in September, a protest against the Acts before the Social Science Congress held at

Bristol resulted in the forming of a local association which was afterwards merged with the Ladies' National Association for the Repeal of the Contagious Diseases Acts, to whose service Mrs. Butler henceforth dedicated herself. Meanwhile, a rival body had already been formed — The Association for the Extension of the Contagious Diseases Act (1866) to the Civil Population of the United Kingdom.[72] It was between these two associations that the ensuing bitter battle over the Acts was mainly fought.

Stated briefly, the arguments against the Acts were partly those which had already been well aired by opponents of government intervention — that is, condemnation of State recognition of vice, interference with civil liberty, and the statistical inadequacy of the evidence in favor of intervention.[73] In addition, the opponents of the Act incorporated new grounds for protest which coincided with the growth of the feminist movement. These were that the Acts were cruel to the women concerned, "violating the feelings of those whose sense of shame is not wholly lost, and further brutalising even the most abandoned" (Butler, p. 19). They also applied solely to women, leaving men entirely untouched, and as such they were the apotheosis of the double standard of sexual morality in Victorian society: "it is unjust to punish the sex who are the victims of a vice, and leave unpunished the sex who are the main cause, both of the vice and its dreaded consequences" (Butler, p. 18). This was not only inequitable, but it was also silly: "What a monstrous absurdity does it not still seem to attempt to check disease common to and propagated by both sexes, by restricting one only. As well might we attempt to stop a river in its course by damming it halfway across."[74] In addition, there were specifically medical objections — the difficulty of distinguishing veneral disease "from numerous afflictions to which most respectable women are subject"; the danger of contamination from infected instruments and, given at certain stages of its evolution, the difficulty of detecting syphilis, thus giving rise to "a false sense of security." Finally there was, given the arbitrary powers of the special plain-clothed police force, always the possibility of arresting an entirely innocent woman and subjecting her to medical examination.

To each of these objections, the supporters of the Acts returned rebuttals. Prostitution was argued to be a permanent feature of society whose consequences could only be abated by state-sanctioned measures. Further, attention to the woman's moral and religious state while in hospital would encourage her to forsake her life of prostitution. Secondly, as the *Lancet* put it, 29 December 1866 (II, 731), prostitutes, far from being degraded by physical examination "readily acquiesce in the arrangements which they seem to understand as intended for their benefit and cheerfully submit to examination." Thirdly, men and women were subject to a double standard since they stood in a different relation to the contraction of venereal disease by prostitution. Again, the *Lancet*, 27 November 1869 (II, 729), argued:

It is only insofar as a woman exercises trade which is physically dangerous to the community that Government has any right to interfere. It does so on the same grounds that it claims to interfere with a railway when in a dangerous condition.... Morally, the male sex may be equally as guilty as the other, or even more so, but in the above respect there is a well defined distinction. Again, the women do not as a rule know the names of their paramours, and even if they did we do not see how they could identify them, so as to identify the sources of contagion. Mistakes would be numerous and the system proposed would not be practicable, nor would it be tolerated. Lastly, there is every reason to suppose ... that a women gives twenty diseases of this sort for every one she receives and more and more she may be quite ignorant that she is the subject of any disease, which is not likely to be the case with a man.

Fourthly, the police, specially selected for their duty and with intimate knowledge of the brothels and their habitués, would be unlikely to arrest an innocent woman. Finally, the statistical evidence for the places to which the Acts had been applied showed their beneficial effects, a fall in the numbers of prostitutes and a reduction in veneral disease rates among the troops.

The controversialists bespattered each other freely with ridicule and denigration made all the more virulent as this was the first major public cause with which women had been identified. What outrage when women spoke in public on matters which were ordinarily considered taboo! From the beginning the *Western Daily Mercury*, in Plymouth, opened its columns to a protracted correspondence on the operation of the Acts. Many correspondents reacted with near hysteria to public meetings attended and addressed by women. On 24 June 1870 a Dr. Preston wrote:

I will pass over Mrs. Josephine Butler's address in public before men ... because I believe that a very large majority of our sex ... can only characterize it as the height of indecency to say the least. But it is my opinion that women are ignorant of the subject — but not Mrs. Josephine Butler and Company — they know nothing about it.... Certainly if such women as Mrs. Butler continue to go about addressing public meetings — they may ultimately do so but at present I venture to say that they are ignorant and long may they remain so. I don't like to see women discuss the matter at all. No men, whomever they may be, admire women who openly show that they know as much on disgusting subjects as they do themselves, much less so those who are so indelicate as to discuss them in public.

What asked the *Western Daily Mercury*, 8 July 1870, were things coming to? "To be obliged to discuss the question in public newspapers is bad enough; to have it expounded by ladies and brought up at the breakfast table afterwards is something so terrible that we shall be excused if we hesitate to express our abhorrence of it in the only terms at our command. The next thing, we suppose, will be to bring home for family reading certain portions of Mr. Mayhew's work on London Labour and the London Poor."

In the end, the Contagious Diseases Acts were suspended and repealed. Why? Tribute must first be paid to women like Mrs. Butler and their male supporters inside and outside of Parliament who steadfastly argued the case against the Acts. In a sense they had a weapon on their side in the nature of the Acts themselves. Being essentially local in their operation limited their effectiveness when all a soldier or a sailor need do, were he sufficiently desperate, was to go elsewhere and especially to London. For this, the only logical remedy was the extension of the Acts to the whole population, but here economic considerations which had favored their introduction, worked against their extension. Sir John Simon as Medical Officer to the Privy Council in 1868 argued that to extend the provisions of the Acts to London alone would, in order to treat the estimated numbers of diseased prostitutes, and taking a conservative view of what that number might be, require the provision of accommodation for 3,000 patients — "nearly equivalent to that which is now given by the twelve general hospitals of London for all bodily diseases put together."[75] This would cost about a half million pounds initially and £100,000 annually, excluding the cost of police arrangements and medical inspectors — "This for London alone! And the requirements of other large towns would probably be of like proportions." Such amounts would be unlikely to be met by voluntary contributions, but would come from national taxes or local rates. Would such provision plausibly be tolerated? Not very likely, suggested Simon, especially when the (to him) doubtful efficacy of hospital detention in limiting venereal diseases was taken into account.[76] It was an argument which was powerful in an age when increases in public expenditure and consequently taxation were regarded as a fiscal sin.

It is difficult to evaluate the effectiveness of the Acts in diminishing the amount of venereal disease or the numbers of prostitutes because of the inherent difficulties posed by the statistical evidence on either topic. Insofar as claims were made for the cure of prostitutes suffering from syphilitic infections, a number of doubts arise. Firstly, given the nature of the disease as it runs its course, how would one know, in the absence of blood tests which were not introduced until 1906 by Wassermann, that the patient was really cured and not merely enjoying a natural remission of external symptoms? Secondly, would not the treatment meted out to the patient, the most common of which were mercurial compounds administered internally and externally, either be ineffective or lead to mercurial poisoning, the effects of which were comparable in horror to those of venereal disease itself?[77] It was not, after all, until Ehrlich's discovery of Salvarsan in 1909 that a more effective specific was introduced into the treatment of syphilis. With such questions in mind one may doubt what medical good the Acts wrought. Their deterrent effect upon women who might otherwise have turned to prostitution is another matter, but again it gives rise to doubts and is incapable of demonstration.

To examine the problems associated with prostitution and its associated diseases is to examine an aspect of life in the nineteenth century which has, as we have argued, been curiously neglected until recently by subsequent historians of that century. It was, after all, a phenomenon which challenged beliefs in the nature of sexual morality and the relations between the sexes; which presented in what was thought to be an acute form manifestations of economic degradation and exploitation and a mirror image, poignantly symbolic, of class relationships. How, if at all, to tackle these problems challenged predominant beliefs in the relationship between the individual and society. To ignore or to minimize the fundamental nature of the problems thus posed and the confusions which clouded attempts to answer them is not only to present an inadequate history of nineteenth-century society, but it is also to place our own society with its comparable problems of sexual morality in a false perspective.

6: Working-Class Women in Britain, 1890-1914

Peter N. Stearns

WOMEN'S HISTORY TENDS TO CONCENTRATE ON WOMEN OF PUBLIC ACHIEVE-
ment and, more particularly, on feminists. Though much useful study
has been devoted to working-class women, it has, for the most part,
focused on woman's place in industry. What follows is an effort to provide a more rounded picture and to suggest a more general evolution of
working-class women, at home and in the factory, in a mature industrial
period. Quite apart from my specific conclusions, I would hope that the
attempt to speculate on developmental stages in women's history might
be applied to other periods and areas. We need a more sweeping con-
ceptual framework in which to fit biographical studies of women and
the surprisingly popular theme of men's opinions of women. In the case
of working-class women, biography is a luxury that can rarely be indulged. And though men's opinions are an important part of the immediate environment in which women shaped their lives, they need
not be studied for their own sake.

The lot of the working-class woman in Britain should have been
improving in the latter nineteenth century. Education increased rapidly
in quantity, and, at least after the mid-nineties, in quality. Working-class
women may have gained more from this than men, if only because they
started from a lower base. By 1900 only a small number of adult women
remained illiterate.[1] Female child labor, the old industrial scourge, was
almost a thing of the past. In textiles, still the biggest user of such labor,
the number of girls under 15 employed in England and Wales was only
62,843 in 1891; a decade later it had dropped a full third, to 41,404.[2]
Real wages had increased rapidly since mid-century, bringing
concrete gains to the working-class family. We must stress at the outset

that it cannot be assumed that women share equally in average improvements in standard of living in the working class. Their role in budget allocations did not remain constant. Still, there is no reason to doubt that their diets had improved somewhat[3] and that the worst housing problems had been alleviated. Charles Booth's investigators found that, while most unskilled workers living in central London still suffered overcrowded housing, most factory workers and artisans, many of whom had fled to the suburbs, had won satisfactory conditions.[4] The working-class wife had more rooms to clean, but she had escaped the grinding agony of early industrial housing. Living standards remained limited and after 1900 their improvement slowed or even reversed, but there was a margin over mere subsistence.

An even more striking measurable change in the life of working-class women was the rapid decline in family size. Certain groups of workers had reduced family size before; textile workers began the process in the 1850's. After 1900 the birth rate declined much more rapidly. Indeed the working class reduced its family size as rapidly as the middle class after that date, whereas in the previous fifty years the gap between the two classes had widened steadily.[5] Among certain groups of workers, including miners and metallurgical workers, the average number of children born to a family fell by nearly 35 per cent between 1900 and 1911. For textile workers, printers, and construction workers the drop was around 20 per cent, but families had been smaller to begin with.[6] This dramatic change reduced the physical hardship and the responsibilities of the working-class wife. Women among the urban poor had traditionally sought to avoid too-frequent pregnancy. Many more of them now learned how to do so and in this one respect their role in family decisions must have increased.

Changes in women's conditions were by no means uniform. We must distinguish at least three groups. At one extreme was the artisan group — printers, workers in precious metals, bookbinders, many skilled construction workers. The artisan's daughter was carefully raised in a suburb and surrounded by suburban furnishings. She was taught to play the piano, along with other graces. She married relatively late — around age 24 — and could expect to have only two or three children. Her career reflected the high living standards of this traditional aristocracy of labor and the essentially middle-class aspirations those living standards then allowed. In many important ways, including marriage age and family size, the artisan's daughter resembled the middle-class woman. Her life had its own special stresses, but it cannot realistically be described as a part of working-class history.[7]

At the other extreme were the traditional poor, about a quarter of the total urban working class by most estimates. These people were on the margins of subsistence. At the same time their women maintained many traditional expectations that often helped perpetuate poverty, but may have eased its burdens. Most notably they did not rapidly reduce their family size.

This leaves the big group in the middle, the bulk of the factory labor force. It would be futile to pretend that its exact size can at this point be determined, for its definition depends not so much on financial situation as on women's outlook and their position in the family. Some poor women, though still on subsistence living standards with a weekly income of about a pound a week, were doubtless entering the group because of changing attitudes. At the upper end of this group, where weekly income exceeded forty shillings, it was increasingly possible to pass into something like the artisan's style of life. Yet we find individual cases of women in families earning up to three pounds a week who maintain the characteristics of the proletarian center. The material position of the proletarian woman was improving. Her standard of living was at least a bit above the poverty line, but her overall situation did not advance as significantly as general trends, including the declining birth rate, suggest. There is evidence, in fact, that it deteriorated psychologically.

A group of Birmingham brassworkers visited Berlin in 1909 and came away singing the praises of the German housewife. German women were better cooks than British women and they wasted less. The whole family was better fed, and they taught their daughters how to cook.[8] Ernst Dückerstoff, a German worker and an ardent anglophile who wrote about his experiences in Britain during the 1890's, did not admire working-class women. British housewives were "not fond of hard work." The evidence? Again, wastage of food; also unwillingness to sew and repair clothes. More interesting still, wives often slept late and took no care of their appearance. Somewhat smugly he stated: "The German woman dresses more simply and neatly and is much more industrious."[9] Lady Florence Bell returned a similar report after investigating textile- and metalworkers' families in Middlesborough. Working-class wives — and most of them were above the admittedly minimal poverty line of the period — slept late and often let their housewifery deteriorate. They were desperately unhappy.[10]

It seems a bit presumptuous to try to judge working-class outlook in the past, and especially so when one is claiming that the inability to cope was not simply the product of poor material conditions. The evidence is impressionistic and comes largely from male sources, but it suggests that there was at the turn of the century a surprisingly unhappy transition period for working-class women. A number of factors worked against the improvement of their lot, while other factors that ought to have brought improvement had ambiguous implications.

Life for the working-class woman had traditionally been bad. Claims of sloppy housework, for example, arise almost with industrialization itself and can easily be explained by the conditions of the time. Wives who worked faced an almost impossible burden in keeping up with domestic chores. Interestingly, however, both earlier in the nineteenth century and at the century's turn, evidence indicates little difference in the quality of housekeeping between working and nonworking wives.[11] Much of the low level of working-class housekeeping during the early industrial revolution can be attributed to poverty. Crowded housing and meager diets made domestic chores difficult. There was little precedent in eighteenth-century rural society for the domestic skills needed in the city. Daughters had learned little before their marriage, while the steady drop of the working-class marriage age plunged more and more ill-prepared teen-agers into the responsibility of running a household. Efforts, from mid-nineteenth century onward, to compensate for inadequate domestic training through education were ill-conceived and ineffective.[12]

Much of the reported sloppiness of working-class wives around 1900 was, no doubt, a heritage of past problems combined with continued poverty. Even with great changes in conditions, the hand of tradition remained strong. Many observers noted the frequency of deaths of children within the working class and the impact this had on women. Charles Booth commented on the repeated funeral processions through working-class districts of London, which spiced the life of those not immediately involved.[13] Many of the women who did manufacturing work in the home, though particularly those who were single and had no other income, actually faced increasing material misery. Pay fell. Suicide was frequent.[14] Housekeeping deficiencies were not the responsibility of women alone, because husbands often had very narrow views of their own well-being, particularly with regard to diet. They stuck to the tried and true – "My husband, he'll eat nothing but boiled bacon, or a chop, or a bit of fat beef over pertaters, and if it won't run to that, 'Gimme a bit of braun cheese 'n I'll know weer I am' he'll say."[15]

As more and more women gained relative affluence, their housekeeping abilities may have improved, and this would account for the impression held by many contemporaries that working-class house-keeping in general was getting better.[16] A survey in Birmingham, though small and badly conducted, claimed that women in families with incomes of over 25 shillings a week, whether they worked or not, generally had tidy homes.[17] This is not consistent with the findings of Mrs. Bell and others, who reported inability to cope well above the 25-shilling level — the figure is interesting because it exceeds by five shillings the poverty line around 1900[18] and suggests that there was a large group of women capable in sheer economic terms of doing somewhat better than they did, but who were blocked by their traditions of poverty. There is no question that the original economic causes of poor housekeeping were receding more rapidly than the symptoms, and that most proletarian women were not improving their housekeeping at all despite an improvement in the standard of living.

In fact, by 1900, the direct correlation between poverty and housekeeping must be questioned. There is, in the first place, the almost universal impression that working-class wives on the continent, despite obviously lower standards of living, coped more successfully. British working-class wives were surprisingly ill-adapted, and the quality of their housekeeping is less interesting than the fact that it apparently expressed a sense of hopelessness and despair that was not simply economic. Indeed, women among the very poor in Britain were in many ways better adjusted than average working-class women.

There is substantial agreement about the characteristics of women among the many students of London's turn-of-the-century poor. The women had great responsibility. Whether they earned a salary of their own or not, they handled most of the family's money and were responsible not only for food shopping, but for paying the rent, buying clothes, keeping up insurance payments and overseeing school expenses for their children. On the other hand, bourgeois observers frequently noted areas in which working-class women could have managed better on their admittedly limited means. They did not use food wisely; many either bought precooked meat and ate it cold or wasted meat by cooking it too rapidly. Some of the poorest seemed inclined to skimp on food more than on other necessities — "I have to go without food to live, or only a bit of bread."[19] Less surprisingly their knowledge of proper health care was slight. They pinned their faith on herbalists and patent medicines and doctors were shunned. Insurance was purchased to cover burial expenses more than to tide the family through an illness.[20]

There was an ambiguous attitude toward children. Without question working-class women had more than they wanted. Babies were breast fed for two years or more, partly to save money on food, but more to delay the next pregnancy.[21] Many parents allowed older children to sleep with them — yet another symptom of the combination of poverty and traditionalism. Above all, the mothers among the London poor expected some of their children to die. Their concern was to provide a proper funeral, and only if they could not, did they sense that anything was improper about the death.

Many women among the poor were resigned to their lot. Their expectations were extremely limited. Their concern for better food was minimal. There was more interest in furniture, and many brides continued working only until they had furnished their apartment. Some talked of better housing, but they were accustomed to meager accommodations and to the smells and noise of the slums. Many London workers continued to live in the central city even when they worked at some distance. Their immobility may have reflected their general resignation but it may also have been the result of the influence among the poor of women who were responsible for the family's housing and who were particularly attached to their neighborhoods.[22] Only about clothing was there any real sense of rising expectations on the part of the London poor. The women seldom got new clothes and had to spend a great deal of time repairing the clothes they had. They were of necessity prepared to sacrifice, like the woman who professed not to need new shoes, which she could not afford anyway, because "there was no need for her to go out if the weather were not fine."[23] Yet they were conscious of their appearance, often, for example, wearing long skirts specifically to conceal worn-out shoes. Pretty clothes were an aesthetic outlet and the interest in dress was definitely spreading after 1900.[24]

Apart from the interest in clothes, however, women could not think much beyond what they had. One woman, treated to a theater performance of *Little Lord Fauntleroy,* was astonished to learn that people lived like that — and more than a little shocked. Doubtless had she been exposed to many such shows her outlook would have changed, but there was no money for theater tickets and her one treat seemed too unreal to color her attitudes. There was no really active desire for different surroundings. Improvement meant only a bit more money and security, a bit less work to do, and perhaps the bliss of having fewer children. These were narrow views indeed — the dullness of slum mothers appalled social workers — for the adjustment to poverty depended on limited horizons. Within them, however, many poor women coped well. They kept themselves as neat as possible, and they were meticulous housekeepers, spending a great deal of time cleaning.[25]

They also carefully schooled their children in their own culture: the purpose of life was to endure, and there was no room for hope.

Husbands gave purpose to the married women among the poor, and wives slaved to make their men content. They took their responsibility for the household very seriously — to the point of hiding from their husbands the full impact of the family's poverty. Their policy stemmed from the necessity in poor families to keep husbands healthy and if possible happy. A woman in York expressed the almost universal attitude: "If there's anything extra to buy, such as a pair of boots for one of the children, me and the children goes without dinner — or mebbe only 'as a cup o'tea and a bit o'bread, but Jim ollers takes 'is dinner to work, and I never tell 'im."[26] The concern for the husband extended to death. Widows went to relatively great expense for the husband's funeral. One widow proudly told Lady Florence Bell that she "buried him with ham" — that is, she had served ham sandwiches after the husband's funeral.[27] Along with their limited expectations women among the big-city poor knew what their role was: they were meant to please husbands.

The comforts of this culture of poverty were not shared by all poor women. Most obviously, unmarried women engaged in the impoverished and impoverishing home industries could not compensate for their material misery and were clearly aggrieved, though often unable to translate their grievances into positive goals. Possibly the poor in factory cities, where an urban culture of poverty had less traditional basis, were less resigned to their situation than their counterparts in London. But many married women among the urban poor were adjusted to their lot — a negative, even a horrible adjustment in many ways, but one which meant that they avoided the extremes of despair of many factory workers' wives who had lost their traditional resignation without being able to fulfill their new desires. We may feel that the discontent of these women was far more admirable than the resignation it replaced — certainly it was a necessary preliminary to a better life. But it did leave proletarian women confused and unhappy. The despairing women that Mrs. Bell writes about did not come primarily from the poorest families (neither did those described by Ernst Dückerstoff).

Most proletarian women retained important traces of the culture of poverty, particularly in their dependence on marriage and male dominance. Where traditionalism went far enough, a life style rather comparable to that of the urban poor could persist even in families well above the poverty line. Mining families, to use the most important example within the proletariat, continued to offer a rather traditional focus for women's lives, particularly in villages remote from urban centers. Traditionalism in this case had rural rather than urban roots, but it produced a somewhat comparable result. The women seemed resigned to poor conditions, particularly in housing; for despite their relatively high earnings mining families, particularly in Wales and Scotland, found it difficult to acquire decent dwellings.[28] Alone among proletarian families, miners' wives rivalled the unskilled urban poor in the number of children they bore. With 3.6 children in 1911, despite the rapid reduction in birth rate, the average miner's family still stood out as the only large category of industrial workers whose families averaged over three children. Many of the miners' wives — most, in fact, who married before 1900 — had not sufficiently escaped from tradition to arrange a reduction in their family size. Only the younger generation was rapidly awakening to an interest in birth control, which older miners considered "unnatural and wicked." Hence the continued resemblance to the urban poor, whose families in 1911 averaged 3.9 children.[29] As with the urban poor, miners' families had a high child mortality rate — almost 50 per cent higher than most factory workers (other than those in textiles). The average miner's wife had to bear about four and a half children to achieve the average family size even in 1911. Clearly, older wives, who started their families before the birth rate dropped, spent much of their adult lives bearing and raising children.

Relationships with husbands were crucial, and here women in the mining villages had worked out their own pattern. They married earlier than any other segment of the population. Often their early marriages regularized illicit relations.[30] Women from miners' families in the mid-1880's married at the average age of 22.5, compared to 23.7 for both artisans and laborers. This was the first sign of a dependence on husband and family that persisted through life. The men in mining towns were extremely family centered. Along with an interest in beer and sports they maintained a variety of family recreations, from taffy making to chapel attendance.[31] Labor protest among miners had the same overtones of family solidarity. Women backed the strikes. In 1909-1910 one of the bitterest mining strikes of the period, in South Wales, occurred in part because of women's grievances. A new eight-hour-day law had prompted mine owners to set up multiple work shifts. One of the leading causes of the strike was that housewives had to prepare meals at all hours of the day, because sons and husbands rarely managed to work the same shift. Women took an unusually prominent role in the strike, stoning shops and policemen.[32] Clearly, women in mining villages had outlets which the urban poor lacked. In another aspect of husband-wife relations, however, normal practice in the mining villages resembled that among the urban poor. The miner's wife handled most of the family's earnings. In many villages the man gave all his money to his wife, receiving back an allowance for his own use, called the "tip-up." The transaction was often completed outside the front door of the cottage, so that neighbors could guarantee fair play. In other instances miners gave their wives all their regular pay, keeping any bonuses back for themselves. Control over the budget was a vital element in the working-class woman's life, for it reflected her place in the family and determined how well she could carry out her responsibilities. Mining women, like the urban poor, usually had substantial power.[33]

Horizons in the mining villages were assuredly narrow, which is why the women preserved a rather traditional family focus so long. Lack of job opportunities even before marriage served, rather like extreme poverty in the big cities, to limit expectations among women. But because there was little sense of alternatives there was little visible despair, and active participation in their husbands' labor protest gave women an outlet many of their urban sisters lacked. Life for married women in the factory cities was not significantly less narrow than that in the slums or the mining villages. But expectations here were changing, while the behavior of husbands toward wives, never particularly enlightened, worsened in a number of respects — hence the deepening unhappiness of many proletarian wives.

New attitudes came from many sources. Slight improvements in living standards could whet the taste for more. Education played an obvious role. These and other direct causes of rising expectations deserve further investigation in the study of working-class women. Certain other developments, however, may have been even more important, leading to a break with tradition and a concomitant confusion over what the proper role of the wife should be.

The decline in the birth rate and the fact that obligatory schooling kept children out of the house for much of the day gave women more free time. Both developments could be troubling. Several investigators reported that children came home from school only to criticize their parents (and their mothers above all) for their backward ways.[34] One claimed further that parents, especially mothers, were losing control over their male children, who spent most of their time in school or on the streets.[35] Certainly many women chafed at the small number of children they now had, for the break from tradition here could be particularly painful. A working-class novel discussed a wife whose only child was growing up. Because she could not afford another, the woman

Women in the Victorian Age

became more and more despondent, feeling that she "needed" another baby to be happy. Even women who wanted a smaller family suffered from an inability to develop alternate ways of proving their importance, particularly in the eyes of their own husbands, many of whom remained suspicious of the propriety of family limitation.[36]

The decline in child mortality among factory workers' families also had ambiguous implications. It encouraged women to make an increasing emotional investment in each child, and indeed occurred in part because women's outlook changed and they took better care of their children. But child mortality had not yet declined enough to protect more than a bare majority of working-class families against an infant's death. The figures in 1911 show that for all wage earners, 13.3 per cent of the children died before their first year, but this included skilled workers and agricultural laborers whose rates were much lower. Workers with intermediate skills had a 12.2 per cent rate, textile workers a 14.8 per cent rate, the unskilled 15.3 per cent, miners 16.0 per cent.[37] A large minority of women in the factory cities still lost a child, but what was new was that increasing numbers of women were seriously distressed by infant deaths. They were not comforted by traditional resignation; a good funeral did not settle the matter for them. Lady Florence Bell found women in Middlesborough evenly divided between those who thought the death of children inevitable and those whom it threw into despair. The latter group was growing more rapidly than child mortality was falling.[38]

Perhaps the greatest source of new attitudes resulted from dramatic changes in the experiences of women between school and marriage. Again, the implications for the married women were decidedly troubling, for the simple fact was that life for young, unmarried women became more varied and interesting; yet most of them married at about the same age their mothers had, and the role of the married woman changed little if at all.

Work outside the home, usually in factories, became the norm for girls in their late teens and early twenties. Between 1891 and 1911 the number of women in manufacturing and transport work rose 40 per cent from 1,710,313 to 2,398,310. This was almost double the increase of women in the overall population (which was 24 per cent) and more than double the increase of women over 15. The total number of women employed rose far less dramatically, by 21 per cent — that is, it merely kept pace with population growth. Traditional nonindustrial employment stagnated. Domestic servants of all types, including charwomen and hotel workers, rose only from 1,715,236 to 1,736,986, while the number of servants per se declined by about 30,000. Employment in textiles increased rather modestly, but the number of women in food processing and clothing manufacture soared. Although the totals were still small, the percentage of women in the labor force in printing, chemicals, shoemaking, and metalwork rose rapidly, and their numbers easily outdistanced the increase in men employed.

Most of the women workers flocking into industry were unmarried. Employment of married women increased, but far less rapidly than the overall rate of female employment. Indeed it barely kept pace with the growing numbers of married women. Between 1901 and 1911, for example, the increase in employment of married women in textiles was 8 per cent, of all women 10 per cent; in metalwork, 36 per cent compared to 40 per cent. By 1911 54 per cent of all unmarried women over 10 were employed. Census figures do not give comparable breakdowns for unmarried females before 1911, but there is no question of the upward trend. Furthermore, the rate of employment for unmarried females over 15 was still more striking. Again, absolute precision is impossible from the census figures, but even if we generously assume that a fifth of the age group 10-15 was employed, that still leaves a full 77 per cent of unmarried women over 15 employed. In the working classes the rate was higher still. Obviously there was a virtual revolution in the life style of working-class women before marriage, while the employment situation of married women evolved but slightly.[39] Only in the textile cities had comparable patterns developed earlier in the industrialization process.

Young women who shifted to factory work from other jobs understood the importance of the new employment opportunities. Former servants were particularly enthusiastic about higher factory wages and increased freedom. Above all, they welcomed factory work because they found "more life" there.[40] Far more women simply experienced the joy of at least a partial escape from their parents and from chores of caring for younger brothers and sisters.[41] They had money to spend and they could indulge new and old expectations. Their spending not surprisingly reflected some of the vague impulses of poor women generally. In particular, they ignored food, except perhaps for candy (many were undernourished), while they spent a great deal on clothing. Their interest in spending on recreation was not as high as among single men, but it rose rapidly. Music halls and picnics commanded a significant share of their budgets.[42]

Of course most of their earnings were paid to their parents for board and room. It is notable, nevertheless, that they kept a significant portion for their own use (their counterparts on the continent normally turned over all their pay to the family fund). Daughters, at least, were winning a new role in the family. One female weaver living with her parents earned 13/6½ a week and paid 8 shillings to her parents for board and room. She spent 1/8¾ on dress, 1d. on amusements, 3½d. on holidays and picnics, and 3d. on educational and cultural materials. Another young woman, earning 15/6¼ a week, gave her parents 7/9½, spending 1/8½ on clothing, 2¼d. on amusements, 4d. on holidays and picnics, and a full 10¾d. on education. Obviously many young women not only indulged their taste for clothing and amusement but also saved for the future (for marriage above all) and bought books and newspapers. The overall pattern that emerges from a large sample of the budgets of unmarried female workers in 1910 suggests that 55 per cent of all earnings went to their parents for board and room; 14 per cent for clothing; 10 per cent for amusements, picnics, and holidays; 8 per cent for cultural expenses; leaving 15 per cent for savings.[43]

The rapid spread of factory employment for working-class women had its disadvantages. Employment at low pay convinced many women that they were inferior and confirmed others in their sense of apathy and hopelessness. Some were aware that the general public regarded working women with disfavor. In a strike in Liverpool in 1890, female clothing workers paraded calmly in the streets in their best dresses to show that they were respectable. They had been moved to strike only because successful agitation by Jewish tailors in the city for a reduction of hours of work prompted them to realize that "what a foreigner could do a woman could."[44]

Most of the young women in the factories were satisfied with material conditions rather than downcast. In terms of their only gradually evolving material expectations they found it easy to accept their salary levels. Only the massive inflation after 1910 brought large numbers of them to a consciousness of economic grievance. Their most commonly expressed complaints concerned personal relations on the job. Female shoeworkers in Knighton Fields conducted a rash of strikes in 1913 against their forewoman's "nagging."[45] The factory girls questioned by Charles Booth's researchers rarely criticized their pay or conditions, but they did condemn those foremen who "treated us like animals" and who were often immoral.[46] At the same time, many women found individual remedies for problems at work. Many changed jobs often. Many were frequently absent, which helped compensate for the strenuous pace of work. Above all, the problems they did perceive on the job were less acute than those they encountered at home. An extensive investigation of women at work in the early 1890's produced evidence of varied grievances, but the sense of satisfaction was more pervasive, with women time and time again citing the conviviality they enjoyed on the job. Not surprisingly, the report noted that women in many companies complained more about their home life than about their work conditions.[47]

The spread of factory employment for young women provided spending money and social contacts outside the home, but the grievances it produced, though too personalized to produce much collective protest, suggest that a new concern for freedom and dignity was developing among young women around the turn of the century. This concern could easily be aimed at fathers or husbands; without question it was often turned against male-dominated labor unions. In 1906 female textile workers in Denton rejected a union membership campaign fearing that they might "lose our individuality" and noting that the union had repeatedly insulted them and ignored their interests in the past.[48]

Factory girls usually married in their early twenties. Only textile workers, who had the longest experience with employment, carried their sense of independence into their decision to marry. There is evidence that by the early 1900's women in textiles were marrying even later than artisans, a reversal of patterns prevalent just twenty years before. With this exception, young women workers expected to marry soon, just as their mothers and grandmothers had. Their marriage expectations doubtless added to their relative contentment at work, for they did not usually plan to remain workers all their lives. They worked in part to save for marriage. Work in some cases facilitated sexual relations among young workers that led to marriage. A working-class novel describes a common pattern: a girl dated a co-worker for 23 months, and the male was in "no hurry" to marry until he found out he could not honorably delay.[49] Marriages occurred early, often with partially reluctant males and often when the newlyweds were too poor to afford their own housing and so had to live with parents. But the possibly bad start was not the main problem. The fact was that working-class marriage was not flexible enough to accommodate the girl's new if vague aspirations. It obviously reduced her spending money; virtually no working-class family could afford to give the wife the five to ten shillings a week for her own purposes that she had enjoyed while single. The wife's social contacts were drastically curtailed. Her role as mother, as we have seen, may have caused new uncertainties. Above all, her husband's conception of her role as wife remained traditional at best and in some cases grew more limited.

The workingman's world was a man's world. The image of virility crops up constantly, to the point that one wonders if some were not protesting too much. A group of strikers agrees not to return to work until blackleg laborers are fired, "for this could be contrary to our manhood."[50] A bookbinder on strike tells an employer trying to lure him back, "I am a. man, sir."[51] Autobiographies by workers covering this period rarely mention women. Although it is often assumed that working-class children until recently had much warmer relationships with their mothers than with their domineering fathers,[52] this is not apparent in autobiographies of the time, where normally only fathers are given any space.[53]

There are ample signs that the working class had absorbed much of the middle-class pedestal image of the woman, despite its glaring inappropriateness to a life of toil. Sailors in Cardiff attacked Chinese laundries suspected of white slaving. Their leader noted, "They knew for themselves that these slips of growing white womanhood became the body slaves of the laundry lords."[54] *The Ragged Trousered Philanthropists* makes the image clearer. Women appear only rarely in the book but those who do are faultless, though in one case a woman is led astray by a man appropriately if unsubtly named Slyme. Their men commiserate with their physical sufferings but rarely pay much attention to them and, with the exception of the socialist protagonist, despair of understanding them. Much more is made of the men's love for their children, who in all significant cases are boys. A man separated from his wife finally decides to return, for the following reason: "The money he earned seemed to melt away almost as soon as he received it; to his surprise he found that he was not nearly so well off in regard to personal comfort as he had been formerly."[55] The author, a construction worker, disapproves of this selfishness, but his own image of women is almost as wooden.

The working-class wife was not supposed to work, at least outside the home. To do so would offend her husband's manhood, for it would demonstrate his inability to provide for her. It was firmly established in working-class culture that only the sick or the depraved sent their wives out to work, and indeed outside of the textile towns only women whose husbands were ill or injured or drunkards or otherwise unemployable normally worked. One survey of Northampton and Reading revealed but a single family in which a man was earning money and the wife also worked.[56] In 1901, in towns such as Swindon and Newcastle, less than 10 per cent of all married and widowed women worked; London, Sheffield, Birmingham, and Manchester fell into the 10-20 per cent range; and only the textile and shoe towns exceeded these figures. In all these cases the majority of the "married" women in the work force were widows. Overall, in 1901, 13 per cent of all married women and widows in the cities were employed. In 1911 the figure had risen, to 14.8 per cent, and for this year it was broken down — 30.1 per cent of all urban widows were employed, 10.3 per cent of all urban married women.[57] Working-class figures were higher, of course, but work for the married woman whose husband was alive was nonetheless a rarity.

Textiles were an exception — in cities like Blackburn close to 40 per cent of all married women and widows worked in 1901, and by 1911 the figure approached 50 per cent. Women in many of these towns could not conceive of confining their lives to home and children. As one put it, "It 'ud give me the bloomin' 'ump."[58] They stayed on in the factory after marriage out of habit and a genuine desire to avoid boredom and loneliness. No direct evidence has yet been uncovered to determine whether women in textiles were more contented than their counterparts elsewhere, but all indications point to a changing life style that must have been more fulfilling. Relatively small families and later marriage were both causes and symptoms of greater independence. Rising levels of employment for married women meant precious social contacts outside the home as well as greater income. In cotton textiles the union movement, which actively recruited women and placed some on governing committees, provided yet another outlet and another indication of relative equality between men and women.

In all industries other than textiles, working-class traditions were undented. Male reluctance to allow wives to work outside the home was in no sense new. It was a peasant-derived reaction to the shock of industrial life. In Germany unskilled workers who came from countryside to city in this same period returned their wives to the home as soon as their own wages reached bare subsistence,[59] just as British workers had done earlier in the nineteenth century. But there was something distinctive about the persistence of the tradition in Britain. German workers with more factory experience or higher skill increasingly abandoned their hesitation; keeping wives home became less important than seeking a better standard of living. Hence the number of married women in German industry almost doubled between 1895 and 1907.[60] British husbands were far slower to change. Their culture of maleness and the ideas about women's role that they could absorb from the middle class held them back. Of course many of their wives doubtless did not want to work, but there was an anomaly, nevertheless. Women who had worked with some satisfaction before marriage and who were burdened

Women in the Victorian Age

with fewer children were still confined to the home. The small general increase in the number of married women working after 1900 was due less to a change in men's attitudes than to the compulsion of rising prices (which forced some husbands to let their wives work) and, above all, to sheer population growth.

The male attitude toward women was also expressed in the labor movement, outside of cotton textiles. In most industries unions long preferred to ignore women workers. The pottery workers' union in North Staffordshire, for example, had long resented women and made no effort to organize them. A rival union formed in 1906-1907 temporarily recruited a number of women. Only in 1911 did the main union add an organizer for women and undertake a major recruitment campaign — which quickly succeeded. Unions in printing, bookbinding, and shoe manufacture pursued similar policies. The national tailors' union and the Amalgamated Society of Engineers, both faced with growing numbers of women in their industries, long discouraged women from joining their ranks, and many strikes were conducted against women workers, particularly by skilled bookbinders and printers.[61]

These policies were neither sensible nor inevitable. Continental trade unions admitted women much faster than those in Britain, as many British organizers noted. Though strikes against women workers were not unknown (particularly among French printers), they were far less common than in Britain. British workingmen did not think women should work. As more and more did so, if only before marriage, men's attitudes stiffened. Outright competition with women on the job merely added to the tension — "Another thing is women . . . there's thousands of 'em nowadays doin' work wot oughter be done by men."[62] At the same time the neglect of women by the union movement added to the workingman's belief in female inferiority: women were too docile, too easily deceived, and the proof was that they resisted the unions.[63]

Several developments more directly affected male-female relationships. A large minority of working-class families took in boarders. This was not a new phenomenon, but its importance increased. In Middlesborough, for example, about a third of all working-class families took in lodgers.[64] A railroad worker expressed a common sentiment: "If a railway man has no children to work for him, he can only live decently by taking in a lodger."[65] Here, obviously, was a desirable compromise for a husband who needed more money — he could avoid the indignity of having his wife work. But the lodger could seriously disrupt family life; his presence reduced the benefits of more spacious housing, and both husband and wife might resent the presence of an intruder. To one woman who took in a boarder after a pleasant first year of marriage, "it seemed that the happiness of the past twelve months had suddenly come to an end."[66] Opportunities for rivalry and for accusations of infidelity were frequent.

Concern about the household budget easily turned into quarreling between husband and wife. This was not a new problem, but it was particularly acute in Britain because working-class men were only vaguely aware of their wives' difficulties in making ends meet while firmly convinced of their responsibility to do so. The problem grew around 1900 when men's expectations about the quality of their diet and clothing were increasing; and it was certainly heightened by inflation after 1900. Workers only gradually became aware of the rise in prices. Many doubtless attempted to keep their wives on a fixed household budget, and could only blame them as they realized that their living standard was deteriorating. One of Robert Tressell's characters started an argument that must have raged frequently in millions of working-class homes: "I never interfere about anything, because I think it's your part to attend to the house, but it seems to me you don't manage things properly."[67]

The most concrete change in the relations between wife and husband, and a clear deterioration in the position of the proletarian wife, concerned the allocation of the family budget. Interpretation of general budget figures, though admittedly a chancy undertaking, suggests that men's interests predominated over women's among that group of workers whose earnings fell between subsistence and relative affluence at the end of the nineteenth century — the group bringing home 21 to 40 shillings a week. In families who moved out of the subsistence category, spending on key food items (particularly meat) and on recreation rose more rapidly than overall income, which meant that spending on clothing, and to a lesser extent on housing, lagged and that women's main consumption interests were not being served.[68] We know that women were not getting anything like an equal share of the new recreational spending and the same thing was probably still true of food. What seemed to be happening was that as wages advanced men took the bulk of the gain for themselves and abandoned the traditional pattern of turning most of their income over to their wives for family use. One worker in Middlesborough, who did not tell his wife what he made, which was two to three pounds a week, put 30 shillings aside for his wife and spent the rest. His wife was required to pay his insurance fees out of her share because they were for her benefit. Another worker, earning 50 to 68 shillings a week, gave his wife 28 shillings a week for household

Women in the Victorian Age

expenses. This was the common pattern among workers with earnings above subsistence, except in mining villages.[69] Doubtless many men used part of their share to buy things for their wives, though again the impressionistic evidence suggests they were more likely to shower their children with presents.[70] Women were not necessarily aggrieved by their fixed allowances and their ignorance of what their husbands earned or did with their earnings,[71] but their economic role in the family declined. They were not sharing fully in advancing working-class prosperity and the change in budget allocations left them ill-prepared to cope with inflation after 1900. Although some said they did not object to the new system, it must at the least have confused the younger wives who had controlled a modest income of their own before marriage.

The increase in men's control of the budget meant also that as their recreational patterns became increasingly diverse, their wives' opportunities changed little if at all. It cannot be definitely claimed that men were sharing fewer activities with their wives than before, but it is clear that the lot of married women was worsening at least to the extent that their new expectations and their experience of wide social contacts before marriage were given no new outlet.

The tensions men felt on the job were mounting at the end of the nineteenth century and they were prone to take some of this out on their wives, or to seek diversions from which their wives were excluded. Job tensions were not new, but the introduction of new machinery into engineering and other industries and the still more widespread effort to step up the pace of work – attested by the concerted attempt to spread the piece rate — suggests a substantial aggravation of the problem. Belief that work was becoming less enjoyable, indeed positively unpleasant, was widespread and frequently expressed.[72] On the continent similar tensions induced men to turn to their families for comfort. In Germany family strolls and gardening overwhelmingly predominated as recreational interests.[73] British miners showed similar interests, but most factory workers did not. Factory earnings were higher than on the continent, so there was more margin for innovation, but traditional attitudes, including the belief in their special manhood, were inhibiting. Perhaps factory workers also sensed that all was not well with their women. In any case, their effort to compensate for hardships on the job, fully understandable in itself, largely excluded their wives. Alfred Williams, a worker in a railroad machine shop in Swindon, describes one reaction to the pressures of work. His workmates are consumed by their jobs. They dislike Sundays because they can think of nothing to do and have no energy anyway, so they stay in bed. Women do not enter this picture of working-class life. If they too stayed in bed, Williams did not find the fact worth mentioning.[74]

More commonly, men developed their own separate recreational patterns. Drinking, although declining slowly within the working class, largely separated the sexes — to a greater extent than earlier in the industrial revolution. Men rarely took their women to pubs. And men were developing new passions, particularly for sports, which they also found inappropriate for women. Their free days were spent at football games or at the races, while the women stayed home. Their increased share of the budget was devoted to these contests and to betting on the results. Family recreations were rare, except in more traditional centers such as the mining villages.[75]

Here, then, was the framework for the lives of married working-class women: their role in the family was in many ways declining, but they were still confined to the family; new material expectations, particularly with regard to clothing, were imperfectly realized (most could not dress nearly so well as when they were single); poverty and their husbands' budget control combined to frustrate them, and many were acutely embarrassed about their appearance; the pleasures which single working girls derived from contacts with a broader social world were largely denied them, if only because their husbands did not take them out and they were not supposed to go out alone. Many women were bored and confused. They might have read at home, and doubtless increasing numbers did as the quality of education improved. But surveys of working-class wives indicated that they still read less than their husbands. They looked at the *News of the World* on Sunday with particular interest in news of crime and betting. They read some other newspapers and novels occasionally, though a significant minority disliked reading of any kind. Their relations with their neighbors were often distant. Improved housing allowed them to avoid some of the bitter daily quarrels characteristic of earlier industrialization, when they had to share kitchens and other facilities. But rivalries persisted (many women measured themselves against their neighbors by the cost of the clothes they hung out to dry).[76] There was a very small increase in the number of married women working, and for those who did not work betting was the only significant new interest. Bookmakers called door to door in many working-class neighborhoods, bringing a bit of excitement at least, plus some hope for relief from a tight household budget — "But that £5 we won at the new year, it did fetch us up wonderful."[77] Small wonder that many wives slept late and let themselves go to seed.

Conditions at the turn of the century formed only a transition period in the history of working-class women in Britain, though one wonders how long those transitional conditions left their mark. Fuller participation in the labor movement, which began to develop in strikes and trade unions around 1910, helped women to become more articulate and changed men's opinions of them. Wider employment opportunities for married women played a still greater role in this process. More recently, a reduction of tensions on the job encouraged men to rethink their attitudes toward their wives.[78] An ultimately hopeful evolution did begin in the painful weaning of working-class women from traditional resignation.

Observers who compared British working-class women with their continental counterparts, to the disadvantage of the former, were doubtless correct. Women in France and Germany, poorer and newer to industrial cities, preserved more traditional resignation, even aided in France by greater religious instruction as children.[79] Their husbands shared at least part of the British distaste for working wives, but their economic situation limited their expression of it, and more married women had an outlet in a job. In other words, differences in the stage of industrialization explain some of the particular problems of women in the British working class. But other factors are suggested as well. British men had long expected more of women domestically than had men on the continent. British women in many regions baked bread at home; continental women bought it.[80] British women packed meals for their husbands to take to work; continental workmen ate in restaurants.[81] There were no reports from the continent that women sacrificed their own diet to keep their husbands happy, as was common among the British urban poor.[82] Nor did continental men refer so frequently or explicitly to their manhood in strikes and personal contacts. As we have seen, male-female relationships on the continent, from family reaction to trade-union organizing, differed from those that developed in Britain. There is reason to believe that some aspects of the situation of British working-class women were distinctively British. We come back to the widespread impressions of sloppy housekeeping, which arose early in the nineteenth century and seemed so unusual to observers familiar with the working classes of many continental countries. British women were held to unusual household responsibilities by husbands who seem to have had a somewhat unusual notion of women's role. Women, very early, may have vented their frustration, individually and ineffectively, by skimping on some of their essential chores.[83]

The ordeal of working-class women around 1900 may thus relate to problems of and attitudes toward Victorian women more generally. One comparative problem is already familiar, though largely unexplored — why the unusual virulence (the word is used advisedly) of feminism in the Anglo-Saxon countries. We need better comparative studies of working-class women involving more work on continental women, and also a more coherent inquiry into the relationship between middle-class and working-class views of women in Britain. One thing is certain: if British workingmen had added some middle-class notions about women to their own culture, working-class women were not able to join their wealthier sisters in complaint. Long deprived, they were demoralized further by the changes in their lives at the end of the Victorian era. Though no longer traditionally resigned, they were far from possessing the ability to protest as women.

7: The Debate over Women

Ruskin vs. Mill

Kate Millett

ONE OF THE MORE REMARKABLE ACCOMPLISHMENTS OF THE NINETEENTH century consisted in its ability both to initiate and, ultimately, to withstand the inception of a sexual revolution, commonly known as the feminist movement. Little enough came of it finally, as the current resurgence of women's liberation would remind us, but the great Victorian debate on Woman did seem in its early fervour to be capable of challenging the most basic of civilization's socio-political institutions — patriarchy itself, together with its ancient relationship of dominance and subordinance between male and female.

Had the older, cynical expressions of male supremacy continued to carry much weight, a first phase of sexual revolution might never have taken place. But the struggle was carried out between two opposing camps, rational and chivalrous, and each of them claimed to have at heart the best interests of both sexes and the larger benefit of society. It is revealing to compare two of the central documents of sexual politics in the Victorian period — Mill's *Subjection of Women* and Ruskin's "Of Queen's Gardens."[1] Compressed within these two statements is nearly the whole range and possibility of Victorian thought on the subject.

In Mill one encounters the realism of sexual politics, in Ruskin its romance and the benign aspect of its myth. Much of the negative portion of Victorian sexual myth is included in Ruskin by implication. His virtuous matron relies for her very existence on that spectral figure of the temptress which is her complement in the period's dichotomous literary fantasy — just as in life, the two classes of women, wife and whore, accounted for the socio-sexual division under the double standard. If Mill's essay is commendable for its lucid statement of an actual situation, Ruskin's lecture is significant as one of the most complete insights obtainable into that compulsive masculine fantasy one might call the official Victorian attitude. Its other side, the darker side of the male attitude, can be found in fiction, and especially in poetry. The dark woman, the period avatar of feminine evil, lurks there in subterranean menace, stationed at intervals all the way from Tennyson's verse to the more scabrous pornography of the age. But the daytime lady in "Of Queen's Gardens" is an expression of the more normative beliefs of the Victorian middle class at the moment of their most optimistic and public profession.

It must always be understood that the sexual revolution made headway slowly and against enormous odds of cultural resistance. While the Victorian period is the first in history to face the issue of patriarchy and the condition of women under its rule, it does so in a bewildering variety of ways: courageously and intelligently as in Mill and Engels; half-heartedly as in the tepid criticism of the novelists who describe it; with bland disingenuousness as in Ruskin; or with turbulent ambivalence as in the poets Tennyson, Rossetti, Swinburne, and Wilde. Intermittent degrees and variations on all these patterns are to be found everywhere, and the subject is a vexed and difficult one. Dickens, for example, achieved a nearly perfect indictment of both patriarchy and capitalism in *Dombey and Son* — a novel virtually inspired by the phenomenon of prenatal preference, and a superb illustration of Engels' statements on the subordination of women within the system of property. Yet Dickens did this without ever relinquishing the sentimental version of women which is the whole spirit of Ruskin's "Of Queen's Gardens." It is one of the more disheartening flaws in the master's work that nearly all the "serious" women in Dicken's fiction, with the exception of Nancy and a handful of her criminal sisters, are insipid goodies carved from the same soap as Ruskin's Queens. Indeed, an acquaintance with Ruskin's "Of Queen's Gardens" is a great aid in the study of Victorian fiction.

One is tempted to see in Victorian chivalry a transition phase between the open male supremacy of earlier ages (such as the bullying license of the Regency) and the revolutionary climate of the early twentieth century when feminism was at its height. While one might object that it is to this latter period which Mill and Engels belong in spirit, they wrote in 1869 and 1884 respectively and their very modern books were products of the Victorian era, however advanced or before their time they may appear. The realities they dealt in were ones that impinged on Victorian sensibility very acutely, either directly through the growing feminist agitation for reform, or indirectly in the strictures on women's social and legal disabilities which began to appear in novels. Among the poets the effects of change are mirrored in the unconscious fantasies of a masculine sensibility often guilty, resentful, or at bay, and driven to compensatory myths of feminine evil. Among women writers one sees the new ideas producing a growing restlessness and rebellion at their condition.

Ruskin presented "Of Queen's Gardens" at the Town Hall of Manchester in 1864 before a mixed audience of middle-class men and women. It appeared in book form with the publication of *Sesame and Lilies* in 1865, and was re-issued in 1871 with an additional preface perfumed with Ruskin's middle-aged infatuation over Rose La Touche. Despite the lavish flattery with which he approaches the women in his audience, a group of bourgeoises whom he addresses with grating regularity as "Queens," he had in fact felt and probably smarted under the pressure of feminist insurgence. "There never was a time when wilder words were spoken or more vain imagination permitted respecting this question" he bemoans — the "question" is of course "the 'rights' of women", Ruskin fussily putting the word *rights* in quotation marks.[2]

Assuring us at the outset that he is no crude chauvinist, Ruskin asserts that he is steering a middle course. He seems to direct his efforts against the "left" of feminism, and his refutation is the courtly platitude that women are loved and honored, have nothing to complain of and are even treated as royalty, so long as they stay at home. His strategy appears to be an attempt to subvert the new heresy through the doctrine of the "separate spheres," the period's most ingenious mechanism for restraining insurgent women.

Mill did not speak for queens, nor was he arrested at the nubile level of Rose La Touche. *The Subjection of Women* was written in 1861, three years before "Of Queen's Gardens." But, as Mill took great care in the timing of his books, it was not published until 1869, two years before Ruskin reprinted his own statement. Mill composed his essay in collaboration with his stepdaughter Helen Taylor and claimed that his own part in it was largely inspired by his wife Harriet Taylor. There is no reason to doubt that the knowledge of female psychology which infuses the book required a woman's assistance, but the style and the logic are Mill's own.[3] *The Subjection of Women* is a reasoned and eloquent statement of the actual position of women through history as well as an attack on the conditions of legal bondage, debilitating education, and the stifling ethic of "wifely subjection" within the Victorian period. It is argued as powerfully as the essay *On Liberty* and is as full of Mill's splendidly controlled humanist outrage as any of his statements on slavery or serfdom, to which he draws frequent parallels.

A political realist, Mill was quite aware of the revolutionary character of his thesis:

> That the principle which regulates the existing social relations between the two sexes — the legal subordination of one sex to the other — is wrong in itself, and now one of the chief hindrances to human improvement; and that it ought to be replaced by a principle of perfect equality, admitting no power or privilege on the one side, nor disability on the other.

This was a drastic recommendation to make then, just as it is now. Mill was fully awake to the resistance he would meet, the appalled uproar, the noisy irrationality of the old school, chauvinist or chivalrous, neither dreaming of producing any real evidence for their assertion that things were quite as they should be between man and woman. Mill even predicts the uncritical bigotry of the opposition: "In every respect the burden is hard on those who attack an almost universal opinion. They must be very fortunate as well as unusually capable if they obtain a hearing at all." For all his extraordinary capability, Mill was scarcely fortunate before a male audience: the reaction in the reviews was disastrous; he was denounced as mad or immoral, often as both.[4]

I   The Question of Nature

Reason has always been an intruder in the area of sexual prejudice. Ruskin, who was by no means a stupid man, probably has recourse to less intellectual energy in "Of Queen's Gardens" than anywhere else in his work. In turning his mind toward "Lilies" it was enough for him to rely on sentiment, a vague nostalgia about the heroic middle ages, and saccharin assertions about The Home. Mill himself remarks that one of the most tedious and characteristic mental habits of the nineteenth century is its reaction against eighteenth-century rationalism, and its quirk of trusting instead to "the unreasoning elements in human nature." Ruskin's lecture is a demonstration of the truth of this observation.

If Ruskin may be said to have a thesis, it is altogether a simpler affair than Mill's and calculated to stroke rather than ruffle his listeners. Beginning with the rather complacent assumption that the educated middle classes exercise a "kingship" over the "illguided and illiterate,"

Ruskin's task is simply to divide a little section of the realm off for Queens, or as he is pleased to put it, determine "what special portion of this royal authority, arising out of noble education, may be rightly possessed by women." If there was just an element of pandering to social pretention in the industrialists whom he had earlier addressed as "kings,"[5] Ruskin is quite unrestrained in the unction he directs toward his female hearers, who "if they rightly understood and exercised this royal or gracious influence, the order and beauty induced by such benignant power would justify us in speaking of the territories over which each of them reigned as 'Queen's Gardens'."

In professing that one cannot conclude what the "queenly power of women should be until we are agreed what their ordinary power should be," Ruskin is only saying that the role of the upper and middle class woman is dependent on the inherent nature and abilities of the female herself. Were these equal to the male's she could be a full member of the elite, not just the auxiliary he proposes. It was precisely to avoid the danger of sexual equality within this or any other class, that he and his fellows invented the doctrine of the separate spheres and proclaimed it "Nature." The two great poles of influence in the Victorian period are Mill and Carlyle. Frequently at odds with the rational tradition which Mill represents, Ruskin follows Carlyle and tends to rely more upon emotionalism than reason. And to those under Carlyle's influence, Nature is not only an emotional term, but all too often a convenient apparatus which can be adjusted at random to sanction class, absolutism, feudalism, or any other system chosen for endorsement. Ruskin was never a democrat like Mill.[6] Instead, he combined moral outrage against the plight of the poor with an excited longing for the heroism and grace he found in aristocratic and medieval revivalism — though at his best moments he transcends this snobbery altogether in a splendid compassion for the poor, Biblical in the energy of its denunciation of Philistine avarice.

As he is far too canny to speak openly of sexual status, Ruskin arrives at it inevitably through adhering to traditional sexual stereotype in role and temperament. However old-fashioned his phraseology may appear, his tactic is perennially popular. It re-emerged in the somewhat more sophisticated terms of Freudianism and functionalism during the reaction against sexual revolution which accompanied the decline of feminism between the 1920's and 1960's.

Ruskin immediately renounces all claims to speak of the "superiority" of one sex to another, as if they could be compared in similar things. "Each has what the other has not; each completes the other.

They are in nothing alike, and the happiness and perfection of both depends on each asking and receiving from the other what the other only can give." This sounds fine until one recognizes it to be the threadbare tactic of justifying social and temperamental differences by biological ones. For the sexes are inherently in everything alike, save reproductive systems, secondary sexual characteristics, orgasmic capacity, and genetic and morphological structure. Perhaps the only things they can uniquely exchange are semen and transudate. One would like to be sure that it is not upon this method of barter that Ruskin intends to construct his social economy.

Having through mere assertion "proven" that the sexes are complementary opposites, Ruskin then proceeds to map out their worlds, reserving the entire scope of human endeavor for the one, and a little hothouse for the other:

Now their separate characters are briefly these. The man's power is active, progressive, defensive. He is eminently the doer, the creator, the discoverer, the defender. His intellect is for speculation and invention; his energy for adventure, for war and for conquest. . . . But the woman's power is for rule, not for battle and her intellect is not for invention or recreation, but sweet ordering, arrangement, and decision. She sees the qualities of things, their claims, and their places. Her great function is praise; she enters into no contest, but infallibly adjudges the crown of contest. By her office and place, she is protected from all danger and temptation. The man, in his rough work in the open world, must encounter all peril and trial — to him therefore must be the failure, the offence, the inevitable error; often he must be wounded or subdued, often misled, and always hardened.

Ruskin has not only glossed over the fact of ruler and ruled in pretentious and inflated language, he has also deliberately confused the customary with the natural, the convenient with the inevitable. Mill, on the other hand, is aware that culturally created distinctions of temperament and role underlie and support the invidious distinctions of sexual status, and are indeed the latter's method of inculcation and perpetuation. He also believes that the practice of splitting male and female humanity into two neat little divisions and calling the distinctions in their social and intellectual situation "Nature" is preeminently a political gesture.

To those who might object to his comparison with other "forms of unjust power" Mill answers that the master class have always regarded their privileges as natural; Aristotle could see no harm in slavery — neither could the American planter class. Both justified their injustice on the grounds of nature and insisted that the subordinate group were born to their position and reserved for it by God. Monarchy was often defended on the same grounds as springing from a more ancient patriarchal authority still more "natural": "So true is this that the un-natural generally means only uncustomary, and that everything which is usual appears natural. The subjection of women to men being a uni-versal custom, any departure from it quite naturally appears unnatural."

Ruskin's whole structure of complementary and separate spheres based on constitutional proclivity is undermined by Mill's logical ob-jection that nothing can be known of the inherent nature of a personality so subject to — as to be virtually created by — circumstantial condi-tioning:

> Standing on the ground of common sense and the constitution of the human mind, I deny that anyone knows or can know, the nature of the two sexes, so long as they have only been seen in their present relation to one another. . . . What is now called the nature of woman is an eminently artificial thing — the result of forced repression in some directions, unnatural stimulation in others.

Mill realizes that what is commonly regarded as feminine character is but the predictable outcome of a highly artificial system of cultivation, or to adopt his own metaphor, society's female is a plant grown half in a steam bath and half in the snow. Mill is optimistic that an idolatrous attitude toward the myth of nature is bound to disintegrate before a "sound psychology." Deplorably, such assistance has yet to appear. In the meantime one may do well to rely on Mill's own, for its psychological contribution is the book's great achievement. In fact, Mill's psychology is grounded in a more lucid distinction between prescription and de-scription than one encounters for example, in Freud, and a more in-telligent grasp of the effects of environment and circumstance.[7] Mill is also sensitive to the mechanisms by which conservative thought con-strues the status quo as the inevitable, a fine trait in a social psychologist. Until we undertake "an analytic study of the most important depart-ments of psychology, the laws of the influence of circumstances on char-acter," we are, Mill observes, unlikely to be able to know anything about the innate differences in male and female personality, for "the most elementary knowledge of the circumstances in which they have been placed clearly points out the causes that have made them what they are." Meanwhile, since nothing is known, it is presumption in man to "lay down the law to women as to what is, or is not, their vocation."

II   The Question of Education

Because he understands how conditioning produces a sexual temperament appropriate to sexual role, Mill is in an excellent position to understand how woman is the product of the system which oppresses her: how all her education, formal and informal, is dedicated to perpetuating it. He also believes "the mental differences supposed to exist between women and men are but the natural effects of the differences in their education and circumstances, and indicate no radical differences, far less radical inferiority of nature." Mill's description of the education assigned to woman tallies exactly with Ruskin's. There is however, one alarming difference: Ruskin finds it a very good thing, whereas Mill despises it as a minimal literary acquaintance with decorative culture deliberately designed to be superficial – in Mill's own cutting phrase, "an education of the sentiments rather than of the understanding" – calculated to render women fit for submission, vicarious experiences, and a service ethic of largely ineffective philanthropy.

Since he has delineated their sphere, it remains for Ruskin to "fit" women for it. Whereas Mill is eager to train women in every branch of arts and science, to open professional learning to them so that the world's available talent might be doubled, Ruskin would not be so precipitate: "We cannot consider how education may fit them for any widely extending duty until we are agreed what is their true constant duty." Translated (it is continually necessary to translate chivalrous sentiment), this only means that women should not be educated in any real sense at all, least of all for the sake of education itself. Instead they should be indoctrinated to contribute their "modest service" to the male. Ruskin's formula is an education deliberately inferior by any standard, and Ruskin's standards are high in the case of young men. In the preceding lecture "Of King's Treasuries," he had derided short-sighted parents who aspired no further than adjusting their heirs to "their station in life." Though he rails at the pragmatic middle class for its unimaginative vocational interests (a low instinct for which he expresses an unqualified contempt) he feels it imperative that the education of women be no more ambitious than merely habituating them to their "duties."

Ruskin believes in the "subjection of wives" – and says so. In general the task of the woman is to serve man and the family through "womanly guidance," to exercise some vague and remote good influence on everyone, and to dispense a bit of charity from time to time. It is to this end that education should prepare a woman. As a theory of education it is nearly an exact parallel of Rousseau's, save for its greater emphasis upon good works. But Ruskin also furnishes definitive propositions about female education; it is to be directed toward making women wise, "not for self-development, but for self-renunciation." This is surely graphic enough. As woman's chief duty is "goodness" the whole force of her education is sentimental rather than intellectual. It is sufficient that she be well-intentioned and a model listener: "A man ought to know any language or science he learns, thoroughly: while a woman ought to know the same language or science only so far as may enable her to sympathize in her husband's pleasures, and in those of his best friends."

Ruskin solicitously warns women away from accomplishment. They may get a smattering of information, but they are given orders to halt at the point of difficulty: "understand the meaning, the inevitableness of natural laws; and follow at least one of them as far as to the threshold of that bitter valley of humiliation, into which only the wisest and bravest of men can descend."[8] Theology is explicitly forbidden for woman, Ruskin apprehending that serious female interference might be fatal to the interests of a patriarchal religion. Here a certain personal hostility lurking behind the chivalrous posture obtrudes itself.[9] Ruskin irritably complains that while women generally admit they have no aptitude for the hard sciences, they plunge right into divinity, "that science in which the greatest men have trembled and the wisest erred." A passage of invective follows castigating those impious females who, as Ruskin puts it, crawl up the steps of God and attempt to divide His throne with Him.

Much of Ruskin's educational program is eked out of the Lucy poems of William Wordsworth, from whence he appears to have procured a recipe for the "delicate strength" and the "perfect loveliness of a woman's countenance," which are the end products of a salutary acquaintance with sun and shower. Joan of Arc, he serenely informs us, was entirely educated by Nature. An obsessive reference to organic phenomena is typical of his statements on women: boys must be "chiseled" into shape, but females, Ruskin is assured, grow effortlessly like flowers. Even chance exposure to classical libraries has no effect on them as blossoms do not give themselves to the contaminations of learning. Together with the graceful studies of music, art, and literature, Nature herself constitutes the fourth branch of female education in Ruskin's pedagogy. Through this study the female will grow in piety, which is well. Piety is less dangerous than theology. Metaphysics and astronomy should be taught to a woman on the following plan: "She is to be taught somewhat to understand the nothingness of the proportion which that little world in which she lives and loves, bears to the world in which God lives and loves." Since it is "not the object of education to turn the woman into a dictionary," Ruskin is persuaded that she need not trouble much about geography and history. Her historical studies should be confined simply to an appreciation of the romantic drama and the demonstrations of religious law afforded by the past.

In Mill's opinion, the conventional educational ideal that Ruskin has outlined, with flurried gallantry and protestations of affection, is nothing less than the most ingenious system of mental enslavement known to history:

All causes, social and natural, combine to make it unlikely that women should be collectively rebellious to the power of men. They are so far in a position different from all other subject classes that their masters require something more from them than actual service. Men do not want solely the obedience of women, they want their sentiments. All men, except the most brutish, desire to have, in the woman most nearly connected with them, not a forced slave but a willing one; not a slave merely, but a favorite. They have therefore put everything in practice to enslave their minds. . . . All women are brought up from the very earliest years in the belief that their ideal of character is the very opposite of that of men: not self will, and government by self control, but submission, and yielding to the control of others.

It is hard to believe that Mill and Ruskin are discussing the same subject — or, that since each claims to have the best interests of womanhood at heart — that one of the two does not prevaricate. Both are sincere. Yet Ruskin, whose educational scheme is clearly not the favor he proclaims it to þe, is rather like a paternal racist of the more genial variety, fairly unconscious of the real drift of his statements. Only occasionally does his hostility peek forth, carefully disguised as a moralist's wrath against frivolous "queens" who forsake their heaven of good works to gad about in petty snobbery or vanity. Moreover, Ruskin's purpose is to ennoble a system of subordination through hopeful rhetoric, whereas Mill's purpose is to expose it.

III   The Domestic Question

The disagreement between our authors grows to still greater proportions when they come to discuss two favorite Victorian themes — "The Home" and the "Goodness of Women." Ruskin's passage on the domestic scene, which he presents in the strongest language as the "woman's true place," is a classic of its kind.

This is the true nature of home — it is the place of peace; the shelter, not only from all injury, but from all terror, doubt, and division. In so far as it is not this, it is not home; so far as the anxieties of the outer life penetrate into it, and the inconsistently-minded, unknown, unloved, or hostile society of the outer world is allowed by either husband or wife to cross the threshold it ceases to be a home; it is then only a part of the outer world which you have roofed over and lighted fire in. But so far as it is a sacred place, a vestal temple, a temple of the hearth watched over by household gods, before whose faces none may come but those whom they can receive with love — so far as it is this, and the roof and the fire are types only of a nobler shade and light, shade as of the rock in a weary land, and the light as of Pharos in the stormy sea — so far it vindicates the name and fulfills the praise of home.

And wherever a true wife comes, this home is always round her. The stars only may be over her head, the glow-worm in the night-cold grass may be the only fire at her foot, but home is wherever she is; and for a noble woman it stretches far round her, better than ceiled with cedar or painted with vermillion, shedding its quiet light far for those who else were homeless.

Mill sees it differently. The home is the center of a system he defines as "domestic slavery." Since woman lives under the first as well as the last, or longest, rule of force in the history of tyranny, Mill calmly declares that she is no more than a bondservant within marriage. He then summarizes the history of marriage as based on sale or enforcement; the husband holding the power of life or death over his wife. He has some impressive legal and historical evidence. Although a husband might divorce his wife, a wife could not escape her husband. English law had, indeed, defined the murder of a husband as petty treason (as distinguished from high treason), because a husband stood to his wife in the relation of a sovereign to a subject. The penalty had been death by burning. And at the present, Mill contends, the wife is "the actual bondservant of her husband: no less so, as far as legal obligations go, than slaves commonly so called. She vows a lifelong obedience to him at the altar, and is held to it all through her life by law." As Mill is careful to make clear, English law permitted a husband to exercise what amounted to a total control over his wife's property, so stringent that even under the settlements of the rich, she had virtually no access to it in her own right. Yet her lord might confiscate the income from it if he liked, by force if he chose. Most slaves, Mill argues, had greater rights than wives under the law: the Romans reserved their *pecuniam* to them and some leisure was always permitted. Even female slaves were sometimes spared coercion into sexual intimacy with their masters. Yet no wife is exempt from sexual assault, however much both partners might despise each other. Under the law, as Mill points out, the father owns the children entirely. Should his wife leave him, she is entitled to take nothing with her, and her husband may, if he wishes to exercise his legal rights, compel her to return. Divorce, Mill urges with ironic force, would seem the least concession in a system where "a woman is denied any lot in life but that of being the personal body-servant of a despot."

While admitting that he has "described the wife's legal position, not her actual treatment," Mill argues that law is not custom, but permission. No tyranny exerts its possibilities without mitigation: "Every absolute king does not sit at his window to enjoy the groans of his tortured subjects." But they are within his reach in every legal sense, should he crave them. "Whatever gratifications of pride there is in the possession of power, and whatever personal interest in its exercise, is in this case not confined to a limited class, but common to the whole male sex," Mill remonstrates. One deals here with absolute power, for the law allows it, and while probably not resorted to as frequently as once, it is still there. Fortunately marriages, and the people who contract them, are far better than the law, but every danger yet remains inherent in such law. And one of the main objects of Mill's essay is to argue in the strongest terms for changes in the legal status of women.

In both Roman and American slavery, Mill points out, affection was by no means uncommon. But it is as perniciously naive to judge "domestic slavery" by its best instances, the loving rule and loving submission which Ruskin dwells upon, as it is foolish to neglect its worst occasions. Of those worst occasions, Mill is too acute a student of nineteenth century life to be ignorant. Even Ruskin shows he has heard of them in a reference of tasteless levity to "Bill and Nancy," whom he deliberately misrepresents as sparring partners, "down in that back street . . . knocking each other's teeth out" (in "Of King's Treasuries").

Mill is perfectly aware that among the poor the female is subject to greater indignities than anywhere else, as she is the only creature in the world over whom a man who is himself exploited can claim superiority and "prove" it by crude force.

And how many thousands are there among the lowest classes in every country, who, without being in a logical sense malefactors in every other respect, because in every other quarter their aggressions meet with resistance, indulge the utmost habitual excesses of bodily violence toward the unhappy wife, who alone, at least of grown persons, can neither repel nor escape from their brutality; and toward whom the excess of dependence inspires their mean and savage natures, not with generous forbearance and a point of honor to behave well to one whose lot in life is trusted entirely to their kindness, but on the contrary with a notion that the law has delivered her to them as their thing, to be used at their pleasure, and that they are not expected to practice the consideration towards her which is required from them towards everybody else.

In the nineteenth century, as today, unreported and even unremarked upon assault against women too innured or too intimidated to risk further attack was a frequent incident among the lower classes. Mill urges that as "there can be little check to brutality consistent with leaving the victim still in the power of the executioner," divorce should be permitted upon conviction of assault, lest convictions become unobtainable "for want of a prosecutor, or for want of a witness." Further down the rungs of connubial sensibility: "the vilest malefactor has some wretched woman tied to him, against whom he can commit any atrocity except killing her, and if tolerably cautious, can do that without much danger of the legal penalty." Such occasions were a favorite Victorian theme, particularly in the melodrama. The treatment afforded this subject matter, then as now, is often a curiously hypocritical mixture of prurient delight and moral compunction.

The conditions of any institution are liable to abuse and Mill's contentions are grounded in legal reality. Ruskin's domestic idyll is somewhat more difficult to infer from the facts than Mill's description. Ruskin will trust to chivalry, but Mill regards it as an evolutionary stage, one only slightly improved over the barbarities which preceded it and hardly a reliable deterrent, depending as it does upon the gratuitous good will of an elite. Mill had consulted social history and law; Ruskin trusted to poetry, and his history of women is based on the gossamer of literary idealization. Out of the political wisdom afforded by the portraits of Shakespearian heroines, "perfect women," "steadfast in grave hope and errorless purpose," "strong always to sanctify, infallibly faithful" — together with the tender beauties of Walter Scott's romances — "patient," full of "untiring self-sacrifice" and "deeply restrained affection," Ruskin attempts to recreate the sexual history of the Western peoples. As further evidence, he introduces the posture of the courtly lover sworn to serve and obey a mistress. Then, with impressive bravura, Ruskin declares that ancient Greek "knights" also practiced courtly love, boasting he could quote antique originals to this effect, were it not that his audience might have difficulty in following him. In any case, he will not be so mean with his hearers as to deny them some descriptions of the "simple mother and wife's heart of Andromache," the house-wifely calm of Penelope, the "bowing down of Iphegenia, lamb-like and silent," and Alcestis' self-immolation to save her husband's life. Ruskin rejoices in this piece of "self-sacrifice," presenting it as evidence that the Greek mind had a premonition of the Christian doctrine of Resurrection. The entire "historical" passage in the lecture, lengthy and presumably central to its argument, is hard to account for. It seems at times that no historical misrepresentation can appear too egregious when its subject is woman. Certain of his contentions, Ruskin calls upon his stout middle-class audience to doubt the validity of his assertions.

He appears convinced, and is sure they will be as well, that the poetry to which he has alluded is no less than a true and accurate picture of the condition of women in the societies in which these literary productions originated, since it is inconceivable that great authors "in the main works of their lives, are amusing themselves with a fictitious and ideal view of the relation between man and woman." Nor can this be mere empty abstraction, but must be fact, for Ruskin declares it is "worse than fictitious or idle — for a thing to be imaginary, yet desirable, if it were possible." While insisting that "in all Christian ages which have been remarkable for their purity of progress, there has been absolute yielding of obedient devotion, by the lover to his mistress," Ruskin neatly reassures the nervous suspicion mounting among the burghers who hear him that while this may be all very well for courtship, it is not appropriate for marriage where the proper thing is a "true wifely subjection."

Ruskin codified his social policy in the dogma of separate spheres: the wife shall be subject but will "guide," even "rule," her lord by serving as his conscience. This pretends to forfeit status through semantics. Yet no forfeiture is involved. In maintaining the most traditional sexual roles, Ruskin prudently reserves the world for the male, leaving the female an ancillary circle of housewifely and philanthropic activity. Moreover, the "gallantry" of his enunciations about the "respect" due to "virtuous women" would suggest that status — dignity and equality in human affairs — were not the issue at all. Due to the gratitude of her "lord," the female actually enjoys a higher status than the male. By transposing political position to moral rectitude, we are given to imagine that women are "better" than men. Unless, of course, they are worse — then God help them.

What Mill has to say on the subject is directly at odds with all this. While in the lower classes the ethic of male supremacy may take the form of brutality, in the middle classes it tends toward the rankest hypocrisy. Among the educated "the inequality is kept as much as possible out of sight; above all out of sight of the children," with "the compensations of the chivalrous feeling being made prominent, while the servitude which requires them is kept in the background." But the facts of the situation intrude themselves quickly enough on the minds of young men, however they are raised. If their education is chivalrous they are only being preserved from an actuality they soon enough discover. Mill was raised by a domestic tyrant who encouraged his children to despise their mother. Ruskin's childhood was very different and undoubtedly encouraged him towards a becoming politeness of attitude. Mill was spared the pretention of chivalry: Ruskin appears to have known it so long that he was unable to recognize it for what it was even had he wished to do so. Mill's observations are an interesting glimpse of boyhood's experience: "People are little aware . . .

how early the notion of his inherent superiority to a girl arises in [a boy's] mind; how it grows with his growth and strengthens with his strength; how it is inoculated by one schoolboy upon another; how early the youth thinks himself superior to his mother, owing her perhaps forbearance, but no real respect; and how sublime and sultan-like a sense of superiority he feels, above all, over the woman whom he honours by admitting her to a partnership of his life. Is it imagined that all this does not pervert the whole manner of existence of the man, both as an individual and as a social being? . . . Above all, when the feeling of being raised above the whole of the other sex is combined with personal authority over one individual among them; the situation, if a school of conscientious and affectionate forbearance to those whose strongest points of character are conscience and affection, is to men of another quality, a regularly constituted Academy or Gymnasium for training them in arrogance and overbearingness. . . .

Approval of a particular sort of male ascendency fosters more general notions of superiority (and satisfaction over differential or prejudicial treatment) from earliest youth. In Mill's analysis, the system of sexual dominance is the very prototype of other abuses of power and other forms of egotism. Just as Engels came to see in sexual supremacy and subordination a model for later hierarchies of rank, class, and wealth, Mill had discovered in it the psychological foundations of other species of oppression. "All the selfish propensities, the self-worship, the unjust self-preference, which exist among mankind, have their source and root in, and derive their principal nourishment from, the present constitution of the relation of men and women."

Chivalric code included, marriage *is* actually feudal (Mill hates feudalism) and is seen as little more than a "school of despotism in which the virtues of despotism, but also its vices, are largely nourished." The family can afford no real love to its members until it is based on a situation of total equality among them. The husband, in his position of authority, is less likely to be inspired to affection than to "an intense feeling of the dignity and importance of his own personality; making him disdain a yoke for himself . . . he is abundantly ready to impose on others for his own interest and glorification." With an admirable touch of candor, Mill admits that no man would wish for himself the conditions of life he chivalrously consigns to women: the pastoral coign of a Queen's Garden would appall any man confined to it, perhaps Ruskin most of all. The single concession Ruskin's sphere theory makes to its rule that male "duties" (meaning privileges) are "public" (war, money, politics, and learning), whereas female "duties" (meaning responsibilities) are "private" (that is, domestic), is in the realm of philanthropy. In pursuit of its kind offices, Ruskin is inclined to permit woman a narrow latitude to step beyond her sphere, never into the great world of nineteenth-century reform, but into the little world of the homes of what were then known as the "honest poor." There, while sewing garments and exchanging recipes, the respectable wife might make some miniscule restitution for the ravages her masculine class-counterpart had been busy accomplishing all day through his prerogatives of politics, money, and technology.

Ruskin, who had concocted a scheme whereby English boys might be "knighted" and English girls "invested" with the official title of "lady" under the auspices of a national chivalry movement something like the boy scouts, has a similar inspiration for the adult middle class. The word "lady," he tells them, means "bread-giver" or "loaf-giver"; "Lord" means "maintainer of laws." Roles should be determined accordingly. Under the euphemism of "maintainer of laws," the male appropriates all power. The "loaf-giving" lady dispenses charity. In its pseudo-medieval character, the whole thing is not only depressingly fantastical, it is singularly inappropriate to the conditions of nineteenth-century industrialism, whose nearly infinite economic injustices Ruskin felt so keenly. These could scarcely be ameliorated by the trifling charities of a middle-class housewife posing as a medieval almsgiver.[10]

Ruskin's typically Victorian insistence that social responsibility is a female province is somewhat ridiculous in the light of two considerations: first, as dispossessed persons themselves, both legally and economically, women were quite unable to give any really material help to other dispossessed groups; secondly, the device enabled men, and especially men of the ruling class, to ignore or deputize their own enormous responsibilities to the poor whom they oppressed — instead of ending such oppression, they could alleviate it with charitable solace.

Like many Victorians, Ruskin believed women to have finer instincts, since men are "feeble in sympathy" and can even "bear the sight of misery" and "tread it down" "in their own struggle." Mill answers this cherished sentimentality with a certain ironic logic:

[women] are declared to be better than men; an empty compliment which must provoke a bitter smile from every woman of spirit, since there is no other situation in life in which it is the established order, and considered quite natural and suitable,

that the better should obey the worse. If this piece of talk is good for anything, it is only as an admission by men, of the corrupting influence of power . . . it is true that servitude, except when it actually brutalizes, though corrupting to both, is less so to the slaves than to the slave-masters.

The philanthropy which Ruskin advocates for women as their sole opportunity outside the Home, is to Mill's better understanding of social economy merely "an unenlightened and short-sighted benevolence" which is pernicious to those it pretends to serve in sapping "the foundations of the self respect" which is the only pride left the independent poor and their only route of escape. The paternalism of any charity-and-gratitude system is humiliating to the poor — far more than Ruskin would permit his queens to realize. Mill says:

A woman born to the present lot of women, and content with it, how should she appreciate the value of self-dependence? She is not self-dependent; her destiny is to receive everything from others, and why should what is good enough for her be bad for the poor? Her familiar notions of good are of blessings descending from a superior. She forgets that she is not free, and that the poor are. . . .

Considerably beyond chivalrous compliment, Mill is perfectly aware of how adverse an effect feminine influence can have: "He who has a wife has given hostages to Mrs. Grundy." Herself the victim of a narrow and superficial education, woman is often just as likely to exert an influence that is petty, family-centered, and selfish.

As to the feminine self-sacrifice which so enthuses Ruskin, it is in Mill's eyes only a despicable self-immolation, both wasteful and tasteless. Because it is not reciprocal, the "exaggerated self-abnegation which is the present artificial ideal of feminine character" produces only a false altruism. Looking beneath the surface of chivalrous blandishment, Mills has detected expediency, even duplicity: "We are perpetually told that

women are better than men by those who are totally opposed to treating them as if they were as good; so that the saying has passed into a piece of tiresome cant, intended to put a complimentary face upon an injury, and resembling those celebrations of royal clemency which, according to Gulliver, the King of Lilliput always prefixed to his most sanguinary decrees.

But if we are to accept Ruskin's vision, the grief of the world is on the heads of women, so powerful are they in their secluded bowers, those shadowy corners of "higher mystery" where masculine power "bows itself and will forever bow, before the myrtle crown and the stainless sceptre of womanhood." Carried aloft by his chimera of woman's power, Ruskin insists that "there is not a war in the world, no, nor an injustice, but you women are answerable for it; not in that you have provoked, but in that you have not hindered." There is a certain humor in the proclamation that woman, confined throughout history to a vicarious and indirect existence, deprived of a deciding voice in any event, with so much of the burden of military, economic, and technological events visited upon them, with so little of their glory, are nevertheless accountable for morality on the planet.

Ruskin then launches into a peroration on flowers, whose subject, though he can never bring himself to say so in English, is prostitution, the cancer in chivalry's rose. He begins prosaically enough: "the path of a good woman is indeed strewn with flowers, but they rise behind her steps, not before them." He then takes off in ecstasy, and orders the good women of England, presumably the matrons snugly seated before him in Manchester's Town Hall, to go out into the "darkness of the terrible streets" on a mission to rescue certain persons there whom he refers to in cipher as "feeble florets." The plan is that the matrons will plant and establish the harlots in "little fragrant beds." Perhaps more in line with his general intentions, is the injunction to "fence them, in their trembling from the fierce wind."[11]

However buried in flowers, the overtones of sexuality in the last passage provoke still others: Ruskin quotes from Tennyson's vaguely erotic lyric "Come into the garden Maude," and transforms the unbalanced young man who is actually the speaker in the poem into a slightly eroticized Christ, and one with whom the lecturer appears to identify in the most curious, oblique, and oddly personal manner. Having run off into a rather self-indulgent pietism Ruskin concludes the lecture in a paroxysm of Dissenting fervor:

Oh you queens, you queens! among the hills and happy greenwood of this land of yours, shall the foxes have holes, and the birds of the air have nests; and in your cities shall the stones cry out against you, that they are the only pillows where the Son of Man can lay his head?

The salvation of the world which, he is assured, should come from its subject women is a concoction of nostalgic mirage, regressive sexuality, religious ambition, and simplistic social panacea. It is the very stuff of the era's pet sentimental vapors enshrined in notions such as "the angel in the house," "the good woman who rescues the fallen," and so on. It is the fabric of dreams. But the dreams of an age are part of its life (although, perhaps just as often, a species of death).

By comparison, Mill's conclusion is not only more rational but full of a new and promising vigor. He urges the complete emancipation of women not only for the sake of the "unspeakable gain in happiness to the liberated half of the species, the difference to them between a life of subjection to the will of others and a life of rational freedom," but also for the enormous benefit this would confer on both sexes and on humanity: "We have had the morality of submission and the morality of chivalry and generosity; the time is now come "for the most fundamental of the social relations" to be "placed under the rule of equal justice." In Mill's tones one hears the energy and cry of revolution; in Ruskin's, only reaction tactfully phrased.

Except for adjustments in diction and phrasing, the debate has scarcely changed in a hundred years. Ruskin is merely updated in Erik Erikson's popular rationalization that women are destined to a life of "Inner Space" and Mill's demand for an end to sexual hierarchy is repeated in the statements of the Women's Liberation movement. It would appear that, together with the anguish of more general scientific, moral, and social upheavals, we also share with the Victorians the complexities of sexual revolution.

8: Stereotypes of Femininity in a Theory of Sexual Evolution

Jill Conway

DARWINIAN BIOLOGY RAISED AS MANY QUESTIONS FOR VICTORIAN SOCIAL theorists as it appeared to settle. In particular it left unclear the significance of sex-differences in the evolution of higher forms of life. When we realize that it was not until 1901 that sex-linked characteristics were understood to be tied to the sex chromosomes, and not until 1903 that the working of hormones in human physiology was understood we began to see why for some forty years the exact nature of sex-differentiation and its psychic accompaniment was a subject of intense, though inconclusive, debate.[1] These biological questions were of significance in many areas of scientific enquiry but they loomed largest in the developing study of sociology, a study for which the groundwork was laid in the same forty-year period between the publication of *The Origin of Species* and the development of modern genetics. Early sociologists working in England or North America derived their ideas from Comte or Spencer, the two pioneers of the discipline who, whatever their differences, were agreed in deriving the principles of social organization from biological models.

The guiding rule of the early social sciences was Comte's classification, wherein knowledge progressed from the most abstract disciplines of mathematics and astronomy through physics, chemistry, and biology until scientific method was sufficiently refined to comprehend the complex phenomena of social life. It was a dictum which required sociologists to develop their discipline upon the basis of a biology in which the significance of sex-differences was far from clear.

In English thought Herbert Spencer's attempt to derive social theory from physics and biology is the most striking example of a sociologist busy at the analysis of human sexuality while lacking the biological concepts with which to go about his work. In the absence of a clear understanding of reproduction or of the precise contribution of male and female to their offspring, Spencer was obliged to conclude (in *The Study of Sociology*) that sex-differences could best be understood by assuming "a somewhat earlier-arrest of individual evolution in women than in men; necessitated by the reservation of vital power to meet the cost of reproduction."[2] Female energy expended in reproduction was not available for psychic and intellectual growth (the deduction followed from the physical law of the conservation and transformation of energy), and reproduction thus limited individual development. However since the male contribution was confined to fertilization, the necessity to reproduce and maintain the species did not impose such strict constraints on male capacities for individual development. In particular the male capacity for abstract reason had been evolved along with an attachment to the idea of abstract justice, and this was a sign of highly-evolved life.

Besides the limiting factor of reproduction, Spencer assumed that there were mental and emotional characteristics acquired by women through their prolonged existence in a male dominated environment. One such trait bound to be environmentally acquired was the desire for approval and the capacity to deceive. A further trait, undoubtedly the product of environmental pressure, was the ability to perceive quickly the emotions of others, hence women's greater power of intuition. Though these temperamental qualities were mutable and could be altered by controlling the human environment so that females would acquire other characteristics, Spencer could see no way to bring his laws of reproduction and individual development into complete harmony except by restraining human sexuality and limiting women's sexual functions (pp. 375-376, 380-381).

By 1882 the stress on the inheritance of acquired characteristics was being modified in England by the publication in translation of August Weismann's early papers. These set out the concept of the continuity of the *germ-plasm* in reproduction and made it the sole transmitter of inherited characteristics, thereby disposing of environmental forces as the major source of variation in species.[3] Much of the writing which followed upon this major modification of Darwinian thought is now forgotten because, in scientific terms, the problems to which it was addressed have been resolved by the study of genetics. However, in the English interpretation of Weismann's *germ-plasm* theory we have a perfect case study of the way in which sexual stereotypes could be adapted to new scientific formulations. The inheritance of acquired characteristics permitted Spencer to explain the existing stereotypes of female character as though these were the forms of femininity evolved by male-domination since primitive times. He could thus give scientific authority to the romantic view of women as intuitive and irrational. Once environmental factors were removed as major sources of variation, evolutionary theorists were compelled to look for other explanations of the supposed psychic differences between the sexes, and other ways to explain the undoubted social fact of the inferiority of women.

An extremely influential, but now forgotten, study of sex-differentiation and its significance in social evolution was the work of the Scottish biologist Patrick Geddes, written in collaboration with his pupil, J. Arthur Thomson.[4] Published in 1889 with the title *The Evolution of Sex* the book contained expositions of the existing state of knowledge on reproduction and sex-differences together with Geddes's own theories about the way in which the social position of women accorded with a vast evolutionary design. In part Geddes's argument seeks to defend Spencer and Darwin on the inheritance of acquired characteristics. In part it attempts to synthesise the growing body of knowledge on cell structure with a new concern for the mechanisms for stability and variation in forms of life. It is thus part of the convergence of several lines of biological enquiry which were to meet in the following decade in the study of heredity.

Geddes had impressive scholarly credentials for attempting a grand scheme of scientific synthesis. He had trained for four years with Huxley at the Royal School of Mines in South Kensington. As a student he had produced a minor correction of the master's work deemed worthy of publication in the *Transactions* of the London Zoological Society. After completing his studies with Huxley in 1877 he had served as senior demonstrator in practical physiology at University College, London, while doing research on the lower forms of life aimed at clarifying the boundaries between botany and zoology. The next year he began training as a field naturalist at the French marine biological station at Roscoff, followed by another two years of work in biology and histology at the Sorbonne and the École de Médicine. After a brief field trip to the zoological station at Naples in 1879 Geddes planned a major expedition to Mexico. This was undertaken to collect biological specimens for the British Association for the Advancement of Science and was to provide Geddes with the field work which he admired so intensely in the career of his intellectual model, Darwin. Shortly after his arrival in Mexico these hopes were permanently blighted by an attack of blindness attributed to lengthy periods of uninterrupted work with microscopes. Though his sight returned, Geddes was not able to use microscopes again for sustained research. The disaster brought about the reorientation of his career toward the interpretation of science for the layman and the synthesis of knowledge from a variety of scientific fields.[5]

His passion for synthesizing had already been demonstrated in his student years by a growing interest in the new science of sociology. As the child of strict Scotch Presbyterians he had been troubled by the apparent conflict between science and religion, and deeply disturbed by Huxley's dismissal of religious belief. In search of a way out of these intellectual difficulties be began to attend the Positivist church on Chapel Street and the week-night meetings of the London Positivist Society. In Paris he followed up his interest in a synthesis of scientific knowledge by attending the lectures of the Société International des études practique de l'Economie Sociale. Founded in 1856 by the social scientist Frédéric Le Play the society was dedicated to the development of scientific methods for the study of social structures and in particular to the study of the interaction of human groups with a given regional environment. These two sources in London and Paris provided Geddes with a knowledge of the developing science of sociology which inspired him to accept Comte's idea that the science of society would bring about the synthesis of scientific knowledge. In 1880 when it became clear that he could no longer be a creative researcher in biology he saw his future in the application of biological method to the study of society.[6]

Thus, while apparently pursuing a conventional scholarly career as a demonstrator in botany and lecturer in zoology at the University of Edinburgh, Geddes was in fact bent on branching out into the science of society. His first steps in the direction of sociology took the form of adaptations of economic theory to biological principles,[7] but his long-term project during the decade of the 1880's was to synthesize what was known about sex-differences and to interpret the social and economic significance of this knowledge. Geddes was convinced that sex differences should be viewed as arising from a basic difference in cell metabolism. The physical laws concerning the conservation and dissipation of energy applied to all living things. At the level of the cell, maleness was characterised by the tendency to dissipate energy, femaleness by the capacity to store or build up energy. From this single factor Geddes was able to depict reproduction and the determination of sex as arising from the general state of nutrition of an organism at the time of fertilization. "Favorable nutritive conditions tend to produce females," he wrote (in *The Evolution of Sex*), "and unfavorable conditions males" (p. 44). Preponderance of waste over new sources of energy would produce an organism with a male or "*katabolic* habit of body." Rich nutrition and abundant supplies of energy produced organisms with an "*anabolic* habit," which were female (pp. 44-45). Many consequences flowed from this division. Male cells had the power to transmit variation along with their tendency to dissipate energy. Female cells by contrast had the power to conserve energy, support new life, and to maintain stability in new forms of life.

In this theory Geddes was addressing himself to the question which Weismann had emphasized, the problem of accounting for the stability of forms of life and their continuity. Geddes's answer was to assume an immutable order and predictability in reproduction arising from cell metabolism. By making sperm and ovum exhibit the qualities of male *katabolism* or female *anabolism* Geddes was able to deduce a dichotomy between the temperaments of the sexes which was easily accommodated to the romantic idea of male rationality and female intuition. This dichotomy of temperament duplicated the dual pattern of cell metabolism, "the hungry, active cell becomes flagellate sperm, while the quiescent, well-fed one becomes an ovum" (pp. 115-117). Male aggression arising from the male tendency to dissipate energy and female passivity flowing from the complementary tendency to conserve resources were thus not merely to be observed in animal and human societies, but were to be found in the very simplest forms of life. In fact the entire evolutionary progression from the lowest organism up to man rested upon these male and female qualities. The lesson which was to be drawn from this picture of reproduction and evolutionary development was clear. Male and female sex roles had been decided in the lowest forms of life and neither political nor technological change could alter the temperaments which had developed from these differing functions.

Cell metabolism and sex differences were of course merely the base upon which Geddes wished to erect a sound and scientifically rigorous social theory. In a chapter of *The Evolution of Sex* entitled "Psychological and Ethical Aspects" Geddes sketched out the implications for future social development of the scheme he had propounded. He was a Victorian moralist and optimist who saw both psychic and ethical growth arising from evolutionary processes. In the scientific study of sexuality he saw no evidence leading to the deflation of romantic ideas about love. On the contrary, proper study of the role of sex differences in evolution showed that mankind was journeying toward a utopia of the emotions in which all humanity would experience the transports of romantic attachment celebrated in poetry and art. A rare Eloise and Abelard merely prefigured the emotional range to be developed by the entire human race. The deepening of the capacity for passionate feelings was to be accompanied by a parallel development in the sense of moral order so that the new sexual paradise did not threaten Victorian ideas of decorum. Such a pattern of development brought together harmoniously the chivalric tradition of romantic love and the potentially disturbing idea that human sexual appetites were mere animal instincts. While the romantic hero and heroine might be subjected to critical comment in the literary culture of the closing decades of the century, Geddes was hard at work shoring up a highly idealized picture of romantic love in his study of social evolution. Neither social realism nor the revived critical current of classicism entered into his treatment of future sexual relationships.

Although he cheerfully acknowledged, as did Freud, that sexual attraction originated in "an organic hunger" he could see no reason for a reductive view of the psychic accompaniments of physical appetite (p. 246). This assertion was based upon his belief that in higher organisms all the social emotions derived from reproduction. The prolonged care of an offspring which was a characteristic of the higher forms of life was accompanied by the psychic evolution of altruism from which the entire range of social feelings was developed. Altruism arising as it did from a biological function was as deeply rooted in human nature as the egoism which drove individual organisms in their "struggle for survival." For Geddes this meant that sexuality in humans was not associated with dominance and lust, but entirely with the rise of the social emotions. In society in his own day he saw a situation in which egoism and altruism were kept in precarious balance in the human psyche. For the future, however, he predicted a great increase in altruistic feelings to be brought about by the elevation of women in a society formerly ordered by male egoism. Females, through their nurture of the young, had unrivalled opportunities to develop their capacites for social feeling, and Geddes expected that their increased participation in social and political life would result in a redirection of social change toward a cooperative society, provided that it preserved separate sex roles appropriate to male and female temperaments.

By postulating an infinite human capacity for social feeling, Geddes was able to retain both the idea of romantic intensity in individual human relationships and an increasing ability for generalized social sentiments.

For the correct path to the future, however, it was necessary to follow the signs of biology. The growth of feminine altruism might be arrested if women abandoned passivity for masculine activism. To alter the profound psychic differences between the sexes it would be necessary to "have all of evolution over again on a new basis." Indeed to free women from their passivity and to open areas of social activity to them which placed them in competition with men would be socially dangerous. Certainly political agitation for female equality with men was fruitless. "What was decided among the prehistoric *Protozoa*," wrote Geddes," can not be annulled by act of parliament" (p. 247).

Lest women should rail against a biological providence which had given them "habits of body" which could be exploited by stronger men, Geddes hastened to proclaim that the study of sexuality in human societies gave no hint that political or social factors had led to the subjection of women. The situation of women in society was not the result of acquired characteristics. It merely reflected the economy of cell metabolism and its parallel psychic differentiation between the sexes. Women were not confined within the home because of their inferior muscular strength. Nor was their domesticity a reflection of a male conspiracy to monopolise military occupations and political power. On the contrary, even in the most primitive societies there had been no male domination in the allocation of sex roles. An uninformed observer might feel that in savage society there was inequity in a situation which gave menial tasks to women while their men lazed around between hunting trips, but once metabolism was considered as a basic factor determining social structures, it became clear that the male savage rested to accumulate the energy for sudden bursts of hunting, while the female merely kept going at routine occupations. There was no injustice in the routine, since female functions and the need to conserve energy for them made hunting out of the question for women (pp. 248-249).

Beyond the stage of primitive societies, the constitutional differences between the sexes had more profound social ramifications. Male intelligence was greater than female, men had greater independence and courage than women, and men were able to expend energy in sustained bursts of physical or cerebral activity. Men were thus activists and excelled in the species-preserving capacities of egoism. Women on the other hand possessed the social talents. They were superior to men in constancy of affection and sympathetic imagination. They were patient because of their passivity and the need to store energy — not, as feminists claimed, because patience is one of the qualities of the oppressed. Here was the traditional Victorian scheme of sexual temperaments. The male temperament was characterized, said Geddes, by "greater power of maximum effort, of scientific insight or cerebral experiment with impressions." Females had "greater patience, more open-mindedness, greater appreciation of subtle details, and consequently what we call more rapid intuition" (p. 250).

This typology of biologically determined sexual temperaments expressed unaltered the romantic myth of the rational male and the emotional, intuitive female. While preserving romantic images Geddes was able to give scientific authority to views of relationships between the sexes which were being questioned in the debate over the women question. History and anthropology might suggest the possibility of matriarchy, but Geddes's sexes had known the same division of labor since the most primitive single-celled organisms. There was no human guilt to be felt over the inferior position of women. It was a function of natural laws which operated well beyond the boundaries of human society.

When he turned his attention from the *protozoa* to contemporary society the social problem which troubled Geddes most deeply was the impact of industrialization on the roles of the sexes. He was afraid that in industrial capitalist society the laws of biology were being ignored because of the peremptory demands of an unnatural economic system. Women were plunging into the industrial struggle to earn their daily bread. By entering the work force they were competing with men and sabotaging the metabolic economy already defined by nature. Woolly headed social reformers might dream about the arrival of social equality through a redistribution of wealth brought about by paying higher wages for women's work, but such fantasies neglected the hard facts of biology, "it is not for the sake of production or distribution, or self-interest or mechanism, or any other idol of the economists, that the male organism organizes the climax of his life's struggle and labour, but for his mate; as she then, he also, for their little ones. Production is for consumption; the species is its own highest, its sole essential product . . ." (p. 249). There must be an angel in the house busy with her brood of children ready to turn the commercial world of everyday economic laws into something finer. It was upon this kind of cooperation between the sexes that "all progress past or future must depend" (p. 259).

If the sexual stereotypes which Geddes enshrined in his social theory were the conventional ones of Victorian domesticity, he departed from convention on the question of family size. He saw human progress arising from such new forms of cooperation between the sexes as the control of conception to permit smaller broods of children and greater individual development for females. Drawing on Herbert Spencer's *Principles of Biology* (1866), Geddes accepted the idea that advancing evolution was associated with a decline in fertility, because the matter and energy expended in completing and maintaining an individual life could not also be made available for the creation of new generations. Thus individual human development could only be achieved at the expense of fertility. This price Geddes was quite willing to pay for the achievement of better human organisms and an improved human environment. In his discussion of the laws of multiplication in the twentieth chapter of *The Evolution of Sex* he treated in some detail the various artificial means of preventing conception (pp. 270-272). Like all Victorians he feared that the universal adoption of birth-control might open such floodgates of sexuality that the human species might in future breed only virtuosos of the senses. Nonetheless he was convinced that rational attempts to control population were the key to future progress. The risk of increased sensuality was worth taking in view of the possibility of "a conscious and rational adjustment of the struggle [for survival] into the culture of existence" (p. 269).

The control of family size was necessary for both eugenic and economic reasons. Women should not be exhausted physically by annual child-bearing. It was also clear that the exploitive character of capitalism could only be maintained while there was an expanding labour force compelled by population pressure to accept employment at subsistence wages. Eugenics and economics thus both required reduction in family size. Yet fear of sensuality made Geddes reluctant to accept universal use of contraceptive devices. He advocated instead a new psychic development which would bring about a temperance in intercourse for married couples as controlling as the obligation to pre-marital chastity. However, where such new forms of consciousness had not evolved, eugenics required contraception. These might have an evolutionary value of their own because "by the very transition from unconscious animalism to deliberate prevention of fertilization" men and women would be bringing sexuality under rational control (p. 273). From this rationality it was possible that physical appetites might be eroded and relations between the sexes limited to the stimulation of romantic emotions. Sexual intemperance in marriages was to be discouraged by ethical development, otherwise married couples might fall to the "ethical level of the harlots and profligates of the streets" (p. 273). The Victorian fear of ungovernable sexual appetites would be disposed of in Geddes's new eugenic order by changes in social attitude and social structures. Human generative powers would be brought under control, not by economic or political measures, but by the improved education and increasing civic activity of women. Linked with this social change there would be a new economy of the sexes, in which female resources formerly allocated to reproduction would be placed at the disposal of society. Nature decreed that these resources would remain intuitive and sympathetic but human reason could be relied upon to direct them to wider social goals. Naturally the principle which is not articulated in this argument is that male reason would of necessity direct the utilization of feminine capacities. Nonetheless, the new social order derived from studying the laws of evolutionary progress was to be one in which female capacities had a central importance (pp. 273-274).

The new social order would be brought about by transforming relationships between the sexes so that their sensual encounters would be minimized and their sex-linked temperaments given new social expression (here Geddes resembled Freud for he saw progress in culture taking place at the expense of sensual gratification).[8] But, unlike Freud, he concluded that women as well as men were capable of sublimation. This view was derived from his understanding of the role of sex in the evolution of the higher forms of life. "Creation's final law" was not struggle but love, because the social affections were a precondition of progress (p. 286). It followed that the development of female emotive capacities was as essential to social progress as the masculine power of rationality. Geddes differed from Freud in seeing no danger to either sex from the repression of sexual drives. These could always be given adequate expression through generalized social affections. In part this difference can be explained by the social context in which Geddes carried out his study of sexuality. His passion for the study of social structures and family life led him in 1887 to take up residence in a crowded slum quarter of Edinburgh.[9] Residence in poverty-stricken James Court meant that Geddes saw sexuality from the standpoint of the urban poor, rather than from the genteel context of the prosperous middle class. Since women were vital to the economy of the pauper household, Geddes could no more imagine them lacking in social function than he could question their biological function. Passive and emotive they must be, but never dysfunctional.

The Evolution of Sex enjoyed considerable réclame after its publication in 1889. Because of its treatment of the forbidden subject of birth-control it went through three printings and two different editions in Great Britain.[10] It came out the next year in the United States as a volume in the Humboldt Library of Science. Two years later, when a French translation was published, Geddes had become an authority of international reputation on his chosen subject. Besides the impact of his published work Geddes was an influential teacher.

In 1887 he borrowed from the American Chautauqua Society the idea of a summer series of lectures for adult education. In his Edinburgh version of the summer school, the lectures alternated between French and English and the student body was decidedly cosmopolitan. While his courses on evolutionary ethics were scantily attended during the early summer sessions, the program began to attract an average of about 120 students by 1893.[11] Among them Charles Zeublin (the Chicago sociologist) and William James have left records testifying to the impact of Geddes's teaching and to the scientific credentials of his students. When the Edinburgh summer school was abandoned it was replaced by more ambitious schemes for international education. The one which had the most transatlantic significance was the International School which Geddes supervised at the Paris Exposition of 1900.[12] Organized under the joint auspices of the British and French Associations for the Advancement of Science, the school had such distinguished lecturers as Lester Ward and Jane Addams representing American sociology, Henri Bergson teaching evolutionary science, and James Bryce outlining the stages of constitutional development. Though attended only by fellow intellectuals visiting the Exposition, the International School made a deep impression on its small student and teaching body. Geddes, as its organizer, planned the courses offered so that they provided an integrated and synthetic view of the vast array of technological and cultural displays at the Exposition. He hoped that, by pooling the intellectual resources of the United States, France, and Great Britain, new insights could be developed into the emerging character of urban, technological society, and a truly Comtean synthesis of existing knowledge in sociology could be forged. But by 1900 the wave of the future in the social sciences was no longer towards a positivist reliance on biological determinants of social structures and, therefore, the International School was one of the last gatherings of social scientists at which scholars claimed to range over the entire field of biology, cultural anthropology, and social psychology with the confidence that Geddes had exhibited in writing *The Evolution of Sex*. After 1900 the inheritance of sex and sex-linked characteristics became the province of genetics. The question of sexual behaviour was illuminated by developments in endocrinology. And the whole question of cultural evolution was divorced from the single progression from primitive to civilized societies which the positivists had envisioned. Thus, with the closing of the International School in 1900, the synthesis of biological, physical, and sociological ideas which Geddes had been trying to achieve became progressively more outmoded. He was to move on to another career as an expert in regional surveys, town planning, and the study of urban civilizations. Nevertheless, his influence on social thought was far reaching; he had intellectual heirs both in Great Britain and the United States.

In the United States his most important popularizer was Jane Addams. She accepted Geddes's idea of biologically determined masculine and feminine temperaments, and based her hopes for the ethical and social improvement of American society upon the political and social activism of women. Following Geddes to the letter, she expected the collectivization of the competitive industrial order of the United States to come about through the moral insights of women, and she undertook to articulate this feminine consciousness for her fellow Americans. Two of her most widely read books took as their point of departure Geddes's sexually determined temperaments. In *Democracy and Social Ethics* (New York, 1902), she worked a familiar theme from Geddes's evolutionary thought by pointing to the need for a psychic evolution by which the domestic morality of small-town America could be generalized to create a cooperative community appropriate to a democratic society. The agents of this moral change were to be women, whose powers of intuition and empathy could be redirected from family to society. *Newer Ideals of Peace* (New York, 1907) was a further treatise on the possibility of psychic and ethical evolution. In it she examined the possibility that industrial societies had evolved beyond warfare and that heroism should consequently take on new psychic and ethical forms. In accordance with Geddes's view of the female temperament, Jane Addams was finally moved to become one of the founders of the Woman's Peace Party in the United States and to lead its campaign to join with other women's organizations in Europe in attempting mediation between the belligerent powers in World War I. This abortive effort at mediation was based on the assumption that there was a universal feminine temperament governed by the biological function of nurturing life, which could be relied on to harness male aggressions under all circumstances of nationality and international conflict. The messianic hopes of the women's peace movement, which were to prove sadly mistaken during 1915-19, derived directly from the kind of evolutionary speculation which Geddes had publicized with such vigour and effectiveness. They were particularly strong in the United States where the social role of middle-class women could most easily be approximated to Geddes's picture of the *anabolic* female.[13]

In England Geddes found a forum for his ideas in the London Sociological Society, founded in 1903. Among his fellow members were H. G. Wells, Leonard T. Hobhouse, J. A. Hobson, and Graham Wallas. Most members of the society were intolerant of Geddes's positivism and puzzled by his religious orientation, but they all shared his interest in collectivism and the evolution of the social feelings. Leonard Hobhouse developed an interest in the evolution of collective psychic phenomena which shared much of Geddes's evolutionary optimism.[14] The new school of social psychologists abandoned the positivist assumption that biology determined social structures and set themselves to study "the social mind," a collective entity which evolved by its own laws. In his *Mind in Evolution* of 1901 and *Morals in Evolution* of 1906, Hobhouse drew optimistic conclusions similar to those of Geddes about the possibility of human psychic and moral growth.[15] In studying social development Hobhouse laid particular stress on the extent to which human rationality could become a determining factor in evolution. Geddes had introduced this idea in his plea for rational control of sex drives and population growth. Where Geddes had seen creation's final law as one hymn of love, Hobhouse made the evolution of mind with its power of purposive control of human action "the central fact in the history of life on earth."[16] In making rationality replace the social feelings as the major theme in man's evolutionary ascent, Hobhouse was obliged to consider the role of sex and sex-related temperaments in social development. Working from the developing study of comparative psychology rather than from biology, he discarded Geddes's assumption that maternal affections were the origin of social feelings.

Comparative psychologists had developed the concept of "instinct" to distinguish between animal behaviour and feeling directed by human rationality.[17] In the study of instinct Hobhouse found no evidence to suggest that a large-scale transfer of a specialized instinct like maternal feeling could be effected toward more general objects. The data suggested a contrary conclusion that generalized feelings became progressively specialized in a pattern of instinctive behaviour. Maternal and paternal devotion, family feelings in general, were thus not the source of the social affections but simply specialized examples of a tendency which was inherent in mind, the impulse to sympathy which was the basis of all feelings of community.[18] Sympathy was seen to be a universal human attribute, but the generalization did not lead Hobhouse to any revolutionary views about the social role of women. In this matter alone biological determinism remained an unquestioned principle. In the matter of relations between the sexes Hobhouse urged modifications of family and sexual codes to "reconcile" educated women to "motherhood of the healthy and capable as a form of social service." Social structures might evolve according to their own laws but, in the matter of the family, eugenics required the continuation of a sturdy domesticity. The elevation of women, which had been a central theme in sociological thought since Comte first coined the name for his new science, now became their rise to a position of "equality" in marriage and parenthood and in the power of dissolving an unhappy marriage union.[19]

No matter how the new social science changed its methods, biology remained the determinant of female functions, and sex roles were interpreted according to the accepted values of contemporary social convention. Geddes had reflected on the social role of women from the standpoint of the Edinburgh slums, where working-class women had vital economic functions. But Hobhouse worked in the conventional urban middle-class milieu of the modern intellectual where women's function seemed irrevocably maternal and domestic. By these different intellectual paths both arrived at the conclusion that for women biology controlled social destiny.

The significance of Geddes's positivism in the development of English evolutionary thought is that it carried on a European tradition which expected significant social improvement to come about through enlarging the sphere in which women's sex-determined mentalities could operate. Thus, while clinging to the romantic stereotype of women as passive and emotive, Geddes tended to raise in his evolutionary thought important questions about the emergence of women from Victorian domesticity. When the generation of Hobhouse turned away from positivism to study the evolution of human rationality, they kept to the same stereotypes of sexual temperaments that had operated in Geddes's thought. After 1903, however, the significance of so-called feminine temperament ceased to preoccupy social scientists, for in endocrinology there was a simple and easily acceptable answer for most supposed temperamental differences between men and women. Man's evolutionary ascent toward rationality and rational control of social structures became a drama in which male powers of reasoning were the critical forces for social betterment. Thus in the abandonment of positivism there were powerful forces at work which tended toward a conservative view of women and their social position. These forces have operated in the social sciences ever since the turn of the century and they have yet to encounter significant opposition. When social scientists abandoned Comte's hierarchy of sciences they also rejected the concern of the French utopians with sexual liberation, and adopted unquestioningly the Spencerian idea that procreative functions brought about an early arrest in the development of women. This assumption, shared by Freud, has governed the study of women's social role despite the development of an extremely sophisticated technology to control procreation in twentieth century. Geddes through his intellectual links with the French utopians was moved to try to grasp the significance of that technology in 1889, but the persistence of sexual stereotypes has prevented much serious thought on the subject for almost a century.

9: Innocent Femina Sensualis in Unconscious Conflict

Peter T. Cominos

ONE VICTORIAN MODEL, HOMO ECONOMICUS, IS FAMILIAR TO EVERYONE and it may be the only safe ground from which to begin this chapter.[1] Homo Economicus was endowed with constant but conflicting positive and negative economic motives. In the model the positive desire for wealth was opposed by the negative aversion for labor and by the negative desire for the present enjoyment of costly indulgences. Good Homo Economicus resolved his economic conflict positively, that is, virtuously. He habitually practised the ascetic economic virtues, being a paragon of calculation, industry, thrift, sobriety, temperance, and continence. The economic virtues were an outward, visible sign of an inward condition of good character.

The formation of the respectable self-controlled social character depended upon the strengthening of the will. Habitual resistance to the temptation of indulging himself strengthened his power to resist. "Resist manfully," Samuel Smiles exhorted his readers, "and the first decision will give strength for life; repeated it will become a habit." Established habits acted involuntarily and effortlessly upon the individual. Virtuous habits were developed easily in the young and they endured for life. As habits strengthened with age, and the character became formed, deviations from good conduct became increasingly rare. Later *unlearn-ing* was more difficult than early learning. Properly developed, the social character of respectable market-oriented man was suited to the economic role incumbent upon his position in the social system of machine production. "Character" was, as Smiles said, "moral order embodied in the individual."[2] The foundation of the moral order was the individual's power of forgoing immediate gratification of desire for the sake of future good.[3]

The sexual counterpart of Homo Economicus at the market was Homo Sensualis in bed.[4] But this chapter is only incidentally concerned with these two models upon which the social character of the Christian gentleman or manly man was formed. Rather it is concerned with one of their two feminine counterparts in the home, Femina Domestica and Femina Sensualis, the two models of feminine human nature upon which the social character of well-to-do daughters was formed, the so-called womanly woman. Formed upon that model, she could be assimilated into the family as daughter, wife and mother. Femina Sensualis is the subject of this chapter.

Femina Sensualis, like her masculine counterpart, Homo Sensualis, was an inarticulated but real model of feminine human nature. From the model all but opposing sexual motives were abstracted. In Femina Sensualis, the temptation to sinful indulgence of the flesh was presented as a conflict between the highest part of human nature, referred to either as the soul or duty or reason — in reality, conscience — and the lowest part of human nature, the body or appetite or animalism — in reality, the sexual instinct or desire. Unlike Homo Sensualis, in whom the conflict of these same antagonistic sexual motives was always conscious and intense, Femina Sensualis was a dual model, either innocent or tainted, in whom the conflict took place unconsciously for the innocent or consciously for the tainted, but not very intensely. Like the sexual conflict which beset Homo Sensualis, the chaste resolution of the conflict conformed to the normative sexual behavior expected of genteel woman. Chaste behavior was the foundation of that social system of relations and actions known as the genteel family. Female chastity constituted a mode of relatedness to themselves and to their male counterparts that was fundamental to the survival of the genteel family. Thus the social character of the womanly woman, Femina Sensualis, normative behavior, consciousness, and family existence were delicate and inseparable strands making up a generalized pattern of genteel feminine life. The scope of this chapter is restricted to the unconscious conflict of innocent woman.

I   Innocence in the Making of an Unconscious Conflict

Innocent Femina Sensualis waged her battle between sensual desire and duty at an unconscious level. Innocence, as the mechanism of sexual repression, played the key role in making the conflict unconscious.

Respectable Victorians did not understand the mechanism, but they desired the result. For them "innocence" or "pure-mindedness" or "inherent purity" was an exalted state of feminine consciousness, a state of unique deficiency or mindlessness in their daughters of that most elementary, but forbidden knowledge of their own sexuality, instincts and desires as well as the knowledge of good and evil.

According to respectable theory[5] all women had "mercifully" bestowed upon them "a remnant of the innocence of Paradise." Paradisiacal innocence of the knowledge of good and evil disposed young women to preserve their chastity. In the words of a staunch defender of innocence, "purity is an instrument by which the least peril to virtue is instantly detected."[6] The daughter's innate innocence established her first line of defense against the predatory male animal. Exposed to the knowledge of the world, the daughters of the poor, "like their Mother Eve,"[7] were not contented with a little knowledge, but probed as deeply as possible and ate of the fruit of knowledge. Once innocence was lost, the daughter's chastity became vulnerable. In the words of Miss E. M. Sewell, educator and leading militant of innocence, "if a girl's mind is not pure, – if her own instincts are so blunted that she cannot *feel* evil before she can explain it – if she cannot shrink from it without knowing why she does so — may God help her! for the wisest safeguards which the best friends may provide for her will never be sufficient to secure her from danger" (p. 81). This passage unwittingly articulated innocence as the mechanism of sexual repression. Innocence as the respectable state of womanly consciousness was sustained through innocence as the respectable mechanism of repression. Repressive innocence created psychological resistance to the conscious acknowledgment of sexual realities unpalatable to the world of respectability in its mindless innocence. Psychological resistance created insuperable barriers to the re-entry into consciousness of childhood memories and awareness of sexuality. Innocent Femina Sensualis was beset by an unconscious conflict between a repressed conscience and unconscious sexual desires.

Alone the daughters were unable to preserve the innocence of their consciousness. It was the joint enterprise of cooperative daughters and mothers or parents who spared no effort to shield their daughters from a reality which the genteel classes perceived to be sexually contaminated. Podsnappery symbolized the acute consciousness of sex everywhere, taking its most ludicrous form in the draping of naked piano legs. Podsnappery became forever apprehensive about bringing the blush to the cheeks of the celebrated Young Person. The vigilant prudery of Podsnappery performed the task of eternally safeguarding the innocence of the Young Person from the contamination of a reality thoroughly suffused with the fear and hatred of human sexuality.

The world of pornography shared this view of a reality thoroughly sexualized. The pornographic male indulged his insatiable appetite and always hungered for more.[8] He reduced women to the sole function of the totally permissive whore as against the strict and unbending morality of the father-figure.[9] The inwardly respectable male resisted sexual temptation. He desexualized women as an aid to his own continence. He even invented an electric alarm clock in which an erection closed the circuit, awakened the guilt-ridden sleeper, and saved him from the catastrophe of a nocturnal emission.[10] The desexualized repressed daughter internalized a kind of Podsnappian resistance to the acknowledgment of realities whose existence was so unpalatable to the world of respectable culture that they were denied. Early childhood sexual experiences and their memory were such realities. The internal world of the daughter's repression and the external world of Podsnappian demands collaborated to fulfill the cultural expectations of the daughter's innocence of consciousness.

To preserve innocence, the struggle had to begin early. According to the respectable theory, all children were pure and innocent but inherited a fallen nature. "If left to themselves, that nature" speedily developed itself. To stifle that development, God had mercifully aided women "by making a part of woman's nature to shrink from anything which is wanting in delicacy or modesty: but this instinct is very much stronger in youth than it is in infancy and childhood." Scarcely perceptible at first, it needed to be cultivated. Children ought to be punished for doing or saying anything not refined or modest just as they were for lying. While children were still in the nursery, it was advisable for mothers, according to Miss Sewell, to "take the trouble to make and maintain a few regulations which concern their delicacy and purity." Infractions deserved sharp and instant punishment. It was useless to warn, reprove or advise. What was aimed at was not "comprehension, but obedience; only, in order to obey, there must be commands — definite and rendered practicable — which shall be based upon these common rules of decorum that must be observed in after years, and which should be enforced on the nurse as well as the children" (pp. 88-89). While their consciences were dormant and insensitive to the proprieties, it was necessary to teach very young children the morality of the drawing room. If successful in the nursery, the next stage in the impressment of principles of modesty and refinement was in large measure achieved. Then little girls, Miss Sewell announced triumphantly, could even share the same room, for having learnt to be modest in deed, they would, according to expectations, be modest in words.

II The Components of the Conflict: Conscience and Feminine Sexuality

Innocence kept Femina Sensualis in unconscious conflict. The components of that conflict were a negative prohibitive conscience and sexual desire. The formation of the negative conscience may be said to be closely related to the process of making daughters innocent. From a very early age feminine conscience was deeply penetrated with the fear of becoming aware of sensuality, which in itself was bad feminine conscience, for it contradicted the family and cultural goal of innocence. The price of an ostensibly good conscience was the repression of sexual awareness and desires. So-called innocence was tantamount to good conscience although it is clear that girls would always be in doubt about the completeness or thoroughness of their innocence, which in turn induced guilt and anxiety. The loss of pure-mindedness was described in terms of "scars" and "wounds" seen and felt by the unfortunate girl. In a soliloquy written for her by that missionary of innocence, Miss Sewell, the tainted daughter sorrowfully reproached herself: "Oh that I had been warned! that I had not been left to the workings of my own mind! that I had learned in infancy to be ashamed of those things which I felt to be evil, though I knew not why! But I was left without a word of caution, and now I can but struggle to forget, what with that caution I might never have learnt" (pp. 81-82). That is the soliloquy of a daughter who has lost her innocence but not her deep repression, anxieties and guilt, nor her prohibitory conscience.

Sexual instinct was the second component of the unconscious conflict of Femina Sensualis, innocent or tainted. The instinct was of a dual nature. The maternal instinct was alleged to be intense and honorable,[11] but hardly actualized before marriage. Its tremendous power greatly exceeded the desire for physical love in normal women, which was disparaged as a lower order.[12] They were not much troubled with sexual feeling; it was in abeyance. Physical desire was alleged to be exceptionally weak and only became intense when it reached the pathological stage of nymphomania,[13] a form of insanity.[14] It was commonly assumed that men "from the nature of their physical constitution and training" were disposed to exaggerate the physical side of love. Less passionate in temperament and educated to a different ideal or standard, genteel women were disposed to minimize the physical and to exalt the emotional and spiritual side of love.[15] They desired affection, not sensuality; the best mothers and wives knew little or nothing of sexual indulgence. As Acton put it, "Love of home, children, and domestic duties, are the only passions they feel." "As a general rule," Acton continued, "a modest woman seldom desires any sexual gratification for herself. She submits to her husband, but only to please him; and, but for the desire of maternity, would far rather be relieved from his attention" (pp. 102-103).

Femina Sensualis, innocent or tainted, in unconscious or more or less conscious conflict, remained, in theory, untroubled by the debilitating inner struggle that beset Homo Sensualis because of his universally acknowledged but lamented powerful sexual drive. Unlike Homo Sensualis, Femina Sensualis was scarcely racked by an inner struggle; her inner protagonists were so unequally matched. Her elusive conscience shrank from overt battle with an inordinately weak physical desire without knowing why. There was so little to conquer. Here is a passage which sums up perfectly the opposing character of the struggle in Homo Sensualis and Femina Sensualis and exonerates the double standard for men. Nature has "provided women with a natural safeguard against persistent passion which is wholly denied to men. It is relatively less excusable, for a woman endowed with modesty, consecrated with the gift of purity, and provided with the natural relief from the baser and more animal part of her nature to be immoral, than it is for a man to obey the nature of his sex with no established safeguard of modest purity and natural help whatever."[16]

III   The Exclusion of the Weak Ego and the
      Moral Irresponsibility of the Conflict

The ego was excluded from the unconscious conflict which divided Femina Sensualis against herself. Her ego was too weak to mediate between the claims of conscience and of sensuality. In Femina Sensualis the sense of I-ness, of individuality, of apartness, was thwarted in its development. "Women don't consider themselves as human beings at all," proclaimed Florence Nightingale in an impassioned denunciation of the Evangelicals for what she thought was their role in the idolatrous "fetish" worship of the family.[17] So very much in Victorian life was designed to promote womanly self-effacement and absorption into family life. "All the moralities tell women that it is their duty," wrote John Stuart Mill, "and all the current sentimentalities that it is their nature to live for others; to make complete abnegations of themselves, and to have no life but in their affections."[18] Conventional Victorians feared improvement in the lives of women which might strengthen them to stand alone.[19] Women were praised for their "child-like innocence and infantine simplicity."[20] They were brought up to be clinging and dependent and their relatedness to the world was a highly dependent one. When they married, they merged their existence into that of their husbands. It was widely believed that "the wife's true relation to her husband" was that her "whole life and being, her soul, body, time, property, thought, and care, ought to be given to her husband; that nothing short of such absorption in him and his interests makes her a true wife. . . ."[21] Brought up with such expectations, it is not difficult to appreciate why womanly women lacked the ego-strength to enter into the struggle between duty and sensuality.

The exclusion of the weak ego and sexual repression perpetuated a defective sense of responsibility. Moral responsibility presupposed freedom of choice as well as the knowledge of moral alternatives. Victorian culture and the genteel family withheld the knowledge from their daughters and their responsibility for choosing. Innocent daughters were spared the awareness of conflicting motives. Hence there was no conscious conflict for innocent daughters; no conscious choice to be made. A conscious struggle was waged on behalf of their moral purity by overprotective parents and chaperons who were forever cognizant of danger. As a state of repressed consciousness, innocence absolved daughters from the exercise of responsibility.

Innocence was a key device for forming feminine character upon the model of the womanly woman. Mill denounced it as a degrading model, a barrier to the realization of autonomy. He drew a contrast with the masculine model who was taught responsibility for his conduct. Women were taught to believe, Mill wrote, "that their ideal of character is the very opposite of that of men; not self-will, and government by self-control, but submission, and yielding to the control of others" (p. 27). For those who believed that this was the destiny of women it was proposed that the position of the sexes be reversed and that men be placed in relations that required them to be modest and obedient. In a generation every characteristically feminine weakness, it was charged, might well be anticipated to appear in men's character.[22]

IV The Resolutions of Sexual Conflicts in Homo Sensualis
    and Femina Sensualis

The character of the inner struggle between duty and sexual desire was not only acknowledged to be of a significantly different order in gentlemen and ladies, but the respectable resolution of the conflicts in terms of continence and chastity took contrasting forms as well. The moral prescription, like innocence, devised for women to attain virtue markedly deviated from the paths laid out for men. Gentlemen, aware of their sexual impulses, attained to virtue by consciously and deliberately sublimating their desires through work and the cult of athleticism. They need only be made cognizant of the dangers to their perfect continence. Their mortal enemies were luxurious living and idleness. Both were promotive of lust, concluded Dr. Lawson Tait, in monkeys as well as men. Dr. Tait drew that conclusion after reflecting upon the universal practice of masturbation among monkeys in captivity. "I fancy," he wrote, "that it is rather the result of luxury living, their freedom from the strain of earning an honest livelihood in the native circumstances of their wild life."[23] No good Anglo-Saxon wanted Englishmen to look like monkeys, lacking in self-control. Such a place was reserved for the Irish.[24] Gentlemen were, therefore, perennially exhorted to control their impulses by strengthening their will to resist. Habitual resistance to temptation strengthened their character and facilitated self control.

The sins of the flesh scarcely troubled angelic women. The temptation to sexual indulgence in them should not be exaggerated. To do so was to compound the already difficult problem of masculine control. Accordingly, ladies were desexualized to help gentlemen cope with the problem of controlling their own sexuality. Young men had erroneously formed their opinions of women's sexual feelings from what they observed of "loose" or "low and vulgar women," pretty women, not necessarily prostitutes, who liked to attract men of higher social status. "Any susceptible boy is easily led to believe, whether he is altogether overcome by the syren or not," wrote Dr. William Acton, "that she, and therefore all women, must have at least as strong passions as himself." The early experience was corroborated when prostitutes simulated sexual feelings so well that the unsuspecting novice thought it genuine. Dr. Acton wrote to expose the fallacy propagated by "loose" women and prostitutes, and to "vindicate female nature from the vile aspersions cast on it by the abandoned conduct and ungoverned lusts of a few of its worst examples" (1862 ed., p. 102). Although Acton admitted that "all we have read and heard tends to prove that a reciprocity of this sexual desire is, to a great extent, necessary to excite the male. . . ." (1857 ed., p. 57), he nonetheless subscribed to the gentleman's ideal woman. She was passionless. Womanly women, living up to the stereotype, were "afraid to admit they have any desire for sexual pleasure."[25] Understanding their problem in this perspective of their own and women's nature, gentlemen were held responsible for their behavior. In their attainment of virtue through sublimation, not the impulse itself was suppressed, but the immoral action which would follow from its indulgence.

The contrast with ladies is simply marvelous. They were alleged to have no physical desire to control so long as their innate "island of innocence" was kept pure by the proper surveillance of mothers and chaperons and by the sense of shame which every manifestation of their own erotic desire aroused. Theoretically and ideally, gentlemen were to be masters of themselves, responsible and self-controlled; ladies had nothing to master or to be responsible for and were to be controlled or "protected" by others. Thus, in the Victorian battle of the sexes, women were disarmed of the weapon of their sexuality. Gentlemen imposed unilateral disarmament upon them which they simultaneously denied doing through the theory of feminine sexual anaesthesia.

While gentlemen were urged to conquer their sexual instincts by complete sublimation through work, genteel women, barred from work and confined to the family circle, sublimated through religion, "the only channel" through which the sexual emotions could be expressed "freely without impropriety."[26] Women realized ideal-love in the religious sense. In the fifties and sixties the "sanctimonious," as the "Evangelical" type of young lady was called, read little but religious tracts, saintly biographies or the worst class of fiction — religious tales; they flaunted their virtue and piety.[27] Annie Besant, born in 1847, was an excellent representative of the sublimated Evangelical. From the age of eight, her education deepened the emotional and religious side of her character and turned her into a pious Evangelical. Tales of the early Christian martyrs inspired fantasies wherein she vicariously experienced martyrdom, being "flung to lions, tortured on the rack, burned at the stake." She passionately lamented that these heroic religious deeds could not be realized again in her own lifetime. Just as her education precluded the reading of romantic novels, so reveries of romantic love were absent from her daydreams. "No knowledge of evil had been allowed to penetrate" her dreamy life. She was "kept innocent of all questions of sex." In her childhood and youth "the budding tendrils of passion" were entwined about two ideals, Christ and her mother. She longed to spend her time in worshipping Jesus. So far as her inner life was concerned, she was absorbed in that passionate love. The human passion of love was transfigured to an ideal.[28] In the Evangelical version of ideal-love, passion was completely deflected from all other human beings to the love of Christ.

It was not without justification that Geoffrey Mortimer wrote about self-deception as the source of much pietistic emotion. "Ample testimony," he declared, "could be afforded to prove the passion of love and the fervour of religion are closely related" (pp. 52-53). Dr. Maudsley, the pathologist, wrote that religious sublimation was expressed in forms of "mental derangement marked by a strange mixture of erotic feeling and religious visions or delusions" (p. 64).

Repression removed the sexual instinct from awareness, but being irrepressible, not from existence, and it therefore exercised a profound influence upon the repressed daughter. She became subject to motives and desires of which she was not aware. She acted upon motives unconscious of their origins,[29] and was spared the knowledge of knowing what she was doing. The innocent and pietistic woman, as Mortimer pointed out, "imagines that she has subjugated the instinct of her sex; but in reality her emotions have a sexual origin." Mortimer penetrated the evil of disguised motives characteristic of innocently brought-up daughters. "Such minds," he wrote, "are self-deceived as to the sources of their pietistic emotion, yet do not always wilfully deceive others." Mortimer drew attention to the pathogenic power of repressed motives in pathological cases. "In mania, old maids, in whom no one but the neurologist would suspect immodesty, frequently suffer from erotic delusions, suppressed desires leading them to firmly believe that they have been ravished" (pp. 52-53). Repressed Victorian sexuality reasserted itself in indirect ways in the symbolic disguises of dreams and fantasies and in symptoms of commissions wherein acts alien to the actors themselves were carried out.

Innocence was not a perfect guarantee for chastity. Innocent Femina Sensualis sometimes resolved her unconscious conflict viciously. The angelic daughter succumbed to the assault of the aggressive male and committed the unforgivable sin. The innocent were indeed seduced. To explain their seduction without contradicting the theory of innocence and feminine sexual anaesthesia the respectable theory or ideology known as the "seduction of the innocent" was formulated. In the fifties and sixties the responsibility for seduction never rested with the innocent, angelic, non-seductive, non-cooperative, naïve, helpless victim whose famous last words were "I didn't mean to do it." She had no guile and no passion, for women were "mercifully constituted with less temptation to sin than men."[30] The initiative for seduction was entirely the seducer's own although the seduced woman paid the inexorable penalty of social ostracism for her seduction. Among the respectables the principal cause of prostitution was alleged to be seduction which was embodied in the formula, "seduced, deserted by lover, and cast off by relations."[31]

In the early 1890's the theory of seduction was revised. Although much survived of the original theory, the responsibility for seduction was now said to be the work of seductive and cooperative women. Until the young daughter was safely brought to maturity, her virtue was the responsibility of her mother who knew the dangers of life and from what girls ought to be protected. If they fell after that, they were "self-seduced quite as much as betrayed." Where ought the blame to be put? "On those whose nature it is to seek and have when they can, or on those whose duty it is to defend and deny?"[32] The theory was now bereft of any exonerating notion of the feminine lack of guile, of naïveté, and helplessness. In the great majority of cases women were responsible for themselves and mothers for their daughters. Women had the initial advantages bestowed by nature. After all women were angels born; men animals.[33] Whether seduced or themselves seductive and cooperative, the responsibility for purity was entirely feminine, and women had to bear the brunt of the public censure, the penalty, and the guilt alone for its loss.

Why did this reversal of responsibility in seduction occur? The weak and very immature character of the womanly woman of the fifties and sixties was less able to resist the advances of her suitor than her own daughter of the nineties. Her immature inability to say no when motives and desires influenced her action and from whose influences her "in-nocence" kept her unconscious made her vulnerable. She needed to be chaperoned. It is certain that in the nineties the character of well-to-do women was more mature, being less family-locked and having greater associations outside the narrow confines of the family circle. The daughters were then expected to resist temptations. They possessed the strength of character to say no. It is clear by then that they had less "innocence," a subject itself then being widely debated and for the most part repudiated as outmoded.

When Femina Sensualis was tainted or tarnished with the knowledge of good and evil and made conscious of her own erotic desires, she became a model in conscious conflict. Unlike innocent Femina Sensualis, the unmarried daughter as tainted Femina Sensualis resolved her conflict consciously. But like the innocent model, the tainted one worked out her conflict either virtuously or viciously. Deprived of innocence, she was thought to be more vulnerable than her pure-minded sisters, but nonetheless capable of remaining chaste and realizing the chief precept of the code of sexual respectability. Although tainted, she responded positively to the respectable sexual motives lodged in her conscience. According to respectable theory innocence was not exactly irrevocably lost, although its passing left something to be deeply regretted. It lowered the esteem of the daughter in her own eyes as well as others, but the loss was partially recoverable. Once tainted, the young girl could be restored to the state of consciousness akin to innocence. The grace of God and the mother's vigilance did wonders by way of restoration, even though the original and incomparable purity itself was scarred (Sewell, p. 81). When the mask of ideology is removed from the theory, the gnawing negative conscience remained to keep the daughter virtuous; in spite of the tainted consciousness, the psychological resistence, no longer as profound, was sustained; overprotective chaperonage kept vigil over the daughter's chastity, and family-confined existence minimized the need for vigilance.

Like innocent Femina Sensualis as the victim of seduction, the tainted model, though it seems rarely, resolved her sexual conflict unchastely. She acted upon depraved sexual motives and her conscious immoral action represented the chief infraction of the code of sexual respectability. According to respectable theory impure girls and women lost their virtue because delinquent parents, nurses and governesses failed to cultivate their innocence and to check their inherited fallen nature. Their thoughts were allowed to become impure and their latent depravity, no longer thwarted, was affirmed.

It was this contingency and the infraction of the code that the genteel family and Victorian culture viewed with the profoundest apprehension. Conscience, whether innocent or tainted, conscious or unconscious, was the chief internal mechanism in making women conform to the code of sexual respectability. This internal device was buttressed by the perpetual surveillance of the family and chaperons. Conformity to the code was reinforced by four major external mechanisms which may be mentioned in passing: (1) the unbridgeable gulf formed between the chaste and unchaste, (2) the indiscriminate severity of social ostracism imposed upon the unchaste, (3) the efficacy of that sanction upon ladies, and (4) the respectable ideology which held that the loss of chastity totally corrupted feminine character.

Unchastity decidedly turned a Victorian woman into a prostitute. "Literally every woman who yields to her passions and loses her virtue is a prostitute," declared one of the spokesmen for the code of sexual respectability, "but many draw a distinction between those who live by promiscuous intercourse, and those who confine themselves to one man."[34] As yielding only in marriage was sanctioned, any other mode of sexual surrender had, in the nature of existing social arrangement, to be identified with the world of prostitution. Thus it is clear that an unmarried or married woman's known sexual behavior classified her either as a respectable member of the social system of the family or one who had fallen below the line of respectability into the subsocial system of prostitution, the negation of the family.

While wayward genteel women fell into prostitution out of their innocence, weakness, and failure to respond to their innate protective sense of modesty, Dr. Charles Mercier, the "alienist" or psychiatrist, interpreted the deviation of prostitution to be a moral failure of character as well as a mark of insanity. His observation rested upon the correct presupposition that being overwhelmingly non-genteel in their class origins prostitutes ordinarily would not be exclusively confined to the role of Femina Domestica, but would be obliged to work and would therefore need to manifest those outward signs of good inward character, the economic virtues associated with Homo Economicus. As prostitutes conspicuously failed to imbibe the commensurate economic virtues as well as failing to develop the civilized instinct of modesty, Dr. Mercier censoriously charged that prostitutes were atavistic throwbacks defective in that inhibitory power which underlay both the economic virtues and modesty: "they exhibit other forms of vice, showing that generally, their capacity of self-restraint is undeveloped. They are usually drunkards; they are always spendthrift . . . they are thoroughly immoral. . . . It is not that the moral impulse towards lust is greater in them than in most women, but the restraint of modesty is less. Incapable of continuous industry, they are yet under the necessity of making a livelihood, and in the absence of restraint of modesty, they turn to that occupation in which a livelihood can be made without industry" (p. 275). Prostitutes resembled the monkeys and Irish in captivity.

Women were classified into polar extremes. They were either sexless ministering angels or sensuously oversexed temptresses of the devil; they were either aids to continence or incontinence; they facilitated or they exacerbated male sexual control. Although apart, these polarities shared an attitude of disguised masculine hostility toward women. It was a fragment of that antifeminine ideology that represented at the level of consciousness those corresponding relations of domination and dependent submission that characterized family existence. *The*

Whore's Catechism echoed the implicit respectable attitude explicitly and more flagrantly in its aggressiveness for womankind as the following question and answer indicated: "Q. – Have all women a decided penchant to become whores? A. – Yes; all are, or desire to be, whores, and it is nothing but pride or fear that restrains the greater part, and every girl who yields for the first time is from that moment a decided whore. The smock once lifted, she is as familiarized to the game as if she had played it for ten years."[35] As negations, the two polarities of family and prostitution were diametrically opposed in their expressions of hostility. In its disguised hostility the world of respectability admitted and lamented the latent depravity of women, but exalted them in their angelic innocence. Superficially, it placed women upon a pedestal. In its avowed hostility the world of prostitution exalted both the potential and the real depravity, and called innocence fear. It placed women where they belonged; respectable ideology disguised the reality of shared hostility. Pimps, prostitutes and madams could have cared less until, like Mrs. Warren, having acquired the price of their withdrawal, they chose to make a dash for respectability.

Victorian society and the family spawned two kinds of women, the womanly woman and her negation, the whorely whore: the pure and the impure. As we have seen, they were sharply differentiated in their awareness and conduct and in the approval and disapproval and the rewards and punishments which others, especially women, eagerly conferred upon them. The pure woman was innocent, inviolate, inspirational and indulged; the impure woman (less than a woman) was doubtful, detected, detestable and destroyed. No dialectic could join the two; a great and impassable gulf divided them. In summary, the respectable ideal of purity represented unadulterated femininity; her opposite represented the *projection* of those rejected and unacceptable desires and actions that must be destroyed to keep women pure beings. If those thoughts and actions could not be totally suppressed inside the womanly woman, they had to be destroyed in the projected outside version of herself. Mrs. Lynn Linton made the fictional character of Lord Exmour the spokesman for the respectable point of view and the exemplar of projected self-hate when he vented his attitude toward the poor criminal and the prostitute, those personifications which negated the respectable goals of wealth and purity: "I would clear them out like rats."[36] In the lessons which Shaw drew from Ibsen's plays there was a hard kernel of truth. Haute bourgeoisie family relations engendered and projected self-hate. "They hate their neighbours as themselves."[37]

V Femina Sensualis and the Freudian Model:
Sexuality and Domination

Femina Sensualis opposed sensuality by sublimating it. In sublimated Femina Sensualis duty overcame sensual desire and its resistance to sublimation. Victorian culture and feminine existence raised a false opposition between sensuality and sublimation and Femina Sensualis incorporated that false antithesis of motives. In the opposing model created by the late Victorian rebel, Sigmund Freud, the opposition appeared between sexuality, defined as affection and sensuality, and their response to parental authority. The successful resolution of that opposition was the daughter's real existential and psychological problem. She fixated upon the first relation to authority. Tenderness and respect first arose from the daughter's relation to parental authority. They preceded sensuality. They could not be mere sublimations. The daughter's first love was authoritarian. Like liberty, sexuality was a later achievement always in danger of being overwhelmed by the daughter's deeper inclinations toward submission and domination. True sexuality, when attained, became a mode as well as a sign of liberation, a freedom from the parents, a purging of parental influence, severing the umbilical cord of parental authority. The victory was signified by the fusion of the currents of love: affection and sensuality.[38]

As Femina Sensualis established a false antithesis between sensuality and sublimation, the model exalted the frigid division in women between affection and sensuality. Femina Sensualis represented the neurotic failure to fuse affection and sensuality. She was disembodied affection without sensuality. The sensual part belonged to her father. In Femina Sensualis the sexual aptitudes were not detached from the parental models. "Psychically," Freud wrote in reference to "the anaesthetic type of woman," the type "distinctly cultivated" by "civilized education," "psychically, she is still attached to her parents...."[39] Her upbringing thwarted her mature development toward becoming free of parental authority and synthesizing both figures in her conscience. On the contrary, so great was the deference for the figure of the authoritarian father, that the young daughter often formed a neurotic attachment to her father and transferred the feeling to her husband. "The really delightful marriage must be where your husband was a sort of father," remarked Dorothea in *Middlemarch*. Her future husband, Casaubon, was twenty-seven years her senior. That suited her, for she did not wish to marry a husband very near her own age. Casaubon, himself, was pleased with her "ardent submissive affection."[40]

Sexuality was not freed from domination nor the urge toward domination. The failure to resolve satisfactorily the oedipal problem in Femina Sensualis deflected (or perhaps displaced) sexuality toward domination. In Victorian culture affective feelings withheld their co-operation too long from developing sensual feelings. Kept apart, the Victorian family produced frigid women. George Moore delineated the character of one in his "Mildred Lawson." Of her betrothed, Mildred declared, "I like him to like me, but I don't think I shall like him if he made love to me." Desiring only "affection" for herself, she remarks to her betrothed, "I suppose affection would not satisfy you." In fact, Moore makes it abundantly clear that her declarations of affection are rational-izations of her insatiable appetite for conquests and the sadistic torture of her victims once conquered. She reflected upon her behavior:

She remembered how frightened, how delighted she had been, when she discovered that she was a cruel woman. . . . She had thrilled at the thought that she could make a man so unhappy. His grief was wonderful to witness, and involuntary remarks had escaped her admirably designed to draw it forth, to exhibit; she was sorry for him, but in the background of her mind she could not help rejoicing; the instinct of cruelty would not be wholly repressed.

Mildred Lawson pined for the capacity to love, but she believed in-consistently that her chastity was her one indispensable "safeguard." If she were to lose that "there would be no safety for her. She knew that her safety lay in chastity, others might do without chastity, and come out all right in the end, but she could not; an instinct told her." When the story closed, Mildred was in a state of marked depression pathet-ically hoping for a passion for God or man, ". . . give me a passion," she cried, "I cannot live without one."[41] The "unimpassioned woman," as one perceptive writer on the character of the frigid woman styled her, was always characterized by the "absence of deep passion. Love is simply preference; hatred is merely dislike; jealousy is only injured pride."[42] Mildred Lawson committed no great crime or wickedness. Duty, Victorian conscience, as Mill pointed out, inhibited the English from such excesses.[43] But it is also possible to ascribe to duty in the case of the unimpassioned women the failure to integrate love and hate and to overcome ambivalence. Mildred Lawson's love-relations failed to express both libidinal and aggressive impulses in the same activity and within the framework of the same relationship.

Morally irresponsible, bereft of liberty, women sought power over others to "compensate themselves . . . ," as Mill put it, "by meddling for their own purposes in the affairs of others. Hence also women's passion for personal beauty, dress and display. . . . where there is the least liberty, the passion for power is the most ardent and unscrupulous. The desire of power over others can only cease to be a depraving agency among mankind, when each of them individually is able to do without it: which can only be where respect for liberty in the personal concern of each is an established principle."[44] Emancipation from parental authority, the separation of sexuality from domination, was a precondition for the decline of the urge for power and for the maximization of the liberty of adults. Established authority, not only parental or patriarchal, or in a hundred other places, was the fundamental issue confronting Victorian England. The antagonist of authority was liberty.

VI   Emancipation as Self-Sustaining: the Take-off

This chapter has briefly explored the model of innocent Femina Sensualis; her unconscious conflict; the mechanism of her sexual repression, innocence; negative conscience and feminine sexuality as the components of her conflict; the apparent lack of intensity in the conflict; its chaste resolution, the exclusion of her ego from the conflict as mediator between the claims of conscience and of sensuality; the moral irresponsibility entailed in her unconscious conflict; her sublimation through religion; the false antithesis embodied in Femina Sensualis; and finally, her imperfect sublimation and the unconscious urge toward domination and submission. In the pursuit of these aims it is hoped that something has been disclosed about the consciousness, existence and social character of the womanly woman. Her character structure, conscience, psychological needs and character traits corresponded to her family existence. Social character and the family system were seemingly self-perpetuating in an unbroken circle. The family produced a specific type of character and the womanly character perpetuated the family.
    The circle was broken during the late-Victorian period. The consciousness and existence of well-to-do women were increasingly challenged and the womanly woman was turned into a beleaguered model rivalled by a new competitor known as the "new woman." Near the close of the 1870's after a struggle of two decades, the "movement for female emancipation" acquired so much momentum that it was described by a sympathizer as a "self-sustaining agent." It ceased to be something like an episodic movement and became an open-ended process. It conquered a position from which in the nature of things it

could not recede, and from which it was almost impossible that it should not advance.[45] The language as well as the process of emancipation is analogous to the take-off in industrialization. Emancipation was as unsettling of patriarchal relations as industrialization. The growing disjunction between the family and character opened a new chapter in the late Victorian history of the family. By the early nineties the disjunction created the most profound gap of the nineteenth century between mothers and daughters. The older generation of mothers, Womanly Women, were confronted by a new generation of daughters, the New Women.

If this chapter may be permitted the indulgence of a paraphrase on a famous manifesto published in 1848, it may be drawn to a close. The Womanly Woman had nothing to lose but her tightly corseted existence, hang-ups, guilt-feelings, crucified flesh, innocent mindlessness, and self-absorbing roles of daughter, wife and mother. After the take-off into emancipation there was hope of her becoming a human being.

10: The Women of England in a Century of Social Change, 1815=1914

A Select Bibliography

S. Barbara Kanner

THE PRIMARY PURPOSE OF THIS BIBLIOGRAPHY IS TO PRESENT A USEFUL catalog of sources for studying the social position of women in England during the nineteenth century.[1] It has the additional purpose of suggesting that there may be considerable value in patterning fresh alternatives to the popular themes of "emancipation of women" and "feminism" in pursuing the subject. As an illustration, one line of inquiry that appears to warrant greater attention involves a close questioning of the relationships existing between the various social changes that transformed national life in Victorian England and the changes that occurred in the social roles and occupations undertaken by English women during that period. This approach focuses not only upon the description of women's roles and occupations in their immediate milieu, but also upon the meaning and function of these roles in the wider matrix of English society.

This vantage point has been chosen by authors of a very brief list of books. That is, there are few systematic, historically oriented studies that relate changes in English women's status to national socioeconomic phenomena in terms of time, place and circumstances. Three outstanding examples of studies that do approach the subject in this manner are:

1. Ivy Pinchbeck, *Women Workers and the Industrial Revolution, 1750-1850.* 1930; rpr. 1969.[2]
2. Margaret Hewitt, *Wives and Mothers in Victorian Industry.* 1958.
3. Neil J. Smelser, *Social Change in the Industrial Revolution.* Chicago, 1959.

Pinchbeck's study not only demonstrates the relationships existing between changes in women's occupations and the social transformations which accompanied the Industrial Revolution, but also calls attention to how variations in local conditions were relevant to changes occurring in women's status. Hewitt's study concerns the effects of the growth and systemization of the manufacturing industry on the roles of married women employed in the textile trades. Smelser's study is also characterized by this analytic-comparative approach, but his book covers a wider scope of questions relative to changing social roles and has a broader subject base. It is in the chapters tracing patterns of change in family life — especially the division of labor within family units — that he offers interpretations of the shifts in female roles as they became responsive to the practical demands of a particular social environment. These three books, all dealing mainly with the question of employment of working-class women, weigh specific changes in women's roles against concrete, precise and relevant social backgrounds. Still wanting are similar investigations concerning the position of women of the various social classes in categories of inquiry such as national education, administrative and institutional developments, law amendment, technology, politics and social service.

These considerations are of direct pertinence to this bibliography because they help to point up sharp differences of approach among the authors whose works are listed below. Perhaps the greatest of these differences lies in the contrast between the methodological and thematic treatment of Pinchbeck, Hewitt and Smelser on the one hand, and the approach taken by authors of well-known, general surveys of the woman question on the other. One significant difference is that the former deal mainly with factual data and with defining sociological relationships, while the latter appear more concerned with discussing ideas and activities representative of some outstanding individuals and their personal coteries. Secondly, the former group of authors take the stance of objective neutrality, while the latter tend to assume positions of partisanship, favoring or even extolling the changes they describe. In addition, the former focus on one main, carefully defined subject, while the latter prefer general themes — usually "the emancipation of women" or "feminism" as pervasive ideologies or "forces." Contrasts in style follow logically, since most of those who survey the "emancipation" question tend to choose a narrative — often polemical — presentation rather than a systematic analysis. Rarely probing the reasons why events occurred just when they did, or why pressure for change was resisted or how the various phenomena may have been interdependent, the narrators usually detail a general story of a "battle" or "struggle" waged by women and a few male "feminists" against social policies, legal restrictions, repressive attitudes and political exclusions imposed by an intransigent patriarchal society. The titles of a few frequently cited surveys in this category will serve to illustrate this motif:

4. G. W. Johnson, *The Evolution of Woman, from Subjection to Comradeship.* 1926.
5. Ray Strachey, *The Cause: A Short History of the Women's Movement in Great Britain.* 1928; rpr. New York, 1969. Also published as *Struggle.* New York, 1930.
6. Ida B. O'Malley, *Women in Subjection.* 1933.
7. R. Glynn Grylls, "The Emancipation of .Women," and Viola Klein, "The Emancipation of Women: Its Motives and Achievements," in *Ideas and Beliefs of the Victorians,* ed. Harmon Grisewood. 1949.
8. Josephine Kamm, *Rapiers and Battleaxes.* 1966.

Because of the considerable value in their collation of biographical detail and careful descriptions of the events and literature which appear to have marked points at which women's status changed, these books hold deservedly respected places in bibliographies concerning the position of women. It is pertinent, however, to suggest that these sources should be read critically, since they tend to support an assumption, still largely untested, that there existed in England from the late eighteenth century a steady, coherent and consistent continuum of events — comprising a "movement" by mid-nineteenth century — which eventually "led" to women's "emancipation." For example, Grylls (entry 7) suggests that this "movement" consisted of "an educated rank and file," and Johnson (entry 4) describes it as a "general revolt." These interpretations have not yet been subjected to close scholarly review, clarification or criticism.

One example may serve to illustrate why the absence of such a review should be kept in mind by readers of a bibliography concerning Englishwomen's changing roles. Viola Klein (entry 7) upholds the popular contention that "women's emancipation" in the nineteenth century was a strictly middle-class phenomenon. Klein says, "the place in which the Feminist Movement was born was not the factory or the mine, but the Victorian middle-class drawing room" (p. 262). But contradictory evidence is suggested in contemporary literature and related secondary works concerning working-class politics. A good example can be found in the literature of the Chartist Movement which aimed directly, at least before the 1840's, toward universal suffrage and sex equality in education. The goals of female Chartists are discussed in:

9. William Lovett, *Life and Struggles.* 2 vols. 1876 ed. rpr. with an introduction by R. H. Tawney. 1920. For example, pp. 131, 145.
10. "Meeting of Female Chartists" in *The Times,* 20 October 1842.

11. *The English Chartist Circular*, vols. 1-3, 1841-1843. rpr. New York, 1968. Variety of articles.
12. William Slossom, *Decline of the Chartist Movement*. New York, 1916. Especially, pp. 206-208.
13. Hermann Schlüter, *Die Chartisten-Bewegung*. New York, 1916. Chapter 21, book III, part 3. A strong socialist view.
14. E. P. Thompson, *The Making of English Working Class*. New York, 1963. Especially, pp. 414-417, 717-718, 730-731.

These sources point in the direction of activities undertaken before mid-century in behalf of and on the part of English working women which aimed at feminine independence, greater sex equality and participation in political programs. It would seem, then, that there may be value in reappraising English "feminism" as an intellectual and social phenomenon that crossed over class lines.

This leads also to the question of imprecision in the terminology which has been applied to the whole subject of women's position. There has been a trend among authors to employ terms such as "feminist movement" for their individual purposes without necessarily pausing to clarify meanings. A point similar to this was made by J. A. and Olive Banks in their admirable study:

15. *Feminism and Family Planning in Victorian England*. Liverpool, 1964.

Except for this very brief consideration of the question, the terminology has gone relatively unchallenged. As a result, there is an absence not only of clear definitions, but also of verbal indicators to mark off the various aspects and degrees of "feminism" which might separate "radicals" from "moderates" or "mere improvers," and which might clarify contextual differences between the seekers of change in women's status at different points in history. In any event, the value of the popular terminology as semantics that can be useful to the historian is a question that merits examination.

The reasons for the existence of problems connected with semantics and interpretations should also be questioned. Certainly one of them may be traced to the relative silence about changes in women's roles in the well-known, authoritative texts covering the history of England in the nineteenth century. O. R. McGregor makes this point in his valuable bibliographical essay focusing on the "emancipation" question:

16. "The Social Position of Women in England, 1850-1914: A Bibliography" in *The British Journal of Sociology*, 6 (1955).

There is no need here to retraverse the ground that McGregor has already covered, but it is important to point out that fifteen years after his essay his observations about historical texts tend, generally, to hold.

This omission of questions about feminine roles is a curious puzzle when one considers that there is a great deal of evidence pointing to a working together of English law and social policy over a long period of time which tended to relegate the female population into a specially regarded grouping in society – and therefore one warranting study. A second consideration in the puzzle is the easy availability but general neglect of a long catalog of contemporary literature and specialized secondary sources which focus on the question of women's status.

The design and organization of this bibliography, then, has been guided by the purpose of presenting sources on the woman question in the context of at least some of the main lines of nineteenth-century social history. It has been influenced also by the opinion that the contemporary literature should figure prominently, although it requires careful re-evaluation not only for factual accuracy, but also for the degree to which the ideas and opinions may be considered representative of wide public opinion. In making selections of the secondary sources, preference has of course been shown for those works which aim at analysis in a defined context, but the most well-known titles have in any case been included.

Largely because of the limitations of space, both the number of subject categories and the number of entries have been sharply curtailed.[3] In separate sections and subsections, the sources are grouped under seven main headings as follows: I. The Climate of Opinion on Social Roles: Woman's "Nature," "Duties," "Conditions," and "Rights"; II. Population Questions, "Surplus Women," and Emigration; III. Social Questions, "Social Evils" and Social Service; IV. Expansion of Employment; V. Education and Vocational Training; VI. The Law and the Amendment of the Law; VII. Political Activity and Public Service.

Among the main libraries consulted were the University Research Library of the University of California at Los Angeles and, in London, the Fawcett Society Library, the British Museum Reading Room, the London School of Economics, the Institute of Historical Research and the Library of the University of London. The library of the Fawcett Society is devoted exclusively to literature on questions pertaining to women, and its holdings of books, pamphlets and manuscripts number in the thousands.[4]

Consistently helpful reference works included: William F. Poole, ed., *Poole's Index to Periodical Literature, 1802-1906.* 6 vols. Boston, 1887-1906; Walter E. Houghton, ed., *The Wellesley Index to Victorian Periodicals, 1824-1900.* Toronto, 1966; and Judith Blow Williams, *A*

Guide to the Printed Materials for English Social and Economic History, 1750-1850. 2 vols. New York, 1926. Shorter bibliographical works of considerable assistance included O. R. McGregor's bibliographical essay (entry 16); the bibliographies in *The Englishwoman's Review* of December 1889, pp. 529-532; January 1889, pp. 73-80; April 1899, pp. 145-152; July 1899, pp. 223-224; October 1899, pp. 285-292 and July 1900, pp. 217-220; and the bibliographical sections of books dealing with the various subject categories.

The arrangement of the sources is chronological. Names of authors are provided only when the works are signed, or when they have been identified by authoritative references such as the British Museum's *Catalogue of Printed Books, Wellesley Index* or *Poole's Index.* Periodical articles are arranged under the title of the periodical rather than the individual author (or anonymous). Chronological order is maintained within these entries. The categories are of course overlapping, but with careful study of the entries, the reader will soon recognize how the various subjects and sources are related.

I   The Climate of Opinion on Social Roles:
    Woman's "Nature," "Condition," "Duties," and "Rights"

English books dealing with ideas and opinions about the social roles of women have been traced to at least the sixteenth century. The themes of these early works vary from advice to young ladies on how to become "compleat women," to "defences" and "apologies" on behalf of the "goodness" of the sex, to "vindications" of female worthiness, superiority and "rights." As the late eighteenth and nineteenth centuries witnessed rapid changes in social, economic and political life, the question of women's roles became an increasingly frequent and controversial point for public discussion. Polemical writers attempted either to reconcile the traditional and conventional expectations of women to changing social conditions, or to make innovative suggestions for adjusting female roles to new socioeconomic imperatives — some of the latter calling for social and legal sex equality. Journalists reviewed a plethora of literature on the woman question, and the subject increased in popular appeal as the century went on. Examined chronologically, it is possible to gauge continuity and change in the argumentation of the literature, since the polemics were of course affected by the changes in women's position that accompanied the long catalog of social, legal, economic and political reforms enacted throughout the period. The contemporary sources below are illustrative of the books, pamphlets and articles that offered the various shades of opinion. A grouping of secondary works then follows.

17. Jean Jacques Rousseau, *Emilius and Sophia: or, a new system of education*, trans. William Kenrick. 4 vols. 1762. Introduces a concept later known as "the doctrine of female influence."

18. Hannah More: *Essays on Various Subjects, Principally Designed for Young Ladies*. 1777; *Cheap Repository Tracts*. 1795-1798, 1821; *Strictures on the Modern System of Female Education*. 1799, 1834; *Coelebs in Search of a Wife*. 1808.

19. William Alexander, *History of Women from Earliest Antiquity to the Present Time*. 3rd ed., 1782; *Women Physiologically Considered*. 1839.

20. Mary Wollstonecraft Godwin, *Thoughts on the Education of Daughters*. 1787; *A Vindication of the Rights of Women*. 1792.

21. Thomas Grisbourne, *An Inquiry into the Duties of the Female Sex*. 1798.

22. Priscilla Wakefield, *Reflections on the Present Condition of the Female Sex with Suggestions for its Improvement*. 1798.

23. *The Edinburgh Review (ER)*: S. Smith, "Advice to Young Ladies on the Improvement of the Mind," 15 (1810), 299-315; E. G. E. Bulwer-Lytton, "Spirit of Society," 52 (1831), 374-387; T. H. Lister, "Rights and Conditions of Women," 73 (1841), 189-209; M. Oliphant, "Mill's Subjection of Women," 130 (1869), 572-602.

24. *Blackwood's Magazine (BM)*: J. Neal, "Men and Women," 16 (1824), 387-394; J. G. Phillimore, "Women's Rights and Duties," 54 (1843), 373-397; M. Oliphant, "The Condition of Women," 83 (1858), 139-154; W. E. Aytoun, "The Rights of Woman," 92 (1862), 183-201; M. Todd, "Some Thoughts on the Woman Question," 156 (1894), 689-692.

25. William Thompson, *Appeal of One Half of the Human Race, Women, Against the Pretensions of the Other Half, Men, to Retain Them in Political and Thence in Civil and Domestic Slavery; in Reply to a Paragraph of Mr. (James) Mill's Celebrated "Article on Government."* 1825.

26. *Fraser's Magazine (FM)*: "The Female Character," 7 (1833), 591-601; "Woman and the Social System," 21 (1840), 689-702; H. T. Buckle, "The Influence of Women on the Progress of Knowledge," 57 (1858), 395-407; F. P. Cobbe, "Criminals, Idiots, Women and Minors: is the Classification Sound?" 78 (1868), 777-794; M. Oliphant, "Grievances of Women," n.s. 21 (1880), 698-710.

27. *The Westminster Review (WR)*: H. Martineau, "Criticism of Women," 32 (1838-1839), 454-475; M. Mylne, "Woman and Her Social Position," 35 (1841), 24-52; T. H. Rearden, "Mission of Woman," 52 (1849-1850), 352-367; "Capabilities and Disabilities of Women," 67 (1857), 42-59; "Capacities of Women," 84 (1865), 352-380; "J. S. Mill's 'Subjection of Women,'" 93 (1870), 63-89; "Emancipation of Women," 128 (1887), 165-173; and "Changing Status of Women," 818-828; E. Ethelmer, "Feminism," 149 (1898), 50-62; N. Arling, "The Role of the New Woman," 150 (1898), 576-587; "Privilege versus Justice to Women," 152 (1899), 128-141; W. K. Hill, "Equality with Man," 160 (1903), 647-664; F. S. Franklin, "Women and their Emancipation," 161 (1904), 407-419.

28. Elizabeth Sandford: *Woman and Her Social and Domestic Character*. 1831. *Female Improvement*. 1836.

29. Anna Jameson: *Characteristics of Women*. 1832. *Memoirs and Essays on Art, Literature and Social Morals*. 1846.

30. *Monthly Repository* (*MR*): W. J. Fox, "A Political and Social Anomaly," 6 (1832), 637-642; W. B. Adams, "On the Condition of Women in England," 7 (1833), 217-231.

31. Harriet Martineau: *Illustrations of Political Economy*. 9 vols. 1834. Didactic stories often illustrating women's roles. *Society in America*. 3 vols. 1837. Considerable attention to the question of women's status.

32. *Metropolitan Magazine*: "An Outline of the Grievances of Women," 22 (1838), 16-27.

33. Sarah Lewis, *Woman's Mission*. 1839, and numerous subsequent editions.

34. Sarah Stickney Ellis: *The Women of England: Their Social Duties and Domestic Habits*. 1839. *The Mothers of England*. 1843. *The Wives of England*. 1843. *The Daughters of England*. 1845.

35. Mrs. Hugo Reid, *A Plea for Women*. Edinburgh, 1843. Reviewed in *Tait's Edinburgh Magazine* (*TEM*), n.s. 11 (1844), 423.

36. Robert Owen, *The Book of the New Moral World*. 1844. Part 6 concerns women's roles, education and status.

37. *The Quarterly Review* (*QR*): A. W. Kinglake, "The Rights of Women," or "Milnes on the Hareem," 75 (1844-1845), 94-125.

38. Herbert Spencer, *Social Statics*. 1851.

39. Maria Grey and Emily Shirreff, *Thoughts on Self-Culture*. 1854.

40. Frances Power Cobbe, *Essays on the Pursuits of Women*. 1863. Includes "Social Science Congresses and Women's Part in Them."

41. *Cornhill Magazine* (*CM*): R. A. King, "A Tête à Tête Social Science Discussion" (on changing roles of women), 10 (1864), 569-582; H. S. Scott and E. B. Hall, "The New Woman," 70 (1894), 365-368.

42. *Victoria Magazine* (*VM*): 1863-1880. A journal devoted to women's questions. Conducted by Emily Faithfull.

43. Thomas Henry Huxley, "Emancipation — Black and White" in *The Reader*, 20 May 1865. Rpr. in Huxley's *Lay Sermons, Addresses and Reviews*. 1880.

44. John Stuart Mill, *The Subjection of Women*. 1869. Numerous editions.

45. Josephine Butler, ed., *Woman's Work and Woman's Culture*. 1869.

46. William Landels, *Woman: Her Position and Power*. 1870.

47. *The Englishwoman's Review* (*EWR*):[5] T. G. Crippin, "The Testimony of Holy Scripture Concerning the Social Status of Women" (1870), pp. 127-163; "Are Rights and Duties the Same?" (1875), pp. 301-306; "Women's Newspapers, A Sketch of the Periodical Literature Devoted to the Woman Question" (1878), pp. 433-440.

48. *Contemporary Review* (*CR*): "V.", "The Powers of Women and How to Use Them," 14 (1870), 521-539; F. P. Cobbe, "The Little Health of Ladies," 31 (1878), 276-296.

49. Charles Anthony, *The Social and Political Dependence of Women*. 1880.

50. Eliza Lynn Linton, *The Girl of the Period*. 2 vols. 1883. Rpr. from *Saturday Review*, a journal known for its "anti-feminist" bias.

51. Theodore Stanton, ed., *The Woman Question in Europe.* 1884.

52. *Fortnightly Review (FR):* G. Allen, "Plain Words on the Woman Question," 52 (1889), 448-458; J. Adam, "The Place of Woman in Modern Life," 57 (1892), 522-529.

53. *The Nineteenth Century (NC):* C. M. Gaskell, "Women of Today, What is Expected of Them?" 26 (1889), 776-784; E. L. Linton, "Partisans of Wild Women," 31 (1892), 455-464; and M. Caird, "A Defense of the So-Called Wild Women," 811-829.

54. Violet Greville, *The Gentlewoman in Society.* 1892.

55. August Bebel, *Woman in the Past, Present and Future.* 1893.

56. Georgina Hill, *Women in English Life from Medieval to Modern Times.* 1896.

57. David Staars, *The English Woman,* trans. J. Brownlow. 1909.

58. Olive Schreiner, *Woman and Labour.* 1911.

59. W. Lyon Blease, *The Emancipation of Women.* 1913.

60. B. L. Hutchins, *Conflicting Ideals: Two Sides to the Woman Question.* 1913.

61. Havelock Ellis, *Man and Woman.* 1914.

62. Zoë Fairfield, *Some Aspects of the Woman's Movement.* 1915.

63. Victor Gollancz, *The Making of Women: Oxford Essays in Feminism.* 1907.

Secondary Sources

64. Wanda Fraiken Neff, *Victorian Working Women, 1832-1850.* New York, 1929; rpr. 1966. Ideas about women's roles are related to working women's social backgrounds. Reliance on fiction and government documents.

65. George L. Nesbitt, *Benthamite Reviewing: the First Twelve Years of the Westminster Review.* 1934. Discusses policy on women's questions.

66. C. Willet Cunnington, *Feminine Attitudes in the Nineteenth Century.* 1935.

67. Ruby Saywell, "The Development of the Feminist Idea in England, 1789-1833." Unpub. M.A. thesis, University of London, 1936. English "women's rights" literature is related to ideas of French radical philosophers. Details of women's inferior legal and social position are surveyed.

68. Robert P. Utter and Gwendolyn B. Needham, *Pamela's Daughters.* New York, 1937. A literary study analyzing heroines in relation to conventional ideas and expectations of women.

69. Viola Klein, *The Feminine Character: History of an Ideology.* New York, 1949. Helpful bibliography.

70. Aina Rubenius, *The Woman Question in Mrs. Gaskell's Life and Works.* Cambridge, Mass., 1950. Conventional expectations are related to Mrs. Gaskell's interest in working girls, fallen women, et al. Good bibliography.

71. Vera Brittain, *Lady Into Woman.* 1953.

72. Janet Dunbar, *The Early Victorian Woman, 1837-1857.* 1953.

73. G. E. and K. R. Fussell, *The English Countrywoman: the Internal Aspect of Rural Life, 1500-1900.* 1953.

74. Richard K. P. Pankhurst: *The Saint Simonians, Mill and Carlyle.* 1957. Shows how ideas of la femme libre circulated in England. *William Thompson, Britain's Pioneer Socialist, Feminist and Co-operator.* 1954.

75. G. R. Taylor: *Sex in History.* 1954. *The Angel-Makers, A Study in Psychological Origins of Social Change, 1750-1850.* 1958.

76. *Essays in Criticism:* Christopher Hill, "Clarissa Harlow and Her Times," 5 (1955), 315-340. Marriage and property relationships.

77. Patricia Thompson, *The Victorian Heroine, A Changing Ideal.* 1956.

78. O. R. McGregor, *Divorce in England.* 1957. Changing roles of women related to changes in family patterns and laws of divorce.

79. John Killham, *Tennyson and 'The Princess': Reflections of an Age.* 1958. Excellent discussion of the woman question.

80. *Journal of the History of Ideas:* Keith Thomas, "The Double Standard," 20 (1959), 195-216. Female chastity as a socioeconomic value.

81. Keith Melder, "The Beginnings of the Women's Movement, 1800-1840." Unpub. diss., Yale, 1963. Changes in social thought, a factor.

82. Hoffman R. Hays, *The Dangerous Sex: The Myth of the Feminine Evil.* 1964.

83. William O'Neill, *The Woman Movement: Feminism in the United States and England.* 1969. A source book with an introduction.

84. *The Historian:* Glenda G. Riley, "The Subtle Subversion: Changes in the Traditionalist Image of the American Woman," 32 (1970), 210-227. Women's roles related to the function of the family system and to women's ascribed responsibilities as guardians of morality.

85. Cynthia White, *Women's Magazines, 1693-1968.* 1970. Journals for women seen as reflectors of change in women's roles and activities.

86. *Victorian Studies:* "The Victorian Woman: A Special Issue," 14 (1970).

See also entries 1-16.

II Population Expansion, "Surplus Women,"
and Emigration

In 1901 the people of Great Britain were three and one-half times more numerous than they had been in 1801, when the first census was taken. Official census returns provided detailed data covering the numerical distribution of the people by sex, occupation, geographical location, etc. Successive Registrars General reports were supplemented in contemporary literature by the comments of economists, journalists, essayists and social reformers. Writers advanced suggestions for relieving social and economic pressures believed to be concomitant with the population "explosion." Limitation of family size was one suggestion offered, and a number of pamphleteers distributed literature among the working- and middle-class "marrieds of both sexes" containing information about practical "means which prevents too rapid a population."

These birth control methods placed considerable responsibility on the women, so that the advocates addressed wives directly, explaining both social and sexual advantages they might achieve by cooperating in the matter. Thus the literature of birth control is relevant to questions about changing attitudes concerning the position of women.

More directly pertinent perhaps are the writings which discussed the numerical disproportion between the sexes: the "surplus of women." Books and papers not only on population questions but also on employment, education, and political developments often discussed the relevance of female surplus. Referring especially to data in the census returns, questions were raised about the ramifications of having a large single female population seeking gainful employment and financial independence. Writers also advanced opinions about emigration as a possible remedy not only for the shortage of well-paid employment for women, but also for the shortage of husbands — the reverse disproportion of the sexes existing in the colonies. Throughout the period, both voluntary agencies and government offices issued literature to encourage female emigration and to present their programs.

87. *The Census of Great Britain, 1851: the Return of the Registrar General.* 1854. Introduction includes discussion of "excess of females" and possible causes. See also returns for later decades.

88. Edward Cheshire, *The Results of the Census of Great Britain in 1851.* 1853.

89. George Drysdale, *The Elements of Social Science.* 1854. Advocates and describes birth control in relation to population problems.

90. *The British Almanac and Companion.* 1855 and thereafter. Census data presented and evaluated. See especially Charles Mackeson's article: "Occupations and Vital Statistics of England and Wales" (1875), pp. 89-110. Includes critique of census categories with example that in some years "unoccupied women" included those who worked in family businesses. Some women, counted in the "domestic class," were actually "innkeepers, beersellers," et al. In his 1885 review, Mackeson calls "the growth of female industry . . . the most striking figure of the census." In the *Almanac* for 1882, see "The Higher Education of Women" by J. J. Manley, pp. 111-129, for population data related to educational questions.

91. Henry Mayhew, *London Labour and the London Poor.* 4 vols. 1861-1862. Originally articles in the *Morning Chronicle,* 1849-1850. Statistical charts and tables with data relating to women are included.

92. *ER:* H. Martineau, "Female Industry," 109 (1859), 293-336.

93. *English Woman's Journal (EWJ):* J. Boucherett, "On the Obstacles to the Employment of Women," 4 (1860), 361-375; "Statistics as to the Employment of Women," 12 (1864), 400-408.

94. *QR:* J. H. Howson, "Deaconesses for the Church of England," 108

(1860), especially 345-346; R. H. Palgrave, "Census of England and Wales, 1871," 139 (1875), 525-550.

95. *FM:* F. P. Cobbe, "What Shall We Do With Our Old Maids?" 66 (1862), 594-610.
96. W. R. Greg, "Why are Women Redundant?" in *Literary and Social Judgments.* Boston, 1868. Written in 1862.
97. *CR:* J. B. Mayor, "The Cry of Women," 11 (1869), 196-215.
98. Jessie Boucherett, "How to Provide for Superfluous Women," in *Woman's Work and Woman's Culture,* ed. Josephine Butler. 1869.
99. Annie Besant, *The Law of Population.* 1877.
100. *CM:* E. W. E. Whitaker, "The Census of 1881," 43 (1881), 468-478.
101. *WR:* "Excess of Widows over Widowers," 131 (1889), 501-505; A. Kenealy, "New View of the Surplus of Women," 136 (1891), 465-475.
102. Adna Ferrin Weber, *The Growth of Cities in the Nineteenth Century.* 1889 ed. rpr. Ithaca, 1965. Includes consideration of "surplus women," and discusses Karl Bücher's theory of Frauenüberschuss.
103. A. V. Dicey, letter to *The Times,* 23 March 1909. Cautions that granting suffrage to the female majority would "confide to that body" the government of England and the destinies of the Empire.
104. *Quarterly Journal of Economics:* Norman E. Himes, "The Place of John Stuart Mill and Robert Owen in the History of English Neo-Malthusianism," 42 (1928), 627-640. See also Himes' "The Birth Control Handbills of 1823," in *The Lancet,* 213 (1927), 313-316; and his edition of Charles Knowlton, *Fruits of Philosophy.* Mount Vernon, N.Y., 1937. An English birth control text of the 1830's.
105. Edith How-Martyn and Mary Breed, *The Birth Control Movement in England.* 1930.
106. J. A. Field, "The Early Propagandist Movement in English Population Theory," in Field's *Essays on Population and Other Papers,* ed. Helen F. Hohman. Chicago, 1931.
107. Hamilton Fyfe, *Revolt of Women.* 1933.
108. D. V. Glass, *Population Policies and Movements in Europe.* Oxford, 1940.
109. J. A. Banks, *Prosperity and Parenthood, a Study of Family Planning Among the Victorian Middle Classes.* 1954. See also entry 15.
110. Peter Fryer, *The Birth Controllers.* 1965. Excellent study.

Emigration

111. *First Seven General Reports of the Colonial Land and Emigration Commissioners, 1840-1847;* succeeding reports published in separate volumes, 1842-1873. Statistics, maps, charts, explanations, etc.
112. *Colonization Circulars,* 1-32. 1843-1873. Issued by the Commissioners. Advice and information for emigrants.
113. *The Economist:* "Mr. Sidney Herbert's Emigration Scheme," 29 December 1849, pp. 1445-1447. Working-class women and emigration.
114. *Emigrant Tracts.* 1850-1852. Collection of pamphlets containing information about and advice to emigrants.

115. Caroline Chisholm, *Family Colonization Loan Society, A System of Emigration.* 1850; *The A.B.C. of Colonization.* 1850, 1859.

116. *Household Words (HW)*: C. Dickens and C. Chisholm, "A Bundle of Emigrant Letters," 1 (1850), 19-24; R. H. Horne, "Pictures of Life in Australia," 307-310; and S. Sidney, "Family Colonization," 514-515; W. H. Wills, "Safety for Female Emigrants," 3 (1851), 228; S. Sidney, "Better Ties than Red Tape Ties," 4 (1852), 529-534.

117. Sampson Low, Jr., *The Charities of London, Comprehending the Benevolent, Educational and Religious Institutions, their Origin and Design, Progress and Present Position.* 1850, 1852, 1862. Includes organizations and institutions assisting female emigration.

118. Fund for Promoting Female Emigration, *First Report.* 1851.

119. John Hill Burton, *The Emigrant's Manual.* 1851.

120. Eneas Mackenzie, *Memoirs of Caroline Chisholm and Sketches of Her Philanthropic Labors.* 1852.

121. *EWJ*: I. Craig, "Emigration as a Preventive Agency," 2 (1859), 289-297; "Emigrant Ship Matrons," 5 (1860), 24-36; and "On Assisted Emigration," 235-240, 326-335; "A Year's Experience in Woman's Work" (includes discussion of needed administrative reform relative to female emigration), 6 (1860), 112-121; "Emigration for Educated Women," 7 (1861), 1-9; M. Rye, "Female Middle Class Emigration," 10 (1862), 20-30; and "Middle Class Female Emigration Impartially Considered," 73-85; Jane Lewin, "Female Middle Class Emigration," 12 (1864), 313-317.

122. Maria Rye, *Emigration of Educated Women.* 1861.

123. R. Harris, *What Has Mrs. Chisholm Done for the Colonization of New South Wales?* 1862.

124. National Association for the Promotion of Social Science, *Transactions (TNAPSS)*:[6] M. Rye, "Report on Female Emigration" (1862), p. 811; and F. Hill, "The Emigration of Educated Women Examined from a Colonial Point of View," p. 812; E. Layton, "On the Superintendence of Female Emigrants" (1864), pp. 616-618.

125. *EWR*: "Prospects of Female Emigrants to South Australia" (1873), pp. 271-272; "Emigration" (1874), pp. 96-102.

126. *Macmillan's Magazine (MM)*: A. Ross, "Emigration for Women," 45 (1882), 312-317.

127. Fred H. Hitchins, *The Colonial Land and Emigration Commission, 1840-1878.* Philadelphia, 1931. Background for government's role in assisted emigration.

128. Douglas Woodruff, "Expansion and Emigration," in vol. 2 of *Early Victorian England, 1830-1865*, ed. G. M. Young. 2 vols. 1934.

129. R. B. Madgwick, *Immigration into Eastern Australia, 1788-1851.* 1937. Important background.

130. Margaret Kiddle, *Caroline Chisholm.* Melbourne, 1957.

131. Oliver MacDonagh, *A Pattern of Government Growth.* 1961. Administrative reform as an important aspect of emigration.

132. *New Horizons: A Hundred Years of Women's Migration.* 1963. A government publication.

III   Social Questions, "Social Evils,"
      and Social Service

English social questions and "social evils" of the nineteenth century have been generally associated with the unharnessed growth of population, industrialism and cities. The problems of poverty, crime, disease, ignorance and sanitation are described, evaluated and searched for causes in contemporary literature and in related secondary works. "Victorian misery" among the poorer classes has been studied closely, with some authors describing it as a condition witnessed with insensitive callousness by a materialistic middle class and with others presenting it as a phenomenon met by humanitarian efforts for social improvement and utilitarian plans for social efficiency. But specialized attention has not often been given to the women of England who were numerous among the beneficiaries of the various modes of social relief, or who numbered importantly among the workers for social welfare and reform. Treated through voluntary organizations or governmental offices were poor, sick, uneducated, and "fallen" women. Employed in charitable, educational and correctional institutions were women who served as superintendents, matrons, managers, and also as unpaid career administrators and planners. Affluent women undertook roles of patronage.

The following sources represent a small collection out of a large body of literature concerning the social problems and social services in which English women were involved. Since the subject of women and crime is an undoubtedly fertile source for information about attitudes toward women, especially those regarded as social outcasts, the works on this topic are grouped separately. Since Victorian attention to prostitution and "fallen women" is related not only to moral and sexual attitudes and beliefs, but also to economic questions and to elements in social cleavage, this subject is also considered in a separate grouping of sources.

133. Sarah Trimmer, *The Oeconomy of Charity*. 2 vols. 1787.
134. John Brownlow, *A Pocket Guide to the Charities of London*. 1836.
135. London Female Dormitory, *Fifth Annual Report*. 1846.
136. Refuge for the Destitute, *Annual Report*. 1849.
137. Anna Jameson, *Sisters of Charity*. 1855.
138. *TNAPSS*: M. A. Baines, "Ladies National Association for the Diffusion of Sanitary Knowledge" (1858), pp. 531-532; L. Twining, "Training and Supervision of Workhouse Girls" (1859), pp. 696-703.
139. *EWJ*: "Charities for Women," 2 (1858), 217-231; B. R. Parkes, "Ladies Sanitary Association," 3 (1859), 73-85; "The Details of Woman's Work in Sanitary Reform," 217-227, 316-324; "Ladies Institute," 51-53; and

"Charity as a Portion of the Public Vocation of Women," 193-196; "Friendly Societies," 6 (1860), 107-112, 265-272; "Official Employment of Women in Works of Charity," 9 (1862), 361-364.

140. Louisa Twining, *Workhouses and Women's Work*. 1858.

141. National Temperance League, *Woman's Work in Temperance Reformation*. 1868.

142. *MM:* O. Hill, "Organized Work Among the Poor," 20 (1869), 219-226; F. Martin, "The Other Side of the Question" (of training girls to work for the poor), 43 (1881), 461-464.

143. A. V. L., *Ministry of Woman and the London Poor*. 1870.

144. *EWR:* "Homes for Working Girls" (1874), pp. 251-252.

145. Louisa Hubbard, *A Guide to All Institutions Existing for the Benefit of Women and Children*. 1878.

146. Donald Fraser, *Mary Jane Kinnaird*. 1890. Clubs for girls.

147. Harriette J. Cooke, *Mildmay, or the First Deaconess Institution*. 1892.

148. Mary Adelaide, Duchess of Teck, *Sketch of Baroness Burdett-Coutts*. 1893. Work of a great philanthropist.

149. Angela Burdett-Coutts, ed., *Woman's Mission: A Series of Congress Papers on the Philanthropic Work of Women by Eminent Writers*. 1893.

150. Frances Power Cobbe, *Life of F. P. Cobbe*. 1894.

151. J. Deane Hilton, *Marie Hilton*. 1897. Child care for working mothers.

152. A. E. Pratt, *A Woman's Work for Women: Aims, Efforts and Aspirations of Louisa M. Hubbard*. 1898.

153. M. A. Lloyd, *Susanna Meredith*. 1903. Aids feeble-minded girls, prison women, et. al.

154. C. J. Montague, *Sixty Years in Waifdom: The Ragged School Movement in English History*. 1904.

155. Ethel E. Metcalfe, *Memoir of Rosamond Davenport-Hill*. 1904.

156. James M. Fletcher, *Mrs. Wrightman of Shrewsbury: the Story of a Pioneer in Temperance Work*. 1906.

157. Lucy M. Moor, *Girls of Yesterday and Today: the Romance of the Y W C A*. 1910.

158. E. T. Cook, *Life of Florence Nightingale*. 1913.

159. Helen Bosanquet, *Social Work in London, 1869-1912*. 1914.

160. Octavia Hill, *Letters to Fellow Workers, 1864-1911* (extracts), ed. Elinor Southwood. 1933.

161. Rosa Hobhouse, *Mary Hughes*. 1949. Work for the "dispossessed."

162. A. F. Young and E. T. Ashton, *British Social Work in the Nineteenth Century*. 1956.

163. Charles Mowat, *The Charity Organization Society, 1869-1913*. 1961.

164. Kathleen Heasman, *Evangelicals in Action, An Appraisal of Their Social Work in the Victorian Era*. 1962.

165. David Owen, *English Philanthropy, 1660-1960*. Cambridge, Mass., 1962.

Women and Crime

166. *ER:* F. Jeffrey, "Prison Discipline," 30 (1818), especially 479-486;

H. Martineau, "The Convict System," 117 (1863), 241-268; H. Martineau, "Life in the Criminal Class," 122 (1865), 337-371.

167. Elizabeth Fry, *Observations on the Visiting, Superintending and Government of Female Prisoners.* 1819, 1827.

168. Society for the Suppression of Vice, *Report.* 1825.

169. British Ladies Society for Promoting the Reformation of Female Prisoners, *Sketch of the Origin and Results of Ladies' Prison Associations.* 1827, 1840.

170. London Female Penitentiary, *Twenty-Ninth Annual Report.* 1836.

171. Alexander Maconochie, *Thoughts on Convict Management.* 1838. Includes references to women. Basic theories behind penal reform.

172. Sarah Martin, *Prison Journals.* 1844. Includes a brief sketch of her life and parliamentary reports on prisons. See also John Buckle, *Sarah Martin, The Prisoner's Friend.* 1910.

173. *BM:* Archibald Alison, "The Causes of the Increase in Crime," 55 (1844), 533-545; and 56 (1844), 1-14. Applicable to female crime.

174. Mary Carpenter: *Reformatory Schools.* 1851. *Juvenile Delinquents.* 1853. *Our Convicts.* 2 vols. 1864. See especially vol. 2, chapter IV, "Female Convicts."

175. R. W. Vanderkiste, *Notes and Narratives of Six Years Mission Principally Among the Dens of London.* 1852.

176. Matilda Wrench, *Visits to Female Prisoners.* 1852.

177. Reformatory and Refuge Union, *First Annual Report.* 1856-1857. See also succeeding reports; and *Fifty Years Record.* 1906.

178. *TNAPSS:* M. Carpenter, "Reformatories for Convicted Girls" (1857), pp. 338-346; M. Carpenter, "On the Disposal of Girls from Reformatory Schools" (1858), pp. 413-419; R. Hanbury, "Facts and Statistics Respecting London Reformatories, Refuges, Industrial Schools and Penitentiaries" (1860), pp. 480-483; C. Fraser, "Origin and Progress of the British Ladies Society for Promoting the Reformation of Female Prisoners" (1862), pp. 495-501; M. Carpenter, "Treatment of Female Convicts" (1864), pp. 415-422; W. Crofton, "Female Convicts and Our Efforts to Amend Them" (1866), pp. 237-243; J. Nugent, "Incorrigible Women: What Are We To Do with Them?" (1876), pp. 375-377.

179. *EWJ:* "Woman's Work in the Reformatory Movement," 1 (1858), 289-295; "Workhouse Visiting Society," 4 (1859), 185-187; "Female Life in Prison," 10 (1862), 1-8.

180. Walter Lowe Clay, *The Prison Chaplain.* 1861.

181. William Tuckniss, "Agencies for the Suppression of Vice and Crime," in Henry Mayhew (entry 91), vol. 4.

182. Henry Mayhew and John Binny, *The Criminal Prisons of London.* 1862.

183. Frederick William Robinson (A Prison Matron, pseud.): *Female Life in Prison.* 2 vols. 1862. *Memoirs of Jane Cameron, Female Convict.* 1864.

184. *VM:* "Female Convicts," 2 (1863-1864), 518-532.

185. Ellice Hopkins, *Notes on Penitentiary Work.* 1879.

186. Arthur Griffiths, *Secrets of the Prison House.* 2 vols. 1894.

187. *Fortnightly Review (FR):* E. Orme, "Our Female Criminals," 69 (1898),

790-796; M. F. Johnston, "Life of a Woman Convict," 75 (1901), 559-567.

188. *CR:* S. A. Amos, "Prison Treatment of Women," 73 (1898), 803-813.
189. H. Blagg and C. Wilson, *Women and Prisons.* 1911.
190. Constance Lytton, *Prisons and Prisoners.* 1914.
191. Ann D. Smith, *Women in Prison: A Study of Prison Methods.* 1962.
192. Philip Collins, *Dickens and Crime.* 1962.
193. J. J. Tobias, *Crime and Industrial Society in the Nineteenth Century.* New York, 1967.

Fallen Women and Prostitution

194. William Dodd, *The Magdalen Charity.* 1766.
195. Lock Asylum, *Account of the Nature and Intention of the Lock Hospital.* 1802.
196. Guardian Society, *Eighth Report.* 1826.
197. Metropolitan Female Asylum, *Report of the Provisional Committee.* 1830.
198. Michael Ryan: *Lectures on Population, Marriage and Divorce as Questions of Medicine.* 1831. Medical beliefs about sexual life. Offers insight into fears connected with sexual activity. *Prostitution in London, Paris and New York.* 1839.
199. London Society for the Protection of Young Females, *Fourth Report.* 1839.
200. J. B. Talbot, *Miseries of Prostitution.* 1844.
201. Ralph Wardlaw, *Lectures on Female Prostitution.* 1842, 1844.
202. Associate Institution for Improving and Enforcing Laws for the Protection of Women, *First Report.* 1846.
203. Thomas Beggs, *Three Lectures on the Moral Elevation of the People.* 1847. Chapter 8, "Prostitution."
204. *QR:* J. Armstrong, "Female Penitentiaries," 83 (1848), 359-376.
205. *WR:* W. R. Greg, "Prostitution," 53 (1850), 448-506; "History of Government Control of Prostitution," 93 (1870), 119-179; and "How to Deal with Prostitution," 477-535.
206. William Acton: *Prostitution in Relation to Public Health.* 1851. *Prostitution Considered in its Mental, Social and Sanitary Aspects.* 1857; 1870 ed. rpr. 1968.
207. Mrs. Gaskell, *Ruth.* 1853. The fallen woman question. Reviewed in *NBR:* J. F. Ludlow, "*Ruth*, a Novel," 19 (1853), 151-174.
208. *Meliora:* "Prostitution," 1 (1858-1859), 70-79; and 3 (1860-1861), 145-157.
209. T. C. Newby, *Our Plague Spot.* 1859.
210. *The Magdalen's Friend and Home Intelligencer, 1860-1864.* A periodical devoted to questions about fallen women.
211. John R. Blackmore, *The London by Moonlight Mission.* 1860.
212. *CR:* "Regulation, Cure and Prevention of Prostitution," 14 (1870), 220-235.
213. William Logan, *The Great Social Evil.* 1871.

214. Vigilance; afterwards, National Association for the Defense of Personal Rights, *The Protection of Young Girls.* 1882.
215. *The Sentinel,* 1882-1896. Monthly journal "devoted to the exposition and advancement of public morality and to the suppression of vice."
216. Amy Sharp, *The Legal Protection of Young Girls.* 1884.
217. *Pall Mall Gazette,* 6, 7, 8, and 10 July 1885: W. T. Stead, "The Maiden Tribute of Modern Babylon."
218. Frederick Mead and A. H. Bodkin, *The Criminal Law Amendment Act.* 1885.
219. Ladies National Association for the Abolition of Government Regulation of Vice, *Seventeenth Report.* Bristol, 1887.
220. G. Merrick, *Work Among the Fallen as Seen in Prison Life.* 1890.
221. Benjamin Scott, *A State Iniquity.* 1890.
222. Josephine Butler, *Personal Reminiscences of a Great Crusade.* 1896.
223. International Congress of Women, *Report, 1899: An Equal Moral Standard for Men and Women.* 1900.
224. William Taylor, *The Story of the Homes: London Female Preventive and Reformatory Institution.* 1907.
225. H. F. B. Compston, *The Magdalen Hospital.* 1917.
226. Geoffrey May, *The Social Control of Sexual Expression.* 1931.
227. J. L. and Barbara Hammond, *James Stansfeld, a Victorian Champion of Sex Equality.* 1932.
228. Irene Clephane, *Towards Sex Freedom.* 1935.
229. Cyril Pearl, *The Girl With the Swansdown Seat.* 1955.
230. Charles Terrot, *The Maiden Tribute: a Study of the White Slave Traffic.* 1959.
231. Nina Epton, *Love and the English.* 1960.
232. *International Review of Social History:* Peter Cominos, "Late Victorian Sexual Respectability and the Social System," three parts, 8 (1963).
233. Fernando Henriques, *The Immoral Tradition: Prostitution and Society.* 1965.
234. Sean O'Callahan, *The White Slave Traffic.* 1965.
235. M. Penelope Hall and Ismene Howes, *The Church in Social Work, a Study of Moral Welfare Work.* 1965.
236. Steven Marcus, *The Other Victorians: a Study of Sexuality and Pornography in Mid-Nineteenth-Century England.* New York, 1966.
237. [H. S. Ashbee], *My Secret Life;* rpr. and ed. G. Legman. New York, 1966.
238. Ivan Bloch, *Sexual Life in England,* trans. William Farsten. 1967.
239. Ronald Pearsall, *The Worm in the Bud: the World of Victorian Sexuality.* 1969.
240. Constance Rover, *Love, Morals and the Feminists.* 1970.

IV The Expansion of Employment

The rapid economic and population expansion of the nineteenth century was accompanied by a dramatic increase in employment opportunities for women. But the availability to employers of a very large female working-class population tended to overcrowd the major fields in which these women were employed, often keeping wages low, working conditions unfavorable and competition high. The outlines of this history are well known. But not as carefully noted is the situation of skilled and comparatively well-paid working-class women who improved their socioeconomic condition and social status. The sources for studying the circumstances of this classification of women workers have tended to remain within the domain of local history.

As for the employable women of the middle classes, they were undoubtedly disadvantaged by what has come to be known as the Victorian "feminine ideal." This popular image included the prejudice that a woman of quality — a lady — lowered or lost her social position if she undertook paid employment. But the rationalization for this went beyond idealization of the "gentler sex." The conventional preference for women maintaining primarily "domestic roles" was closely tied to practical needs, established values, traditional social structure and the law. Contemporary literature dealing with the question of women's work pursues most of these themes. Several sources also detail a concern over "moral dangers" possibly awaiting the women daring to venture into the "mixed assemblies" of the world of work.

This description of the work question, however, is very incomplete — leaving out the considerable number of women who fell into the broad social categories between the extremes, for, by mid-century, class lines were blurring and fluidity was replacing rigidity especially within the various social levels. Female employment appears to have played a role in moving class lines when an increasing number of women responded over the years to the practical labor demands of an expanding society. Meanwhile, articulate men and women addressed themselves to the problem of influencing public opinion to sanction these new feminine roles, and to approve a wider range of occupations. Undoubtedly, these efforts helped toward the eventual social acceptance of Victorian career women.

241. *FM*: "Maid Servants," 28 (1843), 564-572; "Modern Governess System," 30 (1844), 571-583; "Social Position of Governesses," 37 (1848), 411-414; "Ladies as Clerks," n.s. 12 (1875), 335-340.
242. *Christian Lady's Magazine,* ed. Charlotte Elizabeth Tonna, "Helen Fleetwood" serialized 1839-1841, and "Wrongs of Woman" serialized 1841-1843. Didactic fiction based on government reports. Also in *The Works of Charlotte Elizabeth.* 3 vols. New York, 1844-1845.
243. *Nineteenth Century Fiction:* Ivanka Kovačević and S. Barbara Kanner,

"Blue Book into Novel: The Forgotten Industrial Fiction of Charlotte Elizabeth Tonna," 25 (1970), 152-173.

244. *ER:* W. R. Greg, "Juvenile and Female Labour," 79 (1844), 130-156; W. R. Greg, "Review of *Mary Barton*," 89 (1849), 402-435; H. Martineau, "Modern Domestic Service," 115 (1862), 409-439. See entry 92.

245. *QR:* Lady Eastlake, "*Vanity Fair, Jane Eyre* and the Governesses' Benevolent Institution," 84 (1848), 153-185; H. Martineau, "Miss Nightingale's 'Notes on Nursing,'" 107 (1860), 392-422; J. Manners, "Employment of Women in the Public Service," 151 (1881), 181-200.

246. William Shaw, *An Affectionate Pleading for England's Oppressed Female Workers.* 1850.

247. John Milne, *Industrial and Social Employment of Women in the Middle and Lower Ranks.* 1857, 1870.

248. Barbara Leigh Smith Bodichon, *Women and Work.* 1856.

249. Anna Jameson, *The Communion of Labour: a Lecture on the Social Employments of Women.* 1856. Reviewed in *The Economist,* 29 November 1856.

250. Clara Balfour, *Working Women of the Last Half Century* (1856).

251. *NBR:* J. W. Kaye, "Domestic Service, 'Nelly Armstrong,'" 20 (1853), 179-208; J. W. Kaye, "Employment of Women," 26 (1857), 291-338.

252. *TNAPSS:* G. W. Hastings et al., "The Industrial Employments of Women" (1857), pp. 531-548; E. Faithfull, "The Victoria Press" (1860), pp. 819-821; B. R. Parkes, "Condition of Working Women in England and France" (1861), pp. 632-640; R. S. Baker, "Social Results of Employment of Girls and Women in Manufactories and Workshops" (1868), pp. 537-548; "English Matrons and Their Professions" (1874), pp. 25-30; E. Williams, "Protective and Provident Movement Among Women" (1876), pp. 729-733, 945; and W. C. Taylor, "On State Interference in the Industrial Employment of Women," pp. 734-736; "The Duties of Women as Managers of Elementary Schools" (1878), pp. 439-442; and E. J. Watherston, "Industrial Employment of Women in France as Compared with England," pp. 618-631.

253. Angela Burdett-Coutts, *Project for Young Ladies as Schoolmistresses, a Circular.* 1858. Also published in *English Journal of Education,* April 1858. See also Miss Coutts' letter, "A Suggestion for the Daughters of the Middle Classes," in *EWJ,* 6 (1860), 49-53.

254. *EWJ:* B. R. Parkes, "The Profession of the Teacher," 1 (1858), 1-13; "On the Adoption of Professional Life by Women," 2 (1858), 1-19; "Life Assurance Agency as an Employment for Females," 3 (1859), 120-123; and "Female Engravers from the Sixteenth to the Nineteenth Century," 259-270; "Association for Promoting the Employment of Women," 4 (1859), 54-59; "Market for Educated Female Labour," 145-152; and "What Can Educated Women Do?" 217-227; J. Boucherett, "On the Obstacles to the Employment of Women," 4 (1860), 361-375; "Statistics on the Employment of Women," 5 (1860), 1-6; E. and E. Blackwell, "Medicine as a Profession for Women," 145-161; and "A Ramble with Mrs. Grundy" (the *EWJ* press shop) 269-272; "Friendly Societies," 6 (1860), 107-112; S. Gregory, "Female Physicians," 9

(1862), 1-11; Mrs. Jellicoe, "Women's Supervision of Women's Industry," 10 (1862), 114-119; J. Boucherett, "On the Choice of a Business," 145-153; and "Remunerative Work for Gentlewomen," 183-189.

255. Bessie Rayner Parkes (Mrs. Belloc), *Essays on Women's Work.* 1865.

256. *VM:* "Women in the Civil Service," 12 (1868-1869), 438-446.

257. Emily Faithfull, *Woman's Work.* 1871. Especially industrial employment.

258. *CM:* A. Ritchie, "Maids of All Work and Blue Books," 30 (1874), 281-296.

259. R. A. Caplin, *Women in the Reign of Queen Victoria.* 1874.

260. *EWR:* J. Boucherett, "Occupations of Women" (1874), pp. 85-90; H. Blackburn, "Pursuits of Women," pp. 237-246; and "Trade Unions for Women," pp. 281-282; "Women's Protective and Provident League" (1875), pp. 84-85; and "Women in the Civil Service," pp. 197-202, 243-248, 297-301; "Salary No Object" (1878), pp. 107; E. P. R. Laye, "Women and Careers," pp. 193-201; and "Female Clerks," pp. 367-368; "Twentieth Anniversary of the Society for the Employment of Women" (1879), pp. 289-297; "Women in Libraries" (1899), pp. 240-244.

261. Louisa Hubbard, ed., *The Year Book of Women's Work and Guide to Remunerative Employment.* 1875.

262. *Good Words (GW):* A Trollope, "The Young Women at the Telegraph Office," 18 (1877), 377-384; M. Calverley, "Who Teaches Our Little Ones" (certification of governesses), 19 (1878), 390-393; J. Pendleton, "Newspaper Woman," 43 (1902), 57-60.

263. Edwin A. Pratt, *Pioneer Women in Victoria's Reign.* 1879.

264. *CR:* W. Howard, "Ladies and Hospital Nursing," 34 (1879), 490-503; E. Crawford, "Women in Journalism," 64 (1893), 362-371; C. J. Cullingworth, "Registration of Midwives," 73 (1898), 398-402; V. Crawford, "Englishwomen in Agriculture," 74 (1898), 426-435.

265. *NC:* M. E. Harkness, "Women as Civil Servants," 10 (1881), 369-381.

266. Sophia Jex-Blake, *Medical Women.* 1886.

267. Louisa Twining, *Women's Work, Official and Unofficial.* 1887.

268. *WR:* "Nurses and Nursing," 130 (1888), 11-16; "Work and Women," 131 (1889), 270-279; H. M. Browne, "A New Union for Women," 138 (1892), 528-535; E. Holyoake, "Capacity of Women for Industrial Union," 139 (1893), 164-168.

269. *FR:* E. F. S. Dilke, "Benefit Societies and Trade Unions for Women," 51 (1889), 852-856; C. Black, "Organization of Working Women," 52 (1889), 695-704; E. March-Phillips, "Progress in Trades Unions for Women," 60 (1893), 92-104; and E. F. S. Dilke, "Industrial Position of Women," 499-508.

270. Royal Commission on Labour, *The Employment of Women: Reports on the Conditions of Work in Various Industries.* 1893.

271. Emilia F. S. Dilke, *Trades Unions for Women.* 1893.

272. Board of Trade, *Report by Miss Collett on the Statistics of Employment of Women and Girls.* 1894.

273. Women's Industrial Council: *Annual Report.* 1894 and thereafter. *Home Industries of Women in London.* 1897. *Women's Wages in England in*

the Nineteenth Century. 1906. *Interim Reports on Home Industries*. 1906.

274. Agnes Bulley, *Women's Work*. 1894.
275. Margaret Bateson, *Professional Women Upon Their Professions*. 1895.
276. Sidney and Beatrice Webb, *Problems of Modern Industry*. 1898.
277. Women's Institute, *A Dictionary of Employments Open to Women*. 1898.
278. Countess of Aberdeen, ed., *The International Congress of Women, 1899*. 1900.
279. Kathleen Lyttleton, *Women and Their Work*. 1901.
280. Clara E. Collett, ed.: *Educated Working Women*. 1902. *Women in Industry*. 1911.
281. Charles Booth, *Life and Labour of the People of London*. New York, 1902-1904. Multi-volume work.
282. James Ramsay MacDonald, *Women in the Printing Trades*. 1904.
283. B. L. Hutchins: "A Note on the Distribution of Women in Occupations," in *Journal of the Royal Statistical Society*, 67 (1904), part 3. *Home Work and Sweating: Its Causes and Remedies*. 1907. *Working Women and the Poor Law*. 1909. *Women in Modern Industry*. 1915.
284. Sarah A. Tooley, *History of Nursing in the British Empire*. 1906.
285. Central Bureau for the Employment of Women, *The Fingerpost: A Guide to the Professions and Occupations of Educated Women*. 1906.
286. Gertrude Tuckwell et al., *Women in Industry from Seven Points of View*. 1908..
287. Charlotte Perkins Gilman, *Women and Economics*. 1910.
288. Joseph Hallsworth and Rhys Davis, *The Working Life of Shop Assistants*. 1910.
289. William Paine, *Shop Slavery and Emancipation*. 1912.
290. Elizabeth Blackwell, *Pioneer Work in Opening the Medical Profession to Women*. 1912.
291. Edith J. Morley, *Working Women in Seven Professions*. 1914.
292. A. M. Bennett, *English Medical Women*. 1915.
293. C. V. Butler, *Domestic Service*. 1916.
294. Barbara Drake: *The Tea Shop Girl*. 1913. *Women in Engineering Trades*. 1918. *Women in Trade Unions*. 1920.
295. Adelaide Anderson, *Women in the Factory: An Administrative Adventure, 1893-1921*. 1922. Story of the women inspectorate.
296. M. Phillips and W. S. Tomkinson, *English Women in Life and Letters*. Oxford, 1926.
297. Vera Brittain, *Women's Work in Modern Britain*. 1928.
298. Lucy R. Seymer, *A General History of Nursing*. 1932.
299. J. H. Clapham, *An Economic History of Modern Britain, 1820-1929*. 3 vols. Cambridge, 1932-1938; 1952. References to women workers in each volume.
300. R. W. Rich, *The Training of Teachers*. 1933.
301. Dorothy E. Evans, *Women and the Civil Service*. 1934.
302. Hilda Martindale, *Women Servants of the State, 1870-1938*. 1938.

303. Mary P. French, *Fifty Years of Midwifery, the Story of Annie McCall*. 1950.
304. Edith Tancred, *Women Police, 1914-1950*. 1951.
305. E. Moberly Bell, *Storming the Citadel: Women's Entry into Medicine*. 1953.
306. Asher Tropp, *The School Teachers*. 1957.
307. Viola Klein, *Britain's Married Women Workers*. 1965.
308. S. G. Checkland, *The Rise of Industrial Society in England, 1815-1885*. 1966. Important background for women's employment.

V   Education and Vocational Training

In England during the early nineteenth century, education was provided for the affluent classes by private "venture" academies, the old chartered boys' schools and fashionable boarding schools for girls. Children of the other classes were educated in local academies if they could afford them, or in institutions connected with religious establishments, charitable organizations or adult educational programs such as the Mechanics' Institutions. By the end of the era, however, these individual, independent facilities had been supplemented by a large and complex network of state-supported schools within a national system of education. The development of this system has been considered the fruit of a complicated, century-long, controversial education movement.

One aspect of the movement — and considered an important one — was the question of "female education." It is appropriate, then, to view the education of English women in this context. Studies along these lines reveal, for example, that the government and voluntary institutions worked over the years to increase literacy, to improve moral standards and to provide "industrial training" for girls of the impoverished and working classes. In the National Schools of the Established Church poor girls were trained to be schoolmistresses, while others were prepared with skills for alternative employment. In addition, adult education facilities provided a still unestimated number of working-class women with varying degrees of schooling. For these women, education came to signify not only a means to a livelihood and respectability, but also a possible (though mainly unintentioned) way up the social ladder. Comparatively few studies are available concerning working-class female education.

A great deal is known, however, about the history of middle-class women who desired to improve their educational backgrounds either to support their claims to greater social and political equality, or to gain entrance into professional careers. Contemporary sources and a long list of secondary works provide the close details of middle-class female education. They also offer rich biographical information about a leadership of articulate, accomplished women who identified themselves with the goal of opening girls' schools and women's colleges which offered curricula similar to that of educational institutions for men. Gaining entrance for women into the universities was an additional goal they pursued. The sources below record their successes and failures.

309. Catherine Cappe, *An Account of Two Charity Schools for the Education of Girls.* York, 1800.
310. *The Philanthropist:* William Corston, letter, 10 December 1810, "Schools of Industry and Instruction for Female Children," 1 (1811), 173-175.
311. The British and Foreign School Society, *Annual Reports.* From 1811.
312. The National Society for Promoting the Education of the Poor in the Principles of the Church of England: *Annual Reports.* From 1812. *Monthly Paper.* 1847-1876.
313. City of London Society for Promoting the Education of the Poor, *Annual Reports.* From 1816.
314. Anna E. Pendered, *Remarks on Female Education, with an Application of its Principles to the Regulation of Schools.* 1827.
315. Rowland Detrosier, *An Address Delivered at the New Mechanics' Institute.* 1829. Stresses need of instruction for women.
316. *WR:* "Madame Roland and Education of Women," 15 (1831), 69-89; "Education of Women: Admission to Universities," 109 (1878), 56-90; "Higher Education of Women," 129 (1888), 152-162; E. S. Tylee, "Recent Experiments in Co-education," 160 (1903), 313-318.
317. George Combe, *Lectures on Popular Education.* 1833, 1837, 1848.
318. *FM:* "An Inquiry into the State of Girls' Fashionable Schools," 31 (1845), 703-712; "Technical Training for Girls," n.s. 19 (1879), 343-351; "Training Schools for Nurses," n.s. 10 (1874), 706-713.
319. The Ragged School Union, *Annual Reports.* From 1845.
320. *QR:* A. A. Cooper (Lord Ashley), "The Ragged Schools," 79 (1846), 127-141; J. Armstrong, "Vauxhall Factory Schools," 92 (1852), 1-18; J. Davies, "Female Education," 119 (1866), 499-515; M. Burrows, "Female Education," 126 (1869), 448-479; Lady Eastlake, "The Englishwoman at School," 146 (1878), 40-69; P. Gardner, "The Women at Oxford and Cambridge," 186 (1897), 529-551.
321. Harriet Martineau, *Household Education.* 1849.
322. *ER:* H. Moseley, "Educational Census of Great Britain," 102 (1855), 377-403; B. G. Johns, "Education of Women," 166 (1877), 89-114.
323. John Frederick Denison Maurice, *Lectures to Ladies on Practical Subjects.* 1855.
324. Bessie Rayner Parkes (Mrs. Belloc), *Remarks on the Education of Girls.* 1854.
325. Angela Burdett-Coutts, *A Summary Account of Prizes for Common Things.* 1854, 1856. Curriculum in Church Schools for poor girls.

326. *TNAPSS:* M. Carpenter, "Relation of Ragged Schools to the Educational Movement" (1857), pp. 226-232; B. Templar, "Importance of Teaching Social Economy in Elementary Schools" (1858), pp. 320-323; J. S. Howson, "On Schools for Girls of the Middle Class" (1859), pp. 308-316; F. Hertz, "Mechanics' Institutes for Working Women," pp. 347-354; J. P. Norris, "On Girls' Industrial Training," pp. 366-376; and J. G. Fitch, "The Professional Training of Teachers," pp. 411-417; L. O. Hope, "Girls' Schools" (1860), pp. 397-404; M. Carpenter, "On the Principles of Education" (1861), pp. 391-397; M. Carpenter, "The Education of Pauper Girls" (1862), pp. 286-293; various authors, "The Education of Girls" (1865), pp. 268-290; I. M. S. Tod, "Advanced Education for Girls of the Upper and Middle Classes" (1867), pp. 368-379; M. Carpenter et al., "Female Education" (1869), pp. 351-364; D. Beale, "University Examinations for Women" (1874), pp. 478-490; A. Keiller and E. Pechey, "Dangers of Overwork: the Higher Class of Girls' Schools" (1880), pp. 420-454.

327. Emily Shirreff, *Intellectual Education and its Influence on the Character and Happiness of Women.* 1858.

328. *EWJ:* "Why Boys are Cleverer than Girls," 2 (1858), 116-119; "Colleges for Girls," 2 (1859), 361-374; "Aberdeen Industrial Schools," 4 (1860), 335-338; W. B. Hodgson, "The General Education of Women," 5 (1860), 73-85; J. Boucherett, "On the Education of Girls with Reference to Their Future Position," 6 (1860), 217-224; I. Craig, "An Interesting Blue Book," 7 (1861), 217-224, 376-384; "University of London and the Graduation of Women," 11 (1863), 270-275; "University of Cambridge and the Education of Women," 12 (1863), 276-279.

329. James P. Kay-Shuttleworth, *Four Periods of Public Education, 1832, 1839, 1846, 1862.* 1862.

330. Frances Power Cobbe, *Essays on the Pursuits of Women.* 1863.

331. *CM:* H. Martineau, "Middle Class Education: Girls," 10 (1864), 549-568.

332. W. B. Hodgson, *The Education of Girls, and the Employment of Women of the Upper Classes.* 1864, 1869.

333. Emily Faithfull, *The Higher Education of Women.* 1866.

334. Elizabeth Sewell, *Principles of Education.* 2 vols. 1865. Popular text for governess-teachers of upper-class girls.

335. Emily Davies, *The Higher Education of Women.* 1866.

336. *CR:* T. Markby, "The Education of Women," 1 (1866), 396-414; L. Becker, "On the Study of Science by Women," 10 (1869), 386-404; E. Shirreff, "College Education for Women," 15 (1870), 55-66; D. Campbell, "Mixed Education of Boys and Girls," 22 (1873), 257-265; E. Hopkins, "Industrial Training of Pauper and Neglected Girls," 42 (1882), 140-154; H. McKerlie, "Lower Education of Women," 51 (1887), 112-119; J. G. Fitch, "Women and the Universities," 58 (1890), 240-255; W. Besant, "Ragged School Union," 65 (1894), 688-703; M. G. Fawcett, "Degrees for Women at Oxford," 69 (1896), 347-356.

337. George Butler, *The Higher Education of Women.* 1867.

338. M. Johnston, *The Ladies College and School Examiner.* 2nd ed.; 1868.

Includes 600 sample questions for examinations and suggests 100 subjects for themes.

339. *MM:* M. G. Fawcett, "Education of Women of the Middle and Upper Classes," 17 (1868), 511-517; M. B. Smedley, "Workhouse School for Girls," 31 (1874), 27-36; F. Martin, "A College for Working Women," 40 (1879), 483-488.

340. University of London, *Regulations Relating to the Examinations for Women.* 1868.

341. *FR:* M. G. Fawcett, "Medical and General Education of Women," 10 (1868), 554-571; R. Wilson, "Aesculapia Victrix: on the London School of Medicine for Women," 45 (1886), 18-33; A. M. Gordon, "Women as Students of Design," 61 (1894), 521-527; T. Case, "Against Degrees for Women at Oxford," 64 (1895), 89-100; J. R. Tanner, "Degrees for Women at Cambridge," 67 (1897), 716-727.

342. Maria Georgina Grey, *On the Education of Women.* 1871.

343. J. G. Fitch, *Address to the Working Women's College.* 1872.

344. Emily Shirreff, *The Work of the National Union.* 1873. National Union for Improving the Education of All Classes.

345. *GW:* C. Kingsley, "Nausicaa in London, or the Lower Education of Women," 15 (1874), 18-23; M. G. Fawcett, "Old and New Ideals of Education of Women," 19 (1878), 853-860.

346. *EWR:* H. B. Taylor, "Industrial Education for Ladies" (1874), pp. 1-6; J. Boucherett, "Mrs. Nassau Senior's Report on the Education of Pauper Girls" (1875), pp. 49-54.

347. Annie E. Ridley, *Frances Mary Buss and Her Work for Education.* 1895.

348. Blanche A. Clough, *Memoir of Anne Jemima Clough.* 1897.

349. Women's Industrial Council, *Technical Education for Girls.* 1897.

350. Isabel Maddison, *Handbook of Courses Open to Women in British, Continental and Canadian Universities.* New York, 1897.

351. Christina S. Bremner, *Education of Girls and Women in Great Britain.* 1897.

352. Dorothea Beale. *Work and Play in Girls' Schools.* 1898.

353. Countess of Warwick, ed., *Progress in Women's Education in the British Empire.* 1898. Report at the Victorian Era Exhibition, 1897.

354. Alice Zimmern, *The Renaissance of Girls' Education in England: a Record of Fifty Years Progress.* 1898.

355. E. Mackenna, ed., *The Woman's Library.* 3 vols. 1903. Handbooks for self-instruction in various occupations.

356. Sara A. Burstall: *English High Schools for Girls.* 1907. *Public Schools for Girls.* 1911. *Retrospect and Prospect: Sixty Years of Women's Education. 1933. Frances Mary Buss.* 1938.

357. Elizabeth Raikes, *Dorothea Beale of Cheltenham.* 1908.

358. Henry A. Binns, *A Century of Education.* 1908.

359. Emily Davies, *Thoughts on Some Questions Relating to Women.* 1910.

360. Margaret Todd, *Life of Sophia Jex-Blake.* 1918.

361. Muriel Byrne and Catherine Mansfield, *Somerville College, 1879-1921.* 1922.

362. Willystyne Goodsell, *Education of Women, Its Social Background and Problems.* 1923.

363. G. Currie Martin, *The Adult School Movement, Its Origin and Development.* 1924. Chapter 9, "Women's Work."
364. Lillian Faithfull, *In the House of My Pilgrimage.* 1924.
365. Barbara Stephen, *Emily Davies and Girton College.* 1927.
366. Dorothy Gardiner, *English Girlhood at School.* 1929.
367. Cecily F. Steadman, *In the Days of Miss Beale.* 1931.
368. Ruth Young, *The Life of an Educational Worker.* 1934.
369. Mary Agnes Hamilton, *Newnham.* 1936.
370. Annie N. A. H. Rogers, *Degrees by Degrees.* 1938.
371. Margaret Tuke, *A History of Bedford College for Women, 1849-1937.* 1939.
372. Alicia Percival, *The English Miss Today and Yesterday.* 1939.
373. Mabel Tylecote: *The Education of Women in Manchester University, 1883-1933.* 1941. *The Mechanics' Institutions Before 1851.* 1957. See pp. 187-189, 263-267.
374. R. Glynn Grylls, *Queen's College, 1848-1948.* 1948.
375. C. B. Firth, *Constance Louisa Maynard, Mistress of Westfield College.* 1949.
376. M. G. Jones, *Hannah More.* 1952.
377. A. K. Clarke, *A History of Cheltenham Ladies College, 1853-1953.* 1953.
378. Thomas Kelley, *George Birkbeck, Pioneer of Adult Education.* Liverpool, 1957. Considers Mechanics' Institutions as centers for female education.
379. H. G. Burgess, *Enterprise in Education.* 1958. Church's National Schools. See also entry 312.
380. Josephine Kamm: *How Different from Us: Miss Buss and Miss Beale.* 1958.
Hope Deferred: Girls' Education in English History. 1965.
381. Vera Brittain, *The Women of Oxford.* 1960.
382. John F. C. Harrison, *Learning and Living, 1789-1960, A Study in the History of the English Adult Education Movement.* 1961.
383. J. W. Adamson, *English Education, 1789-1902.* 1964.
384. S. J. Curtis, *History of Education in Great Britain.* 1965. Good background survey.
385. Harold Silver, *The Concept of Popular Education.* 1965. Includes discussion of women's education. Bibliography.
386. Honor Osborne and Peggy Manisty, *A History of the Royal Schools for Daughters of Officers of the Army.* 1966.
387. Annie Ridler, *Olive Willis and Downe House.* 1967.
388. J. W. Hudson, *The History of Adult Education.* 1851 ed. rpr. New York, 1969.

VI   The Law and the Amendment of the Law

The legal position of women in England changed considerably over the nineteenth century, thereby affecting traditional female social roles. Each act which amended old statutes and effected new legislation in the categories of property ownership, marriage and divorce, custody of children, crime and punishment, business, employment and enfranchisement, in turn, helped to make modifications in the rights and responsibilities of women in private life and as citizens. The relationship between women's legal and social position, therefore, was both dynamic and reciprocal. Contemporary writers on the various aspects of law reform took a number of approaches to these questions. Authors concerned with ideological matters tended to discuss current legislative proposals in terms of personal and political liberty, individuality and justice. Legal theorists and jurists presented their views and arguments within a more technical and perhaps more utilitarian context, and their treatises reached the public along with the more popular literature on the subject. In general, writers on law reform were concerned with finding legislative remedies for what they described as archaic and irrational legal restrictions on the social and economic development of the nation. They wrote mainly as individuals, but a number of them were represented in the membership and publications of the Law Amendment Society and the National Association for the Promotion of Social Science — organizations which included in their work the support and assistance of programs for amending laws which affected women adversely, and for establishing entirely new legal sanctions for women's wider participation in national life.

It would seem, then, that any consideration of the change in the legal position of women should be made in the context of the general movement for legal reform in England. These relationships are argued, explored or evaluated in the representative sources listed below.

389. William Blackstone, *Commentaries on the Laws of England.* 4 vols. 15th edn.; 1809. See vol. I, chapter 15, "Of Husband and Wife."
390. Caroline Norton [Pearce Stevenson]: *A Plain Letter to the Lord Chancellor on the Infant Custody Bill.* 1839.
    English Laws for Women in the Nineteenth Century. 1854.
    A Letter to the Queen on Lord Chancellor Cranworth's Marriage and Divorce Bill. 1855.
391. John J. J. S. Wharton, *An Exposition of the Laws Relating to the Women of England, Showing Their Rights, Remedies and Responsibilities.* 1853.
392. Barbara Leigh Smith Bodichon, *A Brief Summary in Plain Language of the Most Important Laws Concerning Women.* 1854.
393. *BM:* M. Oliphant, "The Laws Concerning Women," 79 (1856), 379-387; R. Thicknesse, "The New Legal Position of Married Women," 133 (1883), 207-220.
394. *WR:* "Property of Married Women" (a Law Amendment Society Report), 66 (1856), 331-347; "Laws of Marriage and Divorce," 82 (1864),

442-454; "Law in Relation to Women," 128 (1887), 698-710; M. M. Blake, "Women and the Law," 137 (1892), 364-370; "Judicial Sex-Bias," 149 (1898), 147-160, 279-288; "Present Legal Position of Women in the United Kingdom," 163 (1905), 513-539.

395. *ER:* T. E. Perry, "Rights and Liabilities of Husband and Wife," 105 (1857), 181-205; A. Birrell, "Women Under English Law," 184 (1896), 322-340.

396. *NBR:* J. W. Kaye, "The Marriage and Divorce Bill," 27 (1857), 162-193.

397. *QR:* W. E. Gladstone, "The Bill for Divorce," 102 (1857), 251-288.

398. Thomas H. Markham, *The Divorce and Matrimonial Causes Acts of 1857 and 1858, with all the Decisions, New Rules, Orders.* 1858.

399. *EWJ:* "Property of Married Women," 1 (1858), 58-59; and "The New Law of Divorce," 186-189; M. C. Tabor, "On the Condition of Women as Affected by Law," 10 (1862), 124-127.

400. *TNAPSS:* A. Waddilove, "The Law of Marriage and Divorce as at Present Existing in England, Ireland and Scotland" (1861), pp. 191-199; and W. O. Morris, "On the Marriage Question," pp. 199-212; A. Hobhouse, "Is It Desirable to Amend the Law Which Gives the Personal Property and Earnings of the Wife to Her Husband?" (1868), pp. 238-248 and 275-280; M. Burton, "Should the Labour of Women in the Factories be Regulated?" (1877), p. 246 (summary).

401. Jeremy Bentham, *Theory of Legislation,* trans. from the French. 1864. See part 3, chapter 5, "Of Marriage," pp. 215-236.

402. *Meliora:* "The Legal Position of Women and Its Moral Effects," 8 (1865), 93-102.

403. Thomas Chisholm Anstey, *Historic Points in the Laws Relating to Women.* 1868.

404. *Debate on the Second Reading of "The Bill to Amend the Law with Respect to the Property of Married Women." Manchester,* 1868. Speeches of Bright, Lowe, Mill, et al.

405. *The Lords and the Married Women's Property Bill.* Manchester, 1870. Rpr. articles from the daily press.

406. *EWR:* "History of the Married Women's Property Bill" (1873), pp. 177-184; "The Nine Hours Bill, and the Shop Hours Regulation Bill," pp. 209-212; and J. Boucherett, "Legislative Restrictions on Women's Labour," pp. 249-258; "The Night Cometh When No 'Woman' Can Work" (1878), pp. 97-102; "Special Labour Legislation for Women" (1899), pp. 166-168; "Regulation versus Interference" (1900), pp. 1-6.

407. H. Fawcett and Thomas Bazley: *House of Commons Speeches on the Factory Acts Amendment Bill, July 30, 1873.* 1873. *Second Reading of the Government's Factory Bill, June 11, 1874.* Manchester, 1874.

408. M. A. Hardcastle, *Lord Brougham on Factory Legislation.* 1874.

409. Frederick A. Binney, *Marriage Law Injustice; Objections to the Divorce Act with Suggested Amendments.* 1876.

410. Seymour Bushe, *The Legal Position of Women in England and Ireland.* 1878.

411. Elizabeth Wolstenholme-Elmy, *The Criminal Code in Its Relation to Women.* Manchester, 1880.

412. Thomas Barrett-Lennard, *The Position in Law of Women*. 1883. Discusses Married Women's Property Acts of 1870, 1874, 1882.

413. W. A. Holdsworth, *Married Women's Property Act, 1882*. 1882.

414. Frances E. Hoggan, *The Position of the Mother in the Family in its Legal and Scientific Aspects*. Manchester, 1884.

415. *Ward and Lock's Handbook of the Married Women's Property Act*. 1885.

416. Ralph Thicknesse, *The Rights and Wrongs of Women: a Digest*. 1884.

417. Editha Johnson, *Woman and the Law*. 1892.

418. Joseph Bridges Matthews, *Manual of the Law Relating to Married Women*. 1892.

419. C. C. Stopes, *British Freewomen: Their Historical Privilege*. 1894.

420. *FR:* E. March-Phillips, "The Factory Act as it Affects Women," 61 (1894), 738-748; E. March-Phillips, "Factory Legislation for Women," 63 (1895), 733-744; "Marriage Contract in Relation to Social Progress," 83 (1905), 479-485.

421. Arthur Rackham Cleveland, *Woman Under English Law*. 1896.

422. Beatrice Webb: *Women and the Factory Acts*. 1896. *The Case for the Factory Acts*. 1901.

423. Jane Brownlow, *Women and Factory Legislation*. 1896.

424. Jessie Boucherett and Helen Blackburn, *The Condition of Working Women and the Factory Acts*. 1896.

425. Montague Lush, *Changes in the Laws Affecting the Rights, Status and Liabilities of Married Women*. 1901.

426. B. L. Hutchins and M. Harrison, *History of Factory Legislation*. 1903.

427. Women's Industrial Council, *Home Industries of Women in London*. 1906.

428. Gordon C. Whatcat, *Every Woman's Own Lawyer*, 1907.

429. A. Beatrice Wallis Chapman and Mary Wallis Chapman, *The Status of Women Under English Law*. 1909.

430. *Women's Charter: Nine Bills Introduced into the House of Commons*. 1910. Rpr. from the *Daily News*, 15 March 1910.

431. E. C. Harvey, *Labour Laws for Women and Children in the United Kingdom*. 1909.

432. Eugene A. Hecker, *A Short History of Women's Rights*. 1910.

433. Wilfred Hooper, *The Englishwoman's Legal Guide: A Popular Handbook*. 1913.

434. Helena F. Normanton, *Magna Carta and Women*. 1915.

435. Maud Crofts, *Women Under English Law*. 1925.

436. Erna Reiss, *Rights and Duties of Englishwomen: A Study in Law and Public Opinion*. Manchester, 1934.

437. *Women Lawyers' Journal:* M. Fenberg, "Blame Coke and Blackstone," 34 (1948), 7.

438. M. W. Thomas, *Early Factory Legislation*. 1948.

439. Alfred Dunning, *The Changing Law*. 1953.

440. R. H. Graveson and F. R. Crane, eds., *A Century of Family Law, 1857-1957*. 1957.

441. Norman St. John-Stevas, *Life, Death and the Law*. Bloomington, Ind.,

1961; also "Women in Public Law," in *A Century of Family Law* (entry 440).

VII Political Activity and Public Service

Changes in the political and administrative structure and institutions of England during the nineteenth century functioned to fulfill the pressing requirements of the increasingly populous and complex society. As bureaucracy developed to facilitate governmental administration, the recruitment of qualified personnel was extended over the period to increasing numbers of women. In addition to the laws which were already improving women's social and legal status in the areas of property ownership, marital rights and employment, legislation was passed to allow for women's involvement in public service. Over the century, women were enlisted or elected to serve as Poor Law guardians, overseers, churchwardens, governors and medical officers of workhouses, surveyors of highways, inspectors of factories and schools, members of school boards and boards of guardians. Under stipulated conditions, the franchise in municipal elections, and in local government, was legislated to women also. It was the parliamentary franchise that proved to be unattainable until the following century.

National electoral reform legislation from 1832 focused upon questions of male suffrage exclusively, although at least from that date the question of votes for women occasionally appeared in popular literature on political subjects. As in the case of legal reform, arguments on either side of the issue varied from the ideological to the theoretical to the practical aspects of the question. Many of the political and sociological ramifications of extending the parliamentary franchise to women were not explored in contemporary literature, and the many closely related details and questions have yet to receive a thorough evaluation or analysis in secondary sources. But the available literature on the subject does provide essential background covering the polemics of the women's suffrage controversy, the details of various organizations that were established to pursue the goal of enfranchisement or to block it, the personnel of the early suffrage movements and of the militant one organized later in the century, the role of party politics, and some of the other — often equally controversial — issues that became entwined with the main point of votes for women.

442. *The Republican:* "Vindication of Female Political Interference," I, 10 September 1819. Radical views of Richard Carlile.

443. *QR:* J. W. Croker, "Anti-Corn Law Agitation" (criticism of active involvement of women), 71 (1842), especially 261-265; "Society and Politics in the Nineteenth Century," 212 (1910), 309-338.

444. *WR:* H. T. Mill, "The Enfranchisement of Women," 55 (1851), 289-301; "The Claims of Women to the Franchise" (petition presented to the House of Commons by J. S. Mill, 7 June 1866), 87 (1867), 63-79; "Political Disabilities of Women," 97 (1872), 50-60; "Emancipation of Women," 102 (1874), 137-174; "Women Ratepayers' Right to Vote," 122 (1884), 375-381; "Women as Poor Law Guardians," 123 (1885), 386-395; "Women Workers in the Liberal Cause," 128 (1887), 311-318; E. Martyn, "Women in Public Life," 132 (1889), 278-285; "Women's Suffrage," 148 (1897), 357-372; "Women in Local Administration," 150 (1898), 32-46, 248-260, 377-389, and 151 (1899), 159-171; "Registration Reform in Woman Suffrage," 156 (1901), 68-76; "Woman's Lost Citizenship," 159 (1903), 512-522.

445. Archibald Prentice, *History of the Anti-Corn Law League.* 1853; 1968. Work of women in the League defended — and probably understated. See also entry 443.

446. Barbara Leigh Smith Bodichon, *Reasons for the Enfranchisement of Women.* 1866.

447. *VM:* "Employment of Women in the Public Service," 12 (1868-1869), 438-446; "Victoria Discussion Society: Women's Demand for the Privileges of Both Sexes," 15 (1870), 318-356.

448. *MM:* C. Kingsley, "Women and Politics," 20 (1869), 552-561; G. Smith, "Female Suffrage," 30 (1874), 139-150.

449. *CR:* L. E. Becker, "Female Suffrage," 4 (1867), 307-316; E. Pfeiffer, "Woman's Claim," 39 (1881), 265-277; E. Pfeiffer, "Suffrage for Women in England," 47 (1885), 418-435; R. B. Haldane, "Economic Aspects of Women's Suffrage," 58 (1890), 830-838.

450. *Speech of John Stuart Mill on the Admission of Women to the Electoral Franchise, May 20, 1867, in the House of Commons.* 1867.

451. *FR:* R. M. Pankhurst, "Right to Suffrage of Woman Under the Reform Act of 1867," 10 (1868), 250-254; A. Arnold, "Political Enfranchisement of Women," 17 (1872), 204-214; "Woman Suffrage" (includes eight pages of women's signatures to a "Declaration for Suffrage"), 52 (1889), 123-139.

452. Frances Power Cobbe, *Why Women Desire the Franchise.* 1869.

453. *Women's Suffrage Journal, 1870-1890,* ed. Lydia E. Becker.

454. Lydia E. Becker: *Liberty, Equality, Fraternity. A Reply to Mr. Fitzjames Stephen's Strictures on Mr. J. S. Mill's 'Subjection of Women.'* Manchester, 1874.
The Rights and Duties of Women in Local Government. Manchester, 1879.

455. National Society for Women's Suffrage, *Opinions of Women on Women's Suffrage.* 1879.

456. *TNAPSS:* L. Becker, "On the Women's Suffrage Question" (1877), pp. 701-704.

457. *EWR:* "New Objections to Women's Suffrage" (1870), pp. 55-78; and

"Petitions for Extension of Elective Franchise to Women," pp. 198-210; "Election of School Boards" (1871), pp. 1-5; "Public Opinion in the Press on Women's Suffrage" (1873), pp. 29-32 (summary); "The Late School Board Elections" (1874), pp. 6-9; and "Shall a Women House-holders' League be Formed?" pp. 186-188; "Women as Poor Law Guardians" (1875), pp. 157-159; "Pegging Away" (1878), pp. 529-537; "The Issues of Two Debates: Suffrage and Married Women's Property" (1879), pp. 97-103; "Participation of Women in Local Franchises," pp. 206-212; "Three Decades of Progress," pp. 337-344; and "Women on School Boards," pp. 353-359.

458. Louisa Shore, *The Citizenship of Women Socially Considered*. 1874.
459. Women's Local Government Society, *Women and the Municipal Corporations Act of 1882*. 1882; also pamphlets from 1896.
460. W. S. B. McLaren, "The Political Emancipation of Women." 1887. Rpr. *WR:* 128 (1887), 165-173.
461. *NC:* "An Appeal Against Female Suffrage," 25 (1889), 781-788; M. G. Fawcett and M. M. Dilke, "Reply to Appeal Against Female Suffrage," 26 (1889), 86-103.
462. Women's National Liberal Federation, *Quarterly Leaflets*. 1896-1916.
463. M. Ostrogorski, *The Rights of Women*. 1893. Constitutional foundations of the question of enfranchisement.
464. Louisa Twining, *Workhouses and Pauperism, and Women's Work in the Administration of the Poor Law*. 1898.
465. International Congress of Women, *Women in Politics; Report of 1899*. 1900.
466. Helen Blackburn, *Women's Suffrage*. 1902.
467. S. Reddish, *Women and County and Borough Councils: A Claim for Eligibility*. 1903.
468. Keir Hardie: *The Labour Party and Women Suffrage*. 1900. *The Citizenship of Women: A Plea for Women's Suffrage*. 1905.
469. R. J. Campbell, *Women's Suffrage and the Social Evil*. 1907.
470. Women's National Anti-Suffrage League, *The Anti-Suffrage Review*. From 1908.
471. Charlotte C. Stopes, *The Constitutional Basis of Women's Suffrage*. 1908.
472. E. Belfort Bax, *The Legal Subjection of Men: Reply to the Suffragettes*. 1908.
473. *The Englishwoman*. 1909. A Journal for the enfranchisement of women.
474. J. M. E. Brownlow, *Women's Work in Local Government*. 1911.
475. Sylvia Pankhurst, *The Suffragette; the Militant Suffrage Movement*. 1911.
476. F. W. Pethick Lawrence, *Women's Fight for the Vote*. 1911.
477. Margaret W. Nevinson, *Five Years Struggle*. 1912.
478. *The Men's League Handbook on Women's Suffrage*. 1912.
479. Marion Holmes, *A.B.C. of Votes for Women*. 1913.
480. *The Suffrage Annual and Women's Who's Who*. 1913.
481. Almroth Wright, *Unexpurgated Case Against Women's Suffrage*. 1913.
482. *The New Statesman:* "The Awakening of Women," ed. Mrs. Sidney

Webb, 2 (1913), Special Supplement. Introduction by Mrs. Webb, xxiv-xxvi, eleven articles, and bibliography.

483. Emmeline G. Pankhurst: *Suffrage Speeches from the Dock.* 1913. *My Own Story.* 1914.
484. H. M. Swanwick, *The Future of the Women's Movement.* 1913.
485. *Liberal Women's Review:* Vera Cox, "Parliamentary History of Women's Suffrage," July 1914, pp. 29-33.
486. Annie Besant, *Women and Politics: the Way Out of Present Difficulties.* 1914.
487. Charles Seymour, *Electoral Reform in England and Wales.* New Haven, Conn., 1915. Especially, pp. 476-477.
488. J. Ramsay Macdonald, *Margaret Ethel Macdonald.* New York, 1926.
489. Janet E. Courtney, *The Adventurous Thirties: A Chapter in the Women's Movement.* 1933.
490. Philip Snowden, *An Autobiography.* 1934.
491. George Dangerfield, "The Women's Rebellion," in *The Strange Death of Liberal England.* 1935.
492. Emmeline Pethick Lawrence, *My Part in a Changing World.* 1938.
493. Janet Henderson Robb, *The Primrose League.* New York, 1942.
494. Roger Fulford, *Votes for Women: Story of a Struggle.* 1958.
495. A. W. Baldwin, *The Macdonald Sisters.* 1960.
496. Vera Brittain, *Pethick Lawrence. A Portrait.* 1963.
497. David Mitchell, *The Fighting Pankhursts.* 1967.
498. Constance Rover, *Women's Suffrage and Party Politics in Britain, 1866-1914.* 1967.
499. Marian Ramelson, *The Petticoat Rebellion: A Century of Struggle for Women's Rights.* 1967.
500. Hannah Mitchell, *The Hard Way Up.* 1970.

Notes

INTRODUCTION
The Perfect Victorian Lady

1. The phrase "perfect lady" has been defined by C. Willett Cunnington, *Feminine Attitudes in the Nineteenth Century* (London, 1935), pp. 135-136, and by J. A. and Olive Banks, *Feminism and Family Planning in Victorian England* (Liverpool, 1964), pp. 9-11. My own definition differs slightly from both books, but I have found them invaluable in describing the position of the Victorian middle-class woman.

2. Mrs. Ellis, *The Daughters of England* (London, 1845), p. 73.

3. Wanda Neff, *Victorian Working Women* (New York, 1929), pp. 188-189. *Shirley* was published in 1849.

4. "Queen Bees or Working Bees?" Review of a paper read by Miss Bessie Parks to the Social Science Congress, *Saturday Review*, 12 November 1859.

5. See in particular the dialect writings of Ben Brierley (1825-1896), Edwin Waugh (1817-1890) and John Hartley (1839-1915), and any respectable working-class journal.

6. *David Copperfield* (1849-1850), ch. 50.

1: THE VICTORIAN GOVERNESS
Status Incongruence in Family and Society

1. Harriet Martineau, "Female Industry," *Edinburgh Review*, 109 (April 1859), 294 – (authorship per *Wellesley Index*). For governesses in *Punch* see Alison Adburgham, *A Punch History of Manners and Modes, 1841-1940* (London, 1961), esp. pp. 86-87, 99. For a selection of journal articles see Wanda F. Neff, *Victorian Working Women: An Historical and Literary Study of Women in British Industries and Professions, 1832-1850* (London, 1929), notes to ch. V, pp. 269-271.

2. See, for example, "The Profession of the Teacher. The Annual Reports of the Governesses' Benevolent Institution, from 1843 to 1856," *English*

Woman's Journal, I (March, 1858), 5-6, hereafter *EWJ.* See also Martineau, pp. 316-317, 307; Elizabeth Missing Sewell, *Principles of Education, drawn from nature and revelation, and applied to female education in the upper classes* (London, 1865), II, 245-246; and *Once a Week,* III, 271, quoted in Neff, p. 159.

3. Margaret Oliphant, "The Condition of Women," *Blackwood's Magazine,* 83 (February, 1858), 141 and 145 — (authorship per *Wellesley Index*).

4. "The Profession of the Teacher," p. 1. See also: Governesses' Benevolent Institution, London, *Report of the Board of Management for 1851* (London, 1852), p. 146 — hereafter GBI; Bessie Rayner Parkes Belloc, *Essays on Woman's Work,* 2nd ed. (London, 1865), p. 76.

5. Elizabeth Eastlake, "*Vanity Fair, Jane Eyre,* and the Governesses' Benevolent Institution," *Quarterly Review,* 84 (December, 1848), 176 — (authorship per *Wellesley Index*).

6. *Census of Great Britain, 1851,* cited in J. A. Banks, *Prosperity and Parenthood: A Study of Family Planning Among the Victorian Middle Classes* (London, 1965), p. 83. The number of governesses is from J. A. and Olive Banks, *Feminism and Family Planning in Victorian England* (Liverpool, 1964), p. 31.

7. For literary studies see Patricia Thomson, *The Victorian Heroine: A Changing Ideal, 1837-1873* (London, 1956), Ch. II; Katherine West, *Chapter of Governesses: A Study of the Governess in English Fiction, 1800-1949* (London, 1949), Ch. II-IV. On the governess in relation to education and work see: Belloc, pp. 17, 55-56; Rosalie G. Grylls, *Queen's College, 1848-1948* (London, 1948), p. vii and Ch. II; Josephine Kamm, *Hope Deferred: Girls' Education in English History* (London, 1965), pp. 170-173; H. C. Barnard, *A History of English Education: From 1760* (London, 1961), pp. 22, 156 ff.; Stanley J. Curtis, *History of Education in Great Britain* (London, 1965), pp. 171 ff.; Neff, Ch. V.

8. Within this category there were such specializations as the nursery governess and the finishing governess, the former responsible for early education of children and the latter mainly for finishing the training of adolescent girls in the niceties of social life, manners, and culture. For examples of how a family mixed the services of a variety of governesses see Frances Power Cobbe, *Life of Frances Power Cobbe* (London, 1894), I, 38-39, 50-51; Leonard Woolf, *Sowing: An autobiography of the years 1880-1914* (London, 1960), p. 53. The governess should not be confused with the nurse, also called nursemaid or "nanny." The nursemaid, also responsible for child care, was clearly of the servant class. As much overlapping as there might have been in child care duties, the distinction between the two occupations was always clear.

9. I am indebted to Katherine Luomala, "The Native Dog in the Polynesian System of Values," in S. Diamond, ed., *Culture in History. Essays in Honor of P. Radin* (New York, 1960), pp. 195 ff., for this suggestion of a means for displaying a status symbol. See Eastlake, pp. 179-180, who calls the governess a symbol of "fine ladyism."

10. Cobbe, I, 64.

11. "The Disputed Question," *EWJ,* I (August, 1858), 366.

12. Quoted in Kamm, p. 176.

13. Sewell, *Principles,* II, 238, 279.

14. GBI, *Report,* p. 139; "Profession of the Teacher," p. 11. In an earlier era such a woman might go to live with relatives and serve some of the same functions as a governess, but without pay and be, in a truer sense, part of the

family. The job of paid governess may be seen as an institutionalization and movement out of the family of two functions originally performed by the older "extended" family — the education of children, and the support of orphaned or impoverished relatives.

15. "Female Education in the Middle Classes," *EWJ*, I (June, 1858), 224; Belloc, pp. 157-158.

16. Belloc, p. 76; "Profession of the Teacher," p. 6; Eastlake, p. 176.

17. J. A. and O. Banks, *Feminism*, pp. 27-30.

18. For examples that support this stereotype, see: Edmund Gosse, *Father and Son: A Study of Two Temperaments* (London, 1941), p. 20 (financial collapse); Cobbe, I, 51 (orphan governesses). See also: "Going A Governess-ing," *EWJ*, I (August 1858), 396. The GBI, *Report*, pp. 19-27, gives brief histories of needy governesses aided by the society's annuities, nearly all reporting illness or death of father, or financial catastrophe.

19. Martineau, pp. 294 ff.

20. *Governess Life: Its Trials, Duties, and Encouragements* (London, 1849), p. 127; Sewell, *Principles*, II, 259, 275; Eastlake, pp. 179-180; Sarah Stickney Ellis, *The Wives of England . . .* (London and Paris, 1843), pp. 209-210.

21. Eastlake, p. 180; GBI, *Report*, p. 141; "Profession of the Teacher," p. 11; *Governess Life*, p. 71. The thinking is contradictory — the belief that gentle birth would always tell, and that education or "accomplishments" were only a finish and no substitute for good birth, clashes with belief in the possibility of daughters being corrupted by association with those of inferior birth. Belief in the essential identity of good birth and gentle status may have been an effort on the part of those who had arrived to deny their own *movement* into gentility — to suggest, at least, that their gentility was not simply a product of well-spent money.

22. See J. Jean Hecht, *The Domestic Servant Class in Eighteenth Century England* (London, 1956), pp. 29 ff.

23. During 1851, 924 governesses were placed by the GBI (*Report*, p. 15). See also "Going A Governessing," pp. 396-397.

24. Banks, *Prosperity*, pp. 80-81; Martineau, pp. 308-309; Sewell, *Principles*, II, 245. See also GBI, *Report*, pp. 139-140; "Profession of the Teacher," p. 3; Eastlake, p. 180; Neff, p. 158.

25. Banks, *Prosperity*, p. 72, for the cost of board. He finds that an adult daughter living at home cost her father £100 a year (p. 173), and that a married man, wife, one child, and two servants could get by on a minimum of £300 per year (pp. 42-45, 120). Mrs. Belloc, pp. 83, 105, says that £100-£200 a year avoided absolute penury and describes "genteel merchants and second rate professional men" as scraping by on £300-£400 a year with a family and few servants. Cobbe, I, 214, 275, considers an income of £200 a year "narrow" for a woman used to the comforts of middle-class life.

26. GBI, *Report*, p. 139; Sewell, *Principles*, II, 245.

27. Cobbe, I, 38-39; Gosse, pp. 103-105, 107-108.

28. Anne Thackeray Ritchie, *Chapters from Some Memoirs* (London, 1894), pp. 4-5.

29. Louisa Hoare, *Hints for the Improvement of Early Education*, 18th ed. (London, 1872), p. 131; Sewell, *Principles*, II, 217. This notion may be the source of the image of the stern, autocratic governess which seems to have developed in the late Victorian period and afterwards — see K. West for a full discussion. The image of the severe governess is carried to extremes in that

piece of post-Victorian pornography, *Harriet Marwood, Governess* (reprinted, New York, 1967).

30. Letter dated 20 April 1854 in *The Stanleys of Alderley: Their Letters between the Years 1851-1865*, ed. Nancy Mitford (London, 1939), p. 82. See also Sewell, *Principles*, II, 233, 251.

31. Cobbe, I, 38-39, 50, tells of four successive governesses; Dorothea Beall's family's experiences are reported in Grylls, p. 13; Catherine Sinclair, *Modern Accomplishments*, quoted in Alice Zimmern, *The Renaissance of Girls' Education in England* (London, 1898), pp. 16-17, cites an instance of nine governesses employed one after another at a mother's whim to teach one girl.

32. See "Profession of the Teacher," pp. 5-6; Martineau, p. 307; Sewell, *Principles*, II, 245-246.

33. Sewell, *Principles*, II, 240.

34. Eastlake, p. 176.

35. In *Wives*, p. 219.

36. Belloc, p. 74-75.

37. Eastlake, pp. 176-177, 179 (emphasis hers).

38. Sewell, *Principles*, II, 208, 244-245, 257-258.

39. Metaphors of prostitution are not uncommon — see especially "The Profession of the Teacher," pp. 10, 13 — and there are hints that some middle-class women were driven into that older profession — see "A House of Mercy," *EWJ*, I (March 1858), 25; Sewell, *Principles*, II, 245-246. The metaphor of the nosegay comes from Dinah Mulock Craik, *A Woman's Thoughts About Women* (London, 1858), p. 7.

40. John Ruskin, *Praeterita: Outlines of Scenes and Thoughts Perhaps Worthy of Memory in My Past Life* (London, 1949), p. 111. Neff, pp. 165-166, cites other examples.

41. Ruskin, "Sesame and Lilies," in *Sesame and Lilies; The Two Paths; and The King of the Golden River* (London, 1916), p. 60.

42. Sewell, *Principles*, II, 237.

43. See especially *Governess Life* and *Hints to Governesses*, By one of Themselves (London, 1856). Also, Sewell, *Principles*, II, 252.

44. Eastlake, p. 177; Sewell, *Principles*, II, 239; *Hints to Governesses*, pp. 26-27. See the way Amelia's servants treat Becky Sharp in *Vanity Fair*. Neff, pp. 166-168, gives further instances.

45. Eastlake, p. 177. See also "Open Council" (Letters to the Editor), *EWJ*, I (April 1858), 210-211.

46. Sexual relations with servants, such as those described in *My Secret Life*, would have been taboo with the governess. See Steven Marcus, *The Other Victorians: A Study of Sexuality and Pornography in Mid-Nineteenth Century England* (London, 1969), pp. 130-131, 117-118. Physical relations with a woman of the working class seem to have carried no social obligations, while sexual relations with a woman so nearly of one's own class could not be isolated from a whole complex of responsibilities. The sexual tensions may have been one element of what made a governess a better subject for novelists than the lady's paid companion, though the companion was in many respects a similar occupation.

47. Cobbe, I, 51. Sewell, *Principles*, II, 244; also 210, 238; *Governess Life*, p. 15. See Eastlake, pp. 173 ff., for a fierce attack on Jane Eyre's immoral pride.

48. P. 307; also Sewell, *Principles*, II, 245-246.

49. Sewell, *Principles*, II, 211, 250, 258. I have drawn on Max Weber,

From *Max Weber: Essays in Sociology,* ed. H. H. Gerth and C. Wright Mills (New York, 1958), pp. 180-195, for the distinctions between traditional and market relationships.

50. *The Governess; or, Politics in Private Life* (London, 1836), begins with a statement that there are three classes of people in the world, "men, women, and governesses" (p. 1). Some governesses seem to be a fulfillment of the warning, common in the nineteenth century, that work "unsexed" a woman. See for example Belloc, p. 156.

51. Sewell, *Principles,* II, 239-240.

52. For example, in Ruskin, *Praeterita,* pp. 111, 115, and in Augustus Hare, *The Story of My Life* (London, 1896), I, 176, 248, 250.

53. Miss Nightingale in "Cassandra" (fragment from *Suggestions for Thought to Searchers after Religious Truth*), published in Ray Strachey, *The Cause: A Short History of the Women's Movement in Great Britain* (London, 1928), p. 405.

54. Eastlake, p. 178. Charlotte Brontë's *Villette* is the story of a companion who goes abroad to teach.

55. J. A. and O. Banks, *Feminism,* pp. 31, 33.

56. M. S. Rye, "On Female Emigration," *Transactions of the National Association for the Promotion of Social Science* (1862), p. 811, quoted in Banks, *Feminism,* p. 33.

57. GBI, *Report,* pp. 139 ff.

58. Eastlake, p. 181.

59. F. D. Maurice, Charles Kingsley, et al., *Introductory Lectures delivered at Queen's College, London* (London, 1849), p. 3. Some tried to raise the governess's self-esteem by telling her that teaching was a "divine calling." See *Governess Life,* p. 122; Sewell, *Principles,* II, 209.

60. Maurice, pp. 4-5. No doubt the income from fees was a help, too.

61. P. 127; Sewell, *Principles,* II, 259.

62. Eastlake, p. 184. She opposed the examination of governesses for certificates because she felt the true qualification for teaching was personal moral character, which could not be taught or tested. The qualities she names are those of a good Victorian mother.

63. Martineau, p. 330.

64. "The Profession of the Teacher," p. 10.

65. Sewell, *Principles,* II, 232-233; "The Disputed Question," pp. 361-367.

2: FROM DAME TO WOMAN
W. S. Gilbert and Theatrical Transvestism

1. W. S. Gilbert in a speech at the O. P. Club, December 1906, printed in Sidney Dark and Rowland Grey, *W. S. Gilbert: His Life and Letters* (London, 1923), p. 194. They also agreed that no actress in their plays "should be required to wear a dress that she could not wear with absolute propriety at a private fancy ball." Gilbert undoubtedly was speaking of their collaboration from *The Sorcerer* onward, for in their first work, *Thespis,* the roles of Mercury, Sparkeion, and Cymon were all played by actresses, and in their second work, *Trial by Jury,* they had not gained control of their stage and could not hope to impose such a stipulation. In *Princess Ida,* as earlier writers on Gilbert and Sullivan are fond of pointing out, the collaborators broke their own rule and presented three young men who disguise themselves as girls. But the

garments they assume are academic robes, not distinctly feminine garments.

2. *Morning Chronicle*, June 1829, quoted in Charles E. Pearce, *Madame Vestris and Her Times* (London, n.d.), p. 149.

3. Quoted in J. C. Trewin, *Mr. Macready: A Nineteenth-Century Tragedian and His Theatre* (London, 1955), p. 139.

4. Edgar and Eleanor Johnson, eds., *The Dickens Theatrical Reader* (London, 1964), p. 310.

5. *Punch*, I (11 December 1841), 264. Adalgisa was also played by a male comedian, so that the sexes of the entire romantic triangle were reversed.

6. "Sappho; or, Look before You Leap" in *Beeton's Book of Burlesques* (London, 1865), p. 79. This collection was written for performances in private homes and is therefore more decorous than stage burlesques, but even so, Burnand's stage directions stipulate a male Sappho. The description of Minerva is in Erroll Sherson, *London's Lost Theatres of the Nineteenth Century* (London, 1925), p. 225.

7. *Medea; or, The Best of Mothers with a Brute of a Husband*, Lacy's Acting Edition (London, [1856]), pp. 12-13.

8. F. C. Burnand, *Mary Turner; or, The Wicious Willin and Wictorious Wirtue!* Lacy's Acting Edition (London, [1867]), p. 22. There are also references to false teeth, false hair, and dye in the same author's *Fair Rosamund*, in which Robson originally played the Queen.

9. *Conrad and Medora; or, Harlequin Corsair, and the Little Fairy at the Bottom of the Sea*, French's Acting Edition (London, 1873), p. 21. This burlesque-pantomime was originally performed in 1856.

10. V (7 July 1869), 102. These verses also make fun of false hair, tight lacing, powder, and rouge.

11. "Graciosa and Percinet," *The Extravaganzas of J. R. Planché* (London, 1879), II, 309.

12. *The Savoy Operas*, World's Classics Edition (London, 1962), II, 262. All quotations from the Savoy Operas cited in this essay will be found in this two-volume edition, which has been authorized by Miss Bridget D'Oyly Carte.

13. Both Thackeray and Calverley, though gentlemanly, wrote comic verses about plain elderly women. Serious editorials, such as that in the *Graphic*, XVII (9 March 1878), 250-251, objected to the vanity of an old woman who "has been admired in her youth, and cannot bear to lose the admiration of men, so she tries to keep it up by the use of cosmetics."

Margaret Dalziel in *Popular Fiction 100 Years Ago* (London, 1957) points out that the mid-nineteenth-century penny press had only two attitudes towards old maids. "Those who are content to relinquish their hopes of a husband may be pitied — those who continue their efforts are laughed at" (p. 96). Universal scorn was poured on the latter "sometimes in very repulsive terms. She apes the appearance of younger women and adopts a variety of transparent devices to entrap her victim" (p. 112). The spinster's motives are generally inferrable as a desire for money and social advancement.

Dickens, of course, has his Mrs. Skewton, Volumnia Dedlock, and Lady Tippins.

14. Women were also made fun of in non-musical comedies, but there, as the seriousness of the drama or relative realism of the characters increased, the ugly woman was more likely to overhear references to her own deficiencies than to be told them to her face. A characteristic example is Tom Taylor's *Still Waters Run Deep*, in which Mrs. Sternhold overheard Hawksley's slighting remarks on her rouge.

15. "Q" (Thomas Purnell), *Dramatists of the Present Day* (London,

1871), p. 54. Interestingly enough, the great *onnagata* (female impersonator) of the early eighteenth century Kabuki Theatre, Yoshizawa Ayame, insisted that the female impersonator should not "depart from the conduct of a virtuous woman," even to the point of refusing to play a role which might shock such a woman. Charles D. Dunn and Bunzō Torigoe, transl., *The Actors' Analects* (New York, 1969), pp. 55-56.

16. 15 May 1869.

17. For a fuller discussion, see my introduction to *Gilbert Before Sullivan: Six Comic Plays* (Chicago, 1967), pp. 40-41.

18. (London, [1869]), pp. 11-12. The changing fashions in hair colour may be learned from what colour the dame's hair is originally and what colour she dyes it in each case.

19. (Liverpool, 1868), p. 18.

20. Dark and Grey, p. 195.

21. Gilbert had already used this same joke in *La Vivandière* and a variation of it in *A Sensation Novel*. In Samuel's description: "there are the remains of a fine woman about Ruth," Gilbert was adapting a line from Dickens' *Martin Chuzzlewit*, spoken in reference to Sarah Gamp.

22. Raymond Mander and Joe Mitchenson, *A Picture History of Gilbert and Sullivan* (London, 1962), p. 107.

23. 27 January 1887; signed "A Savoyard."

24. When Chappell published separate numbers from *Patience* as sheet music, Hugh Conway wrote new words to Sullivan's music and the song was re-titled "In the Twilight of Our Love." It is insipid enough for the drawing room, although its immediate source would seem to be Byron's "When we two parted." The first verse is typical: "In the twilight of our love,/ In the darkness falling fast;/ Broken by no gleam above;/ What must be our thoughts — the last?/ Silent ere we say 'fare-well,'/ Pausing ere we turn to part,/ Whilst one wish we dare not tell,/ Echoes yet from heart to heart[,]/ Saddest of all sad regret,/ 'Would we two had never met!' "

25. Letter from Sullivan to Gilbert, 1 July 1893, printed in Hesketh Pearson, *Gilbert: His Life and Strife* (London, 1957), pp. 171-172. Sullivan here alleges that Gilbert modified some of Katisha's lines at his request and insists that he has no objection to a dignified elderly lady. His own words, nevertheless, indicate that what really disturbed him was the continuance of passion into middle age.

26. Shaw himself felt no compunction about making a witty comment on the figure and complexion of Sarah Bernhardt in her middle-age.

27. William Empson is one of the few critics who place the "joke of making romantic love ridiculous by applying it to undesired middle-aged women" in the mainstream of Victorian comedy; yet he still says that Gilbert uses this joke offensively for "timid facetiousness." Once again, it is assumed that romantic love can be nothing else than ridiculous in middle age — *Some Versions of Pastoral* (London, 1935), p. 288.

28. *Studies in Literature,* Third Series (New York, 1930), p. 229.

29. *The Thread of Laughter* (New York, 1952), p. 208.

30. *New and Original Burlesques* (Boston, [1932]), p. ix.

31. *Classics and Commercials* (New York, 1950), p. 361.

32. The deleted verses are printed in Harry How, *Illustrated Interviews* (London, 1893), pp. 9-10.

33. Reginald Allen, *W. S. Gilbert: An Anniversary Survey* (Charlottesville, Va., 1963), frontispiece and p. 78.

34. Dark and Grey, pp. 170-171.

3: VICTORIAN WOMEN AND MENSTRUATION

1. See the Grove Press Paperback reprint (New York, 1967), p. 347.
2. "The Social Position of Women in England, 1850-1914: A Bibliography," *British Journal of Sociology*, VI (1955), 59, note 63.
3. *Human Physiology*, fifth edition, (London, 1840), pp. 770-771.
4. The date is supplied by Dr. Mary Jacobi; see our note 7. Raciborski, a Polish exile working in Paris, published, between 1843 and 1868, at least five works dealing with menstruation.
5. Quoted from an undated edition printed in New York by the Truth Seeker Co., p. 24. Background on Knowlton and Drysdale can be found in Norman E. Hines, *Medical History of Contraception* (New York, 1963), pp. 230-233.
6. Frank Harris was therefore repeating the most enlightened advice available when he gave the following lecture on birth control to one of his early conquests: "Your seed is brought down into your womb by the menstrual blood; it lives there a week or ten days and then dies, and with its death your desires decrease and the chance of impregnation. But near the next monthly period, say within three days, there is a double danger again; for the excitement may bring your seed down before the usual time, and in any case my seed will live in your womb about three days, so if you wish to avoid pregnancy, wait for ten days after your monthly flow is finished and stop, say four days before you expect it again; then the danger of getting a child is very slight." From *My Life and Loves* (New York, 1963), p. 121.
7. *The Question of Rest for Women during Menstruation* (New York, 1877), p. 13.
8. P. 101. The first quotation comes from Horatio R. Storer, *Criminal Abortion*, 1868; the second from an address to the Obstetrical Society of London in 1874, reported in the *British Medical Journal*, 16 January 1875.
9. *Anthropological Review*, VII (1869), cxcviii-cxix.
10. *The Other Victorians* (New York, 1966), p. 235.
11. See the unabridged Grove Press reprint, 2 vols. (New York, 1966), Book I, p. 80.
12. *A Private Disgrace: Lizzie Borden by Daylight* (New York, 1967), p. 131.
13. *The Woman Movement*, ed. William O'Neill (London, 1969), p. 170.
14. "Sex in Mind and Education," XXI (1874), 468.
15. "The Lady Novelists," *Westminster Review*, n. s. II (1852), 133.
16. "Mr. Mill on the Subjection of Women," *Blackwood's*, 106 (1869), 314.

4: MARRIAGE, REDUNDANCY OR SIN
The Painter's View of Women in
The First Twenty-Five Years of Victoria's Reign

1. London, Victoria and Albert Museum. Exhibited at the Royal Academy in 1845. Reproduced in Jeremy Maas, *Victorian Painters* (London, 1969), p. 111.
2. In *The Wives of England, their relative duties, domestic influence, and social obligations* (New York, 1844), p. 28.

3. London, Tate Gallery. Reproduced in Raymond Lister, *Victorian Narrative Painting* (London, 1966), p. 83.

4. *The Life and Letters of Sir John Everett Millais* . . . [edited] *by his son John Guille Millais*, I (New York, 1899), 147.

5. *Germ; thoughts towards nature in poetry, literature and art* (1850), p. 134.

6. XII (1850), 235. The painting is in the collection of Her Majesty, The Queen.

7. *The First Cloud*, 1887, London, Tate Gallery. Reproduced in Lister, p. 119; Maas, p. 245; and Graham Reynolds, *Victorian Painting* (New York, 1967), p. 187 (color). *Mariage de Convenance*, 1883, Glasgow, City Art Gallery. Reproduced in Maas, p. 246; and Graham Reynolds, *Painters of the Victorian Scene* (London, 1953), Plate 87.

8. London, Tate Gallery. Reproduced in Lister, p. 92.

9. *Art Journal*, n.s., V (1853), 151. Neither the painting nor a reproduction of it has been located.

10. W. P. Frith: *The Proposal*, 1853?, Sir David Scott. Reproduced in Reynolds, *Painters of the Victorian Scene*, Plate 21. *The Proposal*, 1877, Sir David Scott. Reproduced in Reynolds, *Victorian Painting*, p. 48 (color). Arthur Hughes, *The Tryst*, before 1859, London, Tate Gallery. Reproduced in Reynolds, *Painters of the Victorian Scene*, Plate 52. Frank Stone, *The Tryst*, Thomas Agnew & Sons, London. Reproduced in Reynolds, *Victorian Painting*, p. 107 (color).

11. Birmingham Art Gallery. Reproduced in Robin Ironside, *Pre-Raphaelite Painters* (New York, 1948), Plate 67; Lister, p. 109.

12. Formerly in the Lady Lever Art Gallery, Port Sunlight, Cheshire.

13. Painting or reproduction not located. Reviewed in the *Art Journal*, n.s., IV (1852), 137.

14. William Rathbone Greg, "Why are Women Redundant," *Literary and Social Judgments* (Boston, 1873), pp. 276, 282-83.

15. Painting or reproduction not located. Listed in the *Art Journal*, XII (1850), 49.

16. The first two paintings have not been located, nor have reproductions of them. *The Poor Teacher* exhibited in the Royal Academy in 1843 is in the possession of Miss Diana Anderson; the version reproduced is more properly called *The Governess*. It was exhibited at the Royal Academy in 1845 and contains the added figures of three young girls.

17. *Spectator*, XX, No. 989 (12 June 1847), 571.

18. "Autobiography of Richard Redgrave, A.R.A.," in the *Art Journal*, XII (1850), 49.

19. *Ibid.*

20. Letter of 1 June 1844, quoted in Richard Redgrave, *A Memoir compiled from his diary by F. M. Redgrave* (London, 1891), p. 26.

21. Hugh Macmillan, *The Life-Work of George Frederick Watts, R.A.* (London, 1903), p. 218.

22. Cited in Walter E. Houghton, *The Victorian Frame of Mind, 1830-1870* (New Haven, Conn., 1957), p. 366.

23. London, Royal Academy. Reproduced in *Illustrated London News*, 209, Supplement (9 November 1956), 31.

24. The Rt. Hon. Lord Sherfield. Reproduced in Maas, p. 236.

25. Sir Colin Anderson. Reproduced in Ironside, p. 29 (color).

26. W. Holman Hunt, *Pre-Raphaelitism and the Pre-Raphaelite Brotherhood*, I (London, 1905), 347.

27. Quoted in Walker Art Gallery, *William Holman Hunt: An Exhibition arranged by the Walker Art Gallery* (Liverpool, 1969), pp. 36-37.

28. Diana Holman-Hunt, *My Grandfather, His Wives and Loves* (London, 1969), p. 217.

29. Wilmington, Delaware Art Museum, Samuel and Mary R. Bancroft Collection. Reproduced in Lister, p. 101; and Ironside, Plate 33.

30. London, Tate Gallery. Reproduced in Lister, pp. 55, 57, 59; and Reynolds, *Painters of the Victorian Scene*, Plates 48, 49, 50.

31. London, Tate Gallery, dated 1856. Reproduced in Ironside, Plate 11.

5: VICTORIAN PROSTITUTION AND VENEREAL DISEASE

1. For examples of histories which either do not mention sexual behavior or do so merely in passing see: A. Briggs, *The Age of Improvement* (London, 1959); G. Best, *Mid Victorian Britain, 1851-1875* (London, 1971); S. G. Checkland, *The Rise of Industrial Society in England, 1815-1885* (London, 1964); J. W. Dodds, *The Age of Paradox, 1841-1851* (London, 1953), R. C. K. Ensor, *England, 1870-1914* (Oxford, 1936); H. Perkin, *The Origins of Modern English Society, 1780-1880* (London, 1969), G. M. Trevelyan, *English Social History* (London, 1942); E. L. Woodward, *The Age of Reform, 1815-1870* (Oxford, 1938); G. M. Young, ed., *Early Victorian England, 1830-1865*, 2 vols. (Oxford, 1934).

A conspicuous exception is the treatment given by W. E. Houghton, *The Victorian Frame of Mind, 1830-1870* (New Haven, Conn., 1957), pp. 353-393. More recently, J. F. C. Harrison, *The Early Victorians, 1832-1851* (London, 1971), pp. 115-121, displays awareness of the problem. Within the past few years topics concerning nineteenth-century sexual mores have received attention in the following: H. Grisewood, ed., *Ideas and Beliefs of the Victorians* (London, 1966); V. C. Pearl, *The Girl with the Swansdown Seat* (London, 1955); K. Thomas, "The Double Standard," *Journal of the History of Ideas*, XX (1959), pp. 195-216; P. Cominos, "Late Victorian Sexual Respectability and the Social System," *International Review of Social History*, VIII (1963), pp. 18-48, 216-250; S. Marcus, *The Other Victorians: A Study of Sexuality and Pornography in Mid-Nineteenth-Century England* (New York, 1966); E. and P. Kronhausen, *Walter, the English Casanova* (London, 1967); B. Harrison, "Underneath the Victorians," *Victorian Studies*, X (1966-67), 239-262; F. Henriques, *Modern Sexuality: Prostitution and Society*, III (London, 1968); R. Pearsall, *The Worm in the Bud: The World of Victorian Sexuality* (New York, 1969); K. Chesney, *The Victorian Underworld* (London, 1970), pp. 306-364; C. Rover, *Love, Morals and the Feminists* (London, 1970), pp. 58-85.

2. For the important exception in the earlier novels of Mrs. Gaskell see A. Rubenius, *The Woman Question in Mrs. Gaskell's Life and Works* (Upsala, 1950), pp. 176-216.

3. B. Scott, *A State Iniquity: Its Rise, Extension and Overthrow* (London, 1890), Appendix B. The most reliable account of the Acts is contained in J. L. and B. Hammond, *James Stansfeld, A Victorian Champion of Sex Equality* (London, 1932), pp. 118-259. The Acts are treated briefly, or neglected, in the standard texts: E. Halévy, *A History of the English People in the Nineteenth Century*, 6 vols. (London, 1934), VI, 498-500; W. L. Burn, *The Age of Equipoise* (London, 1964), pp. 159-160; G. Kitson Clark, *An Expanding*

Society: Britain, 1830-1900 (London, 1967), p. 166. A brief factual account is R. L. Blanco, "The Attempted Control of Venereal Disease in the Army of Mid-Victorian England," *Journal of the Society of Army Historical Research*, 45 (1967).

4. Scott, *A State Iniquity*, pp. 381-382.

5. W. Acton, *Prostitution, Considered in Its Moral, Social, and Sanitary Aspects, in London and Other Large Cities, with Proposals for the Mitigation and Prevention of Its Attendant Evils* (London, 1857). The substantially revised second edition was published after the passing of the Contagious Diseases Acts under the title, *Prostitution, Considered in Its Moral, Social, and Sanitary Aspects, in London and Other Large Cities and Garrison Towns, with Proposals for the Control and Prevention of Its Attendant Evils* (London, 1870). The later edition has been recently reprinted but unfortunately not in its entirety, W. Acton, *Prostitution*, ed. P. Fryer (London, 1968).

6. M. Ryan, *Prostitution in London, with a Comparative View of that in Paris and New York* (London, 1839); W. Tait, *Magdalenism, An Inquiry into the Extent, Causes and Consequences of Prostitution in Edinburgh* (Edinburgh, 1840); J. B. Talbot, *The Miseries of Prostitution* (London, 1844). "Prostitution," *Westminster Review*, 53 (1850), 448-506, was reprinted as *The Great Sin of Great Cities* (London, 1853), which the British Museum Catalogue attributes to William Rathbone Greg. Henceforth cited as *WR* (1850).

7. "Paris, Its Dangerous Classes," *Quarterly Review*, 70 (1842), 20.

8. See A Physician [Robert Knox], *The Greatest of Our Social Evils* (London, 1857), pp. 231-232.

9. Richelot, in A. J. B. Parent-Duchâtelet, *De la Prostitution dans la Ville de Paris* II (3rd ed.; London, 1857), 561.

10. P. Colquhoun, *Treatise on the Police of the Metropolis* (4th ed.; London, 1797). These estimates are discussed in L. Radzinowicz, *A History of the English Criminal Law and Its Administration from 1750*, II (London, 1958), 242-246, 276.

11. 3S Hansard *Parliamentary Debates*, XCIX, c.333 (5 June 1848).

12. J. C. Whitehorne, *The Social Evil Practically Considered* (London, 1858).

13. *WR* (1850), 475; "Prostitution in Relation to the National Health," *Westminster Review*, 92 (1869), 185.

14. B. R. Mitchell, *Abstract of British Historical Statistics* (Cambridge, 1962), p. 60, Table C, 1871.

15. The figures before and including the year 1857 are taken from Acton (1857), pp. 15-16. The estimates after and including 1858 are taken from the annual estimates returned by the police (of known prostitutes) and printed in the *Judicial Statistics* (England and Wales), Part I, Police and Constabulary.

16. H. Mayhew, *London Labour and the London Poor*, IV (London, 1861), 213. A similar skepticism was apparent in Acton (1857), pp. 17-18.

17. W. Logan, *The Great Social Evil* (London, 1871), p. 32.

18. H. Robinson, *The Whole Truth and Nothing But the Truth About the Social Evil* (Edinburgh, 1866).

19. Logan, p. 46, quoting the *Report* of the Bradford Chief Constable for 1851, and p. 88, quoting the *Report* of the Liverpool Chief Constable. For further estimates see W. W. Sanger, *The History of Prostitution, Its Extent, Causes and Effects Throughout the World* (New York, 1859), p. 342 (reprinted; New York, 1939).

20. Prostitution and the failure of the police to maintain order were discussed both in editorials and correspondence. See, for example, *The Times,* 24 March 1841; 26 June 1841; 12 November 1847; 19 December 1848.

21. For descriptions of these celebrated vice spots, see Acton (1870), pp. 16-27, and Daniel J. Kirwan, *Palace and Hovel, or Phases of London Life* (1870), ed. A. Allan (London, 1963), pp. 180-187.

22. In July 1885 W. S. Stead exposed the international virgin trade in a series of articles published in the *Pall Mall Gazette* entitled "The Maiden Tribute of Modern Babylon." See C. Terrot, *Maiden Tribute: A Study of the White Slave Traffic of the Nineteenth Century* (London, 1959).

23. See V. C. Pearl, *The Girl with the Swansdown Seat,* and H. Blyth, *Skittles, The Last Victorian Courtesan* (London, 1970), pp. 49-105. Also the letter to the *Pall Mall Gazette,* 16 April 1869, on the English demimonde, quoted in Acton (1870), pp. 299-301.

24. Mayhew's letters to the *Morning Chronicle* in 1849, quoted in WR (1850), 464.

25. *Ibid.,* 470.

26. On the sexual vulnerability of domestic servants see the episodes related by "Walter," the author of *My Secret Life,* ed. E. and P. Kronhausen, I, 41-65; II, 271-315.

27. The relationship between the factory environment and sexual immorality was outlined in F. Engels, *The Condition of the Working Class in England* (1845), trans. and ed. W. O. Henderson and W. H. Chaloner (Oxford, 1958), pp. 167-168.

28. Dr. A. R. R. Preston, letter in *Western Daily Mercury,* 18 May 1870.

29. W. Acton, *The Functions and Disorders of the Reproductive Organs in Childhood, Youth, in Adult Age, and in Advanced Age, Considered in their Physiological, Social and Moral Relations* (4th ed.; London, 1865), p. 112.

30. With special reference to the motivation of prostitutes, see E. Glover, *The Psychology of the Prostitute* (London, 1957).

31. *Lancet,* 14 November 1857 (II, 504).

32. For further condemnation of the seducer and the double standard, see WR (1850), 504; Acton (1857), pp. 173-179; *Medical Times and Gazette,* 23 January 1858, p. 91.

33. "Prostitution: Its Causes and Remedies," *British and Foreign Medico-Chirurgical Review,* XXI (1858), 388-415, 397. Henceforth cited as BFMR.

34. Robinson, p. 23. The same opinion was stated in a letter written by a prostitute to *The Times,* 24 February 1858. This has been conveniently reprinted in E. Royston Pike, *Human Documents of the Victorian Golden Age, 1850-1875* (London, 1967), pp. 339-346.

35. A comprehensive catalog of thirty-nine causes was presented in the evidence to the Select Committee of the House of Lords Appointed to Inquire into the State of the Law Relating to the Protection of Young Girls, P.P. 1882 (344) XIII, Appendix B, p. 53. Among those listed were self-pollution, intemperance, laziness, the evils of hiring fairs and hop-picking, evil language, and the lack of exercise and bathing.

36. Knox, p. 97. The *Western Daily Mercury,* 20 November 1870, records an account of the prosecution of a professional photographer specializing in indecent pictures.

37. 12 and 13 Victoria, c. 76. The act was the result of a series of attempts to strengthen the laws against procuring. Six bills were introduced in Parliament between 1844-1849, supported by public petitions, before the measure was finally made law. The debates are particularly valuable in providing a

guide to the views of the legislature not only on procuring but on the related subjects of prostitution, brothels and seduction.

38. Further evidence on the maintenance of appearances and the postponement of marriage is discussed in J. A. Banks, *Prosperity and Parenthood* (London, 1954).

39. *Lancet*, 5 February 1853 (I, 137). The power of the theories surrounding masturbation and its consequences are indicated in E. H. Hare, "Masturbational Insanity: The History of an Idea," *Journal of Mental Science*, 108 (1962), 1-25; R. H. MacDonald, "The Frightful Consequences of Onanism: Notes on the History of Delusion," *Journal of the History of Ideas*, 28 (1967), 423-431; A. Comfort, *The Anxiety Makers* (London, 1967), pp. 77-122.

40. Letter entitled "The Other Side of the Picture," quoted in Acton (1857), pp. 170-172.

41. O. R. McGregor, *Divorce in England* (London, 1957), p. 36.

42. J. B. Talbot, quoted in WR (1850), 476.

43. For the classic statement of the function of the prostitute in the monogamous family system, see W. Lecky, *History of European Morals*, II (London, 1869), 299-300, quoted in Thomas, p. 197.

44. A clear statement of the laws concerning prostitution is given in T. E. James, *Prostitution and the Law* (London, 1951), pp. 28-51, 144-151.

45. In 1857, following a burst of protest, the police attempted to clear the major streets of London of prostitutes. Such coercive action was strongly condemned by the *Lancet*, 23 January 1858 (I, 95-96), as an "abuse of power, the misrule of the strong," for by repressing prostitution and providing no alternative means of employment, the result would be to force the prostitutes into crime.

46. BFMR (1858), 415. The *Medical Times and Gazette*, 23 January 1858, pp. 90-91, also emphasized the "physico-moral" instruction of the adolescent.

47. BFMR (1858), 400. See also Acton (1857), pp. 161-169. This point of view also found favor with Florence Nightingale in connection with mitigating the consequences of prostitution in the army, and resulted in various schemes to improve the education of the soldier and provide him with some alternative forms of amusement and occupation. See Sir Edward Cook, *The Life of Florence Nightingale* (London, 1914).

48. The nature and extent of these institutions were examined in a number of contemporary articles; see, for example, "Female Penitentiaries," *Quarterly Review*, 88 (1848), 359-376, and "Penitents and Saints," *Christian Remembrancer*, 17 (1849), 1-17. I. Bloch, *Sexual Life in England*, trans. William H. Forstern (London, 1958), pp. 185-191, is a useful summary. On the reclaiming activities of Dickens and Gladstone, see P. Collins, *Dickens and Crime* (London, 1962), pp. 94-116, and R. Deacon, *The Private Life of Mr. Gladstone* (London, 1965). Other societies such as those concerned with needlewomen and female emigration were also facets of this charitable solution among whose purposes was to save women from prostitution.

49. Acton (1857), p. viii. For a biting attack on the futility of the reclamation societies, see *Medical Times and Gazette*, 18 February 1860, pp. 169-170.

50. *Report* of the Commissioners to Inquire into the Regulations Affecting the Sanitary Condition of the Army, the Organization of the Military Hospitals and Treatment of the Sick and Wounded, P.P. 1857-58 (2318) XVIII. A revealing account of the role of Florence Nightingale in this cardinal investigation is given in C. Woodham-Smith, *Florence Nightingale*

(London, 1950). Of the investigations spawned by the Army Sanitary Commission (1857), the *General Report* of the Commission Appointed for Improving the Sanitary Condition of Barracks and Hospitals, P.P. 1861 (2839) XVI, and P.P. 1863 (3084) XIII, provide the statistical details behind the conditions and recommendations of the earlier inquiry. For the evidence see Army Sanitary Commission (1857), XVIII, 6-13.

51. Unless detailed for guard duty, the soldier was usually left to his own devices from 1 P.M. until 9:30 P.M. A useful account of the daily routine of the soldier is given in "Life in a Barrack," *Cornhill Magazine*, VII (1863), 441-456. On the monotony of army life and the inevitable consequences, see *Edinburgh Review*, 106 (1858), 136-144.

52. Copy of *Reports of Captain Jackson, R.A.*, to the Secretary of State for War, Respecting the Present State of Soldiers Institutes in England, P.P. 1862 (126), XXXII, 709.

53. *Report* from an Official Committee on Barrack Accommodation for the Army, P.P. 1854-55 (405), XXXII, 40. See also *The Queen's Regulations and Orders for the Army* (London, 1859), p. 397. On regimental variations see Colonel G. Moncrieff, *Minutes of Evidence,* Q.150. *Report* showing what is the Estimated Equivalent Weekly Wage of a Private Soldier . . . , P.P. 1871 (192), XXXIX, 37, states there was no extra pay for married soldiers although a fuel and furniture allowance was granted.

54. This article was concerned chiefly with the prostitutes who lived in the hedges and ditches around the barracks at the Curragh. On these "wrens" as they were nicknamed, see also G. R. Scott, *Ladies of Vice* (London, 1968), pp. 90-93. For a description of the conditions in the village of Aldershot, see *Reports of Captain Jackson*, pp. 707-710, and J. Walters, *Aldershot Review* (London, 1970), pp. 37-44.

55. Drink and women were denied the sailor while at work and it was only natural that they should be sought when leave, usually with the wages from the voyage, was granted. An attempt to describe the network of brothels and drinking houses established to satisfy this demand in English ports has been made in S. Hugill, *Sailor Town* (London, 1967), pp. 95-136.

56. See below, note 77.

57. Mr. Young, letter to *Lancet*, 19 December 1846 (II, 675). A. Fessler, "Advertisements on the Treatment of Venereal Disease and the Social History of Venereal Disease," *British Journal of Venereal Diseases*, 25 (1949), 84-87, provides some evidence on this system of treatment. The existing facilities were detailed and criticized by Acton 1857), pp. 136-144. In 1857 the London hospitals provided 184 beds for female venereal cases, leaving the vast majority to be treated as out-patients or by other means.

58. The different forms of continental government control, which were also in operation in Malta and Gibraltar, were outlined in T. S. Holland, "The Control of Prostitution," *BFMR*, XIII (1854), 113-126, 440-458. A later account is S. Amos, *A Comparative Survey of the Laws in Force for the Prohibition, Regulation and Licensing of Vice in England and Other Countries* (London, 1877).

59. Review of *The Action of Preventives of Venereal Disease* (London, 1842).

60. W. Acton, "Observations on Venereal Diseases in the United Kingdom," paper read before the Royal Medical and Chirurgical Society, 9 June 1846; it was printed in the *Lancet*, 3 October 1846 (II, 369-372).

61. *Lancet*, 21 January 1854 (I, 77, 88-89); see also 15 January 1853 (I,

62); 5 February 1853 (I, 137); and 9 April 1853 (I, 346-347). The lock wards were opened in 1853, largely due to the efforts of Dr. John Rose.

62. *Lancet*, 7 March 1846 (I, 279); a later statement of this argument was made on 11 July 1857 (II, 39). The theme of syphilitic infection of the innocent was explored later in Ibsen's *Ghosts*.

63. Army Medical Department — *Statistical, Sanitary and Medical Reports*, P.P. 1861 (2853) XXXVII; *Statistical Report* of the Health of the Royal Navy, P.P. 1857-58 (473) XXXIX. Beginning in 1859 the Army Medical *Reports* were published annually, and the annual series for the navy commenced from 1856. They provide a complete record of the incidence of disease and mortality in the armed forces. The value of the naval statistics is discussed in C. Lloyd and J. Coulter, *Keevil's Medicine and the Navy, 1200-1900*, IV (London, 1961), 266-271.

64. For similar views of the financial savings which would result from government action (calculated using a primitive cost-benefit analysis), see *Medical Times and Gazette*, 13 February 1858, p. 170; and C. A. Gordon, "Vice and Disease in Garrison Towns," letter to *The Times*, 23 April 1862. These may be compared with latter day cost-benefit analyses of the problems, e.g., H. E. Klarman, "Syphilis Control Programs," in R. Dorfman, ed., *Measuring Benefits of Government Investments* (Washington, D.C., 1965), pp. 367-414.

65. BFMR (1858), 389. The *Medical Times and Gazette*, 25 February 1860, p. 201, reported that Samuel Solly, a council member of the Royal College of Surgeons, "Far from considering syphilis an evil, he regarded it on the contrary as a blessing, and believed it was inflicted by the Almighty to act as a restraint upon the indulgence of evil passions. Could the disease be exterminated, which he hoped it could not, fornication would ride rampant through the land."

66. For a statement of the failings of the continental control system, see *British Medical Journal*, I (October 3, 1863), 372-374, and BFMR (1858), pp. 405-409. The opposing case was outlined in Holland, "The Control of Prostitution."

67. The annual army and navy medical *Reports* display increasing concern over the incidence of venereal disease. Dr. A. Bryson, commenting on the high venereal rates among the British naval service for 1859, stated: "Portsmouth and Plymouth still maintain an unenviable notoriety for containing a population amongst whom venereal complaints exist to an extent unknown in almost any other town, whether in this country or abroad. It is much to be regretted that the local authorities do not take measures to lessen this evil. . . ." P.P. 1862 (199) XXXIV, 522. Dr. Graham Balfour writing about the venereal rates of the army in 1859 observed that when "the admissions by it are found to equal in number one fourth of the whole force, it surely becomes a question of grave importance by what means these diseases can be diminished." P.P. 1861 (2853) XXXVII, 16.

68. The investigation was undertaken by the Medical Committee under the chairmanship of F. C. Skey, which was examining the nature and treatment of venereal disease. The report on the operation of the 1864 Act and the recommendations of the Committee which were embodied in the 1866 Act were not published until 1867. *Report* of the Committee to Inquire into the Pathology and Treatment of the Venereal Disease, with a View to Diminish Its Injurious Effects on the Men of the Army and Navy, P.P. 1867-68 (4031) XXXVII, 452-482.

69. *Report* from the Select Committee on the Contagious Diseases Act (1866), P.P. 1868-69 (306) VII.

70. This provision attempted to keep women in hospital who were unable to undergo examination due to menstruation. The Aldershot Visiting-Surgeon, John Coleman-Barr, stated that while menstruation prevented examination, it did not hinder the prostitutes' sexual activities. *Report* from the Select Committee (1866), Minutes of Evidence, Q. 601.

71. J. E. Butler, *Personal Reminiscences of a Great Crusade* (London, 1896), p. 14.

72. The Association, primarily of medical men, was formed in 1867 from a Committee of the Harveian Society which had been investigating the question of controlling venereal disease.

73. As outlined in the Woman's Protest of 1 January 1870, Butler, pp. 17-20. For a later statement of the objectives of the Repeal Association, when it had become international in character, see Bloch, pp. 191-193. On the statistical manipulations concerned with the Acts, see B. Hill, "Statistical Results of the Contagious Diseases Acts," *Journal of the Royal Statistical Society,* 33 (1870), 463-485; J. Stansfeld, "On the Validity of the Annual Government Statistics of the Operation of the Contagious Diseases Acts," *J.R.S.S.,* 39 (1876), 540-561; R. Lawson, "The Operation of the Contagious Diseases Acts among the Troops in the United Kingdom," *J.R.S.S.,* 54 (1891), 31-69.

74. C. B. Taylor, *The Contagious Diseases Acts (Women): From a Sanitary Point of View, Showing How and Why Such Despotic Measures Not Only Fail to Repress Venereal Disease but Tend to Increase Its Most Serious Manifestations* (London, 1870), p. 32.

75. *Eleventh Report* of the Medical Officer of the Privy Council, P.P. 1868-69 (4127) XXXII, 12.

76. For Simon's understanding of the problems associated with the medical effectiveness of the Acts as well as the more general arguments, see his evidence to the Select Committee on the Contagious Diseases Acts (1866), Minutes of Evidence, Q. 1292-1308 and Q. 1507-1528.

77. The Skey Committee (1867) provides an accessible collection of the different opinions concerning the origin, nature and treatment of venereal disease. Explanations varied on all aspects of the diseases. A Dr. Macloughlin held the view that there was in fact no such disease as syphilis! On the therapeutic side, while the Committee placed its faith in mercury as the most effective known method of treatment, methods of application were not particularly scientific. Thus Acton, one of the foremost venerealogists, described his procedure, "I take a portion of mercurial ointment as large as the top of my thumb and rub it in" (Q. 3015). The success of mercury may be gauged by the large number of other agents employed such as iodine, sarsaparilla, guaiacum, arsenical compounds, and nitric acid. These were often combined — mercurial compounds, potassium iodide and syrup of sarsaparilla made a potent syphilitic cocktail. Such treatment unless strictly controlled was highly dangerous. Ignorance could prove fatal, as it proved in the attempts to treat and provide immunity by "syphilization," where the syphilitic poison was innoculated into the patient.

6: WORKING-CLASS WOMEN IN BRITAIN, 1890-1914

1. Mrs. Hugh Bell, *At the Works* (London, 1907), p. 162.

2. Board of Trade, *Census of England and Wales, 1901 General Report* (London, 1904), Cd. 2174.

3. This probable improvement, however, left women far below both adequate nutritional standards and men's nutritional levels. See J. C. Drummond and Anne Wilbraham, *The Englishman's Food* (London, 1957).

4. Charles Booth, ed., *Life and Labour of the People in London*, X (London, 1897), p. 39.

5. E. H. Phelps Brown, *The Growth of British Industrial Relations* (London, 1965), pp. 6, 21.

6. *Census of England and Wales*, XIII: *Fertility of Marriage* (London, 1917), Cd. 8678.

7. M. Loane, *Next Street But One* (London, 1907); Sidney Pollard, *A History of Labour in Sheffield* (Liverpool, 1959), p. 123.

8. R. H. Best, W. J. Davies, and C. Perks, *Brassworkers of Berlin and Birmingham* (London, 1910).

9. Ernst Dückerstoff, *How an English Workman Lives*, trans. C. H. Leppington (London, 1899), p. 40 and *passim*.

10. Bell, p. 180 and *passim*.

11. Edward Cadbury, et al., *Women's Work and Wages* (London, 1906); Margaret Hewitt, *Wives and Mothers in Victorian Industry* (London, 1958), pp. 68 ff.

12. Hewitt, pp. 40, 45, 68 ff.

13. Booth, IV.

14. Board of Trade, Select Committee on Home Work, *Report* (London, 1908), HC 246.

15. Loane, p. 28.

16. Pollard; Hewitt.

17. Cadbury, pp. 214 ff.; Bell.

18. By 1914 the poverty line had risen to 24s., due to inflation.

19. Select Committee, p. 92.

20. Loane: *Next Street But One; The Queen's Poor* (London, 1905); *Neighbours and Friends* (London, 1910); *From Their Point of View* (London, 1908); M. S. Pember Reeves, *Round About a Pound a Week* (London, 1913).

21. Reeves, p. 110.

22. Reeves; Loane, *Next Street*.

23. Robert Tressell, *The Ragged Trousered Philanthropists* (London, 1955). Originally published in London in 1914, after the death of the author, Robert Noonan, an Irish carpenter who worked for many years in Hastings. The novel provides excellent insights into working-class life in a backward southern area. See Jack Mitchell, *Robert Tressell and the Ragged Trousered Philanthropists* (London, 1969).

24. Loane, *Neighbors and Friends*.

25. Reeves; Loane, *Next Street* and *Point of View*; Bell.

26. R. Seebohm Rowntree, *Poverty, a Study of Town Life* (London, 1901), p. 55.

27. Bell, p. 76.

28. Phelps Brown, pp. 9, 21 ff.; Wil Jon Edwards, *From the Valley I Came* (London, 1958).

29. *Census*, XIII: *Fertility, passim*.

30. Paul de Rousiers, *The Labour Question in Britain*, trans. F. Herbertson (London, 1898), p. 192; Hewitt, p. 45.

31. Edwards; Wyndham Childs, *Episodes and Reflections* (London, 1930).

32. Public Record Office, HO 210615.

33. Edwards; Phelps Brown, p. 9. Miners too would change, and those

in England probably began to do so even before 1914. D. H. Lawrence, in *Sons and Lovers*, portrays the sort of limited allowance system that, as we shall see, came to predominate in the household budgets of factory workers earlier.

34. Loane, *Point of View*.

35. R. A. Bray, *Boy Labour and Apprenticeship* (London, 1911), p. 100.

36. Tressell, p. 178. On the importance of new status for women accompanying birth limitation, see J. A. and Olive Banks, *Feminism and Family Planning* (Liverpool, 1964).

37. *Seventy-fourth Annual Report of the Registrar-General* (London, 1913), Cd. 6578, p. 88; see Phelps Brown, p. 39.

38. Bell, pp. 180 ff. I am not arguing that this despair was unprecedented, but simply that it increased as part of a less resigned outlook.

39. All figures are for England and Wales only, from the census returns of 1891, 1901, and 1911. For a convenient summary, see *Abstract of Labour Statistics* (London, 1915), Cd.7733, pp. 293-319.

40. Royal Commission on Labour, *The Employment of Women* (London, 1893), Cd.6894, p. 36.

41. Booth, IV.

42. Cadbury; J. B. Firth, "Weavers of Bradford: Their Work and Wages," *The Economic Journal* (1892), pp. 543-549; Booth, IV, 401.

43. Board of Trade, *Accounts of Expenditure of Wage-Earning Women and Girls* (London, 1911), Cd. 5963, pp. 70, 105.

44. Royal Commission.

45. National Union of Boot and Shoe Operatives, *Monthly* (February 1913).

46. Booth, IV, p. 300.

47. Royal Commission.

48. Barbara Drake, *Women in Trade Unions* (London, 1921), p. 40.

49. Tressell, p. 49. On the marriage age patterns in 1911, see Hewitt, p. 45; and *Census*, VII: *Age and Conjugal Conditions*, Cd. 6610, and XIII: *Fertility*.

50. Friendly Society of Ironfounders (Sheffield Branch), Strike Committee Minute Book, 1912-1913; see also London Society of Compositors, *To the Workmen of the United Kingdom* (London, 1892).

51. Frederick Rogers, *Labour, Life and Literature* (London, 1913), p. 43.

52. Ferdinand Zweig, *The Worker in an Affluent Society* (New York, 1961).

53. Admittedly, the worker-autobiographer is an unusual type, likely to have been highly aggressive and perhaps atypical in his focus on the father, but the pattern is interesting nonetheless. For some examples, see Thomas Bell, *Pioneering Days* (London, 1941); John Hodge, *From Workman's Cottage to Windsor Castle* (London, n.d.); George Barnes, *From Workshop to War Cabinet* (London, 1924); Onlooker [A. H. Telling], *Hitherto* (London, 1930); Harry Gosling, *Up and Down Stream* (London, 1927); Robert Smillie, *My Life for Labour* (London, 1924).

54. Edward Tupper, *Seaman's Torch* (London, 1938), p. 51.

55. Tressell, p. 600.

56. A. L. Bowley and A. R. Burnett-Hurst, *Livelihood and Poverty* (London, 1915); see also Cadbury.

57. *Census*, X: *Occupation and Industry* (London, 1914), Cd.7018, *passim*.

58. Mrs. J. R. MacDonald, et al., *Wage Earning Mothers* (London, n.d.). The book was published between 1900 and 1910.

59. Elisabeth Gottheimer, *Studien über die Wuppertaler Textilindustrie und ihre Arbeiter* (Leipzig, 1903); Dora Landé, *Arbeits- und Lohnverhält-nisse in der Berliner Maschinenindustrie zu Beginn des 20. Jahrhunderts* (Leipzig, 1910).

60. Landé, Kaiserliches Statistisches Amt, *Volkszählung* (Berlin, 1909). Between 1895 and 1907, the two census years, the German increase in married women employed in industry was almost two times as great as the increase in female population and 50 per cent higher than the overall rise of women in industry. In 1907 26 per cent of all married women, not including widows and divorcees, worked; this of course reflected Germany's relatively large agricultural population as well as the trends in industry, but even so the contrast with Britain is striking.

61. Drake; W. H. Warburton, *The History of the Trade Union Organization in the North: Staffordshire Potteries* (London, 1931), pp. 213 ff.; Sarah Gillespie, *A Hundred Years of Progress: the Record of the Scottish Typographical Association* (Glasgow, 1953); Alan Fox, *A History of the National Union of Boot and Shoe Operatives 1874-1957* (Oxford, 1958); G. D. F. Cole, *Trade Unionism and Munitions* (Oxford, 1923); Hugh Clegg, et al., *A History of British Trade Unions since 1889*, I (London, 1964), pp. 441 and *passim*. For strikes against women workers: Bookbinders' and Machine Rulers' Consolidated Union, *Trade Circulars,* 1909-1914; J. Ramsay MacDonald, *Women in the Printing Trades* (London, 1904).

62. Tressell, pp. 494-497.

63. Tressell, p. 25.

64. Bell, *passim*.

65. Rowland Kenney, *Men and Rails* (London, 1913).

66. Tressell, p. 133.

67. Tressell, p. 58; see also Edwards on the tension which inflation produced in mining families.

68. Board of Trade, *Report of an Enquiry into Working-Class Rents, Housing, and Retail Prices* (London, 1908), Cd. 3864, *passim*.

69. Bell, pp. 77-80.

70. Alfred Williams, *Life in a Railway Factory* (London, 1915), p. 108; Thomas Bell, p. 16.

71. Bell, pp. 77-80.

72. The new stage of work organization is sketched in David S. Landes, *The Unbound Prometheus* (Cambridge, 1969), pp. 318-320.

73. Adolf Levenstein, *Die Arbeiterfrage* (Munich, 1912), contains a series of polls on workers' recreational preferences.

74. Williams.

75. Bell.

76. Bell, pp. 162, 250, and *passim;* Tressell; Dückerstoff.

77. Bell, p. 257.

78. Zweig, pp. 27 ff.

79. The contrast was vivid to a British worker visiting Paris. See Henry Steele *The Working Classes in France, a Social Study* (London, 1904).

80. Bread baking at home was more common in the North, but was also noted by Rowntree in York and in the London area — see Edward G. Howarth and Mona Wilson, *West Ham* (London, 1907). It was also widely noted in budget studies, as in Board of Trade, *Enquiry*. Comparable budget studies on the continent fail to turn up even scattered home bread baking in the

working class. See, for example, Deutscher Metallarbeiter-Verband, 320 *Haushaltsrechnungen von Metallarbeitern* (Stuttgart, 1909), and W. Morgenroth, *Die Kosten des Münchener Arbeiterhaushalts in ihrer neueren Entwicklung* (Munich, 1914).

81. Bell; Best, et al.; Harold Perkin, *The Origins of Modern English Society: 1780-1880* (Toronto, 1968), pp. 149 ff. The restaurant habit was particularly developed in France, but was common in Germany as well. Maurice Halbwachs, *L'Evolution des besoins dans les classes ouvrières* (Paris, 1933).

82. None of the contemporary inquiries into working-class life on the continent suggest such behavior. Most interesting in this regard is R. Seebohm Rowntree, *Land and Labour: Lessons from Belgium* (London, 1913), where the pattern the author uncovered so clearly in York does not emerge.

83. Obviously these comparable suggestions need more work, for as I have pointed out elsewhere — "National Character and Comparative Labor History," *Journal of Social History* (1970-1971) — many impressions of national working-class characteristics are inexact. Dückerstoff for all his insistence on British women's messiness claimed that their houses were cleaner than those in Germany. Certainly the "sloppiness" of British wives and mothers did not prevent British workers from achieving lower child mortality rates than those on the continent — so the housekeeping differentials may have been exaggerated, though I am certain that at least in food handling and personal neatness they existed. No qualifications seem necessary as to the differences in the attitudes of British male workers and in family recreational patterns. I am not claiming that British working-class wives were less well treated by their husbands in all respects, but certainly the treatment was different.

7: THE DEBATE OVER WOMEN
Ruskin vs. Mill

1. John Stuart Mill, *The Subjection of Women* (1889), reprinted in *Three Essays by J. S. Mill,* World's Classics Series (London, Oxford University Press, 1966). John Ruskin's "Of Queen's Gardens," in *Sesame and Lilies,* first published in 1865, reprinted in an American edition (Homewood Publishing Company, 1902). After having found in "Of Queen's Gardens" a representative, and perhaps even a definitive expression, of the chivalrous position, it is pleasant to discover that so distinguished a Victorian scholar as Walter Houghton is in agreement as to its significance in the period: "This lecture of Ruskin's is the most important single document I know for the characteristic idealization of love, women, and the home in Victorian thought" — Walter Houghton, *The Victorian Frame of Mind* (Yale, 1957), p. 343. In view of the present neglect of his work (Victorian scholars tend to look embarrassed when it is mentioned), it is material to recall that *Sesame and Lilies* was also Ruskin's most popular volume.

2. The preface (1871) refers to further "questions" which have arisen since the lecture "respecting the education and claims of women." These have "greatly troubled simple minds and excited restless ones." Disdaining to pursue such nonsense, Ruskin proceeds to harangue the female reader on virtue, his tone growing didactic ("Take out your Latin dictionary and look out

"sollenis" and fix the word well in your mind"), and even punitive ("Of all the insolent, all the foolish persuasions that by any chance could enter and hold your empty little heart"), etc.

3. The question of Harriet Taylor's contribution to Mill's feminist work is carefully reviewed in Alice Rossi's edition of *The Subjection of Women* (Chicago, 1971), and printed together with Harriet Taylor's articles on women.

4. A reviewer rebuked Mill for his interest in "the strangest" and the "most ignoble and mischievous of all the popular feelings of the age," another was incredulous that Mill could imagine the relations of men and women might ever "work on a purely voluntary principle," while others found the book indecent. Thirty years later it could be anathematized as "rank moral and social anarchy" — see Michael St. John Packe, *The Life of John Stuart Mill* (New York, 1854), p. 495.

5. The preceding lecture "Of King's Treasuries," dealing with education and poverty and addressed largely to men, is excellent and by no means complacent. Nothing could afford a greater contrast than the two pieces.

6. "I am, and my father was before me, a violent Tory of the old school — Walter Scott's school, that is to say, and Homer's" — Ruskin's *Praeterita*. See *The Genius of John Ruskin*, a selection, edited by John Rosenberg (New York, 1963), p. 461.

7. Freud knew and disliked Mill's essay. He had even translated it. He probably did not know Ruskin's lecture but it is easy to see how much more he would have approved it. Freud responded to Mill by arguing that the sexes are inherently different in temperament and then, despite the logical contradiction, by deploring changes in upbringing which might erode these differences. He pays chivalrous compliment to "the most delightful thing the world can offer us — our ideal of womanhood." He is also convinced that "nature has determined woman's destiny through beauty, charm, and sweetness." Yet he jumps from ridiculing Mill and his book ("one simply cannot find him human". . . "he lacked in many matters, the sense of the absurd, for example in that of female emancipation and the woman's question altogether") to a stance of personal defensiveness about his fiancée: "If for instance, I imagined my gentle sweet girl as a competitor it would only end by my telling her, as I did seventeen months ago, that I am fond of her and that I implore her to withdraw from the struggle into the calm uncompetitive activity of my home" — Ernest Jones, *The Life and Work of Sigmund Freud*, I (New York, 1953), 175-176.

8. The rhetorical stress on "wisest and bravest," and the "valley of humiliation" is directly at odds with the earlier statement that "a man ought to learn any language or science he learns thoroughly." This is *any* man, not the "wisest and bravest."

9. Ruskin's mother and Rose La Touche were both religious women.

10. Ruskin appeals to the genteel pretensions of his audience, urging them to pointless and impractical feudal largesse in statements like: "Your fancy is pleased with the thought of being noble ladies, with a train of vassals. Be it so; you cannot be too noble and your train too great; but see to it that your train is of vassals whom you serve and feed."

11. An alliance between whores and ladies, however unlikely, might well be the end of chivalry, which relies, as Mill is careful to point out, on the double-standard for its chief value, "virtuous womanhood." Though undoubtedly sincere, Ruskin can scarcely be taken literally, so little does he appear to apprehend the consequences of his suggestion.

8: STEREOTYPES OF FEMININITY
IN A THEORY OF EVOLUTION

1. See Charles Singer, *A History of Biology to about the year 1900*, 3rd ed. (London, 1958), pp. 542-543, 571-573.

2. New York, 1893, p. 373 — first published in serial form in England and the United States in 1872-73, appearing in the *Contemporary Review* and in *Popular Science Monthly*.

3. August Weismann (1834-1914) of Freiburg was obliged to give up his researches in microscopical biology in 1870 because of failing eyesight. For the remainder of his career his main concern was the general subject of variation. His early papers were translated in 1882 and his ideas were of considerable influence in England in the 1880's. See Arthur Huges, *A History of Cytology* (London, 1959), pp. 80-82; and Singer, pp. 553-557.

4. Patrick Geddes (1854-1932) later Sir Patrick. Scottish biologist and sociologist. The standard biographies of Geddes are Philip Boardman, *Patrick Geddes: Maker of the Future* (University of North Carolina Press, 1944), and Philip Mairet, *Pioneer of Sociology: The Life and Letters of Patrick Geddes* (London, 1957). Patrick Geddes and J. Arthur Thomson, *The Evolution of Sex* (London, 1889). References in this paper are to the New York edition (1890). On the nature of the collaboration between Geddes and J. Arthur Thomson (later Sir Arthur) see Philip Boardman, pp. 120-121.

5. See Boardman, pp. 23-52, and Mairet, pp. 13-30, for Geddes's student career and the crisis of his blindness. On Geddes's studies with Huxley see Patrick Geddes, "Huxley as Teacher," *Nature* CXV (9 May 1925), 740-743.

6. Boardman, pp. 41-43, Mairet, pp. 27-28.

7. See his "Analysis of the Principles of Economics," *Proceedings of the Royal Society of Edinburgh*, XII (1884), 943-980.

8. See Philip Rieff, *Freud: The Mind of the Moralist* (New York, 1959), pp. 161-168, for a summary of Freud's views on culture and sensual gratification.

9. See Boardman, pp. 101-105, and Mairet, pp. 51-54.

10. Boardman, p. 125.

11. Boardman, p. 156, Mairet, pp. 62-69.

12. See Boardman, pp. 222-231, and Mairet, pp. 98-108.

13. On the woman's peace movement see Jane Addams, *Peace and Bread in Time of War* (New York, 1922). On the impact of Geddes and the International School see Jane Addams to Mary R. Smith, Paris, 10 June 1900, and same to same, Paris, 27 June 1900. Both letters in the Jane Addams Correspondence, Jane Addams Collection, Swarthmore College Peace Collection, Swarthmore, Pa.

14. See Boardman, pp. 239-240, and Mairet, pp. 121-123.

15. Hobhouse's *Mind in Evolution* (London, 1901) and *Morals in Evolution: A Study in Comparative Ethics* (London, 1951 [1906]) show him to be working in the collectivist evolutionary tradition of which Geddes was an important early English exponent. Hobhouse was the outstanding scholar of his generation to achieve the synthesis of biology, anthropology, and psychology for which Geddes had striven.

16. *Mind in Evolution*, p. v. See also his *Development and Purpose* (London, 1913), pp. 10-12.

17. For a detailed history of the concept of instinct see *The International Encyclopedia of the Social Sciences* (New York, 1968), vol. 7, pp. 363-371.

In popular usage instinct implies impulse uncontrolled by deliberation. In scientific language the term has had a variety of meanings. Darwin's use of instinct ranged over three possible meanings; the motive force of a behaviour pattern such as migration in birds; the hereditary disposition to a trait; the tendency to sympathy in man. All three uses suggest a behaviour pattern developed in successive generations without mediation of experience. Freud's use of the term was one which always contrasted natural impulse or instinct with acquired or learned features of mental life with which the instincts were in conflict. William McDougall (1871-1938) was the psychologist most influential in defining the concept of instinct for Hobhouse's generation. McDougall's use of the term linked perception, action and feeling in an inherited pattern of responses. The psychophysical phenomenon of instinct had adaptive value, since it integrated responses toward the gratification of a need or goal. Instinct, to paraphrase McDougall, was thus an inherited disposition which determined the possessor to perceive and pay attention to certain objects, to experience emotional excitement of a special quality on perceiving such objects, and to act in regard to them in a certain way. This definition of instinct set out in McDougall's *An Introduction to Social Psychology* (1908) held the field until attacked by behaviourists in the twenties. While behaviourists have questioned the validity of the concept it has been revived by ethologists since the 1930's. A notable aspect of the instincts held to be observable in animals by Konrad Lorenz and Nikolaas Tinbergen has been their stress on the distinct differentiation between the sexes in patterns of instinctive behaviour.

18. Hobhouse restated his ideas on the evolution of social structures in *Social Development: Its Nature and Condition* (New York, 1924), see pp. 150 ff. for a discussion of the origin of social sentiment.

19. Hobhouse, *Social Development . . .* , pp. 120-121.

9: INNOCENT FEMINA SENSUALIS
IN UNCONSCIOUS CONFLICT

1. This chapter was read to colloquia at the University of California, Berkeley, Stanford University, and San Jose College, the University of Warwick, and the University of York. I wish to thank my listeners for their criticisms and especially E. P. and Dorothy Thompson. I should also like to express my gratitude to the Social Science Research Council and the American Philosophical Society for summer grants.

2. Samuel Smiles, *Self-Help* (London, 1859), ch. 12.

3. Charles Mercier, "Vice, Crime, and Insanity," in Thomas Clifford Allbut, ed., *A System of Medicine*, VII (8 vols.; London, 1896-1899), 264.

4. Peter T. Cominos, "Late-Victorian Sexual Respectability and the Social System," *International Review of Social History*, VIII, 1, 2 (1963), 18-48, 216-250.

5. "By the Author of 'Amy Herbert' " [E. M. Sewell], *Principles of Education, Drawn from Nature and Revelation, and Applied to Female Education in the Upper Classes*, II (2 vols.; London, 1865), ch. V, "Purity."

6. W. J. Dawson, "The Ideal Woman," *Young Woman* (1892), p. 42.

7. Mary Jeune, "The Revolt of the Daughters," *Fortnightly Review*, n.s. 54 (1894), 275.

8. Steven Marcus, *The Other Victorians, A Study of Sexuality and Pornography in Mid-Victorian England* (New York), 1966.

9. David Foxam, "Libertine Literature in England, 1660-1745," *The Book Collector*, XII, 1, 2 & 3 (Spring, Summer, Winter, 1963), 21-36, 159-177, 294-307.

10. Peter Fryer, *The Man of Pleasure's Companion, A Nineteenth Century Anthology of Amorous Entertainment* (London, 1968), pp. 147-151.

11. W. Balls-Headley, "The Etiology of the Disease of the Female Genital Organs," in Thomas Clifford Allbut, ed., *A System of Gynaecology* (London, 1896), p. 135.

12. M. D. O'Brien, *The Natural Right to Freedom* (London, 1893), p. 220.

13. Caesar Lombroso and William Ferrero, *The Female Offender* (London, 1895), p. 254.

14. William Acton, *The Functions and Disorders of the Reproductive Organs in Childhood, in Youth, in Adult Age, and in Advanced Life, Considered in their Physiological, Social, and Psychological Relations* (3rd ed.; London, 1862), pp. 101-102.

15. Goeffrey Mortimer, *Chapters on Human Love* (London, 1900), p. 89.

16, Clement Scott, "An Equal Standard of Morality," *Humanitarian* (November 1894), 254.

17. Cecil Woodham-Smith, *Florence Nightingale* (London, 1950), p. 93.

18. J. S. Mill, *The Subjection of Women* (London, 1869), p. 27.

19. Josephine Butler, *The Education and Employment of Women* (London, 1869), p. 17.

20. J. B. Bury, "The Insurrection of Women," *Fortnightly Review*, n.s. 52 (1892), 652.

21. Francis Power Cobbe, *Criminals, Idiots, Women and Minors. Is the Classification Sound? A Discussion on the Laws concerning the Property of Married Women* (Manchester, 1869), pp. 18-19.

22. [Sarah Grand], *Ideala, A Study from Life* (London, 1868), p. 100.

23. Lawson Tait, *The Diseases of Women and Abdominal Surgery, I* (Philadelphia, 1889), 61.

24. L. P. Curtis, Jr., *Anglo-Saxons and Celts, A Study of Anti-Irish Prejudice in Victorian England* (New York, 1968).

25. Havelock Ellis, *Studies in the Psychology of Sex*, III (7 vols.; Philadelphia, 1897-1911), 164.

26. Henry Maudsley, *The Pathology of Mind* (London, 1879), p. 164: "Between the instinctive sexual impulses with the emotional feelings that are connected with them and the conventional rules of society which prescribe the strictly modest suppression of them and any display of them, a hard struggle is not infrequently maintained."

27. "The Author of 'The English Matron,'" *The English Gentlewoman, A Practical Manual for Young Ladies on their Entrance into Society* (3rd ed.; London, 1861), pp. 47-49. First edition published in 1845.

28. Annie Besant, *Annie Besant, An Autobiography* (London, 1893), pp. 42-43, 65-67, 71.

29. For a fascinating account of the way repressed sexuality influenced feminine dress, see C. W. Cunnington, *Feminine Attitudes in the Nineteenth Century* (London, 1935).

30. M. D. Mulock, *A Woman's Thoughts about Women* (London, 1858), p. 286.

31. Rev. G. B. Merrick, *Work Among the Fallen, as Seen in the Prison Cell* (London, 1890), p. 36.

32. E. L. Linton, "The Partisans of the Wild Women," *Nineteenth Century*, 31 (1892), 460.

33. Clement Scott, "An Equal Standard of Morality," *Humanitarian* (November 1894), 255.

34. B. Hemynge, "Prostitution in London," in Henry Mayhew, *London Labour and the London Poor*, IV (4 vols.; London, 1851-1862), 215.

35. Cited in Fryer, p. 70, quoted from [Denon, Dominique Vivant, Baron], *The Voluptuous Night: or, The non plus ultra of pleasure.* "By Mary Wilson, Spinster" (London, "Printed by Sarah Brown, Princes Place, Pimlico, 1830" [i.e., c. 1890]). This translation of Denon's *Point de lendemain* (a work printed in *Mélanges littéraires ou Journal des dames*, puin 1777, and sometimes attributed to Claude-Joseph Dorat) was originally issued by George Cannon in 1830. *The Whore's Catechism* appended to it is a translation of "Mlle. Theroigne de Mericourt," *Catéchisme libertin, à l'usage des filles de joie et des jeunes citoyennes qui se décident à embrasser cette profession* ("Luxuriopolis," 1791).

36. Mrs. E. Lynn Linton, *The True History of Joshua Davidson*, I (2 vols.; London, 1872), 173.

37. George Bernard Shaw, "The Quintessence of Ibsenism," in *Major Critical Essays* (London, 1948), p. 103.

38. Philip Rieff, *Freud, The Mind of the Moralist* (New York, 1961), ch. V.

39. Sigmund Freud, *Collected Papers*, trans. Joan Riviere, II (3 vols.; London, 1955), 93.

40. George Eliot, *Middlemarch* (London, 1952), pp. 12, 41, 44, 51, 63-64.

41. George Moore, "Mildred Lawson," in *Celibates* (London, 1895), pp. 42, 62, 280, 92, 147, 152-154, 156, 157, 247, 312.

42. Furneaux Jordan, *Character as Seen in the Body and Parentage; with a Chapter on Education, Careers, Morals and Progress* (London, 1890), p. 15.

43. J. S. Mill, *Inaugural Address* (London, 1867), pp. 88-89.

44. J. S. Mill, *The Subjection of Women*, pp. 181-182.

45. A. Orr, "The Future of English Women," *Nineteenth Century*, 2 (June 1878), 1010.

10: THE WOMEN OF ENGLAND IN A CENTURY OF SOCIAL CHANGE, 1815-1914

A Select Bibliography

1. This chapter is an excerpt from a larger bibliographical work, "The Victorian Woman in English Social History."

2. Place of publication is London unless otherwise stated.

3. Entries for periodicals and their contents are severely reduced, considering the great number available. Among the categories not included here are: Family Patterns and Child Training; The Woman Question in Fiction; Women's Affairs and the Daily Press; Women Travelers and Adventurers: and Victorian Biography.

4. I would like to express appreciation to Miss Mildred Surry, Librarian of the Fawcett Library, for her valuable assistance in locating sources. At the University of California, Los Angeles, I wish to thank Mr. Robert Collison,

Head, Reference Department, University Research Library, for his suggestions and interest in the project, and also Professor D. C. Moore, Department of History, for reading the manuscript.

5. Volume numbers are not included since editions vary greatly.

6. The dates provided here refer to the year the paper was presented to the Association rather than the date of publication, one year later.

The Editor and Authors

PETER T. COMINOS, Associate Professor of History, Tulane University. Author of "Late-Victorian Sexual Respectability and the Social System," in *International Review of Social History* (1963).

JILL CONWAY, Assistant Professor of History, University of Toronto. Author of a study of Jane Addams and of articles on other women reformers.

S. BARBARA KANNER, Instructor in English History, University of California, Los Angeles, Extension Division. Fellow, American Association of University Women. Co-author, "Blue Book into Novel: the Forgotten Industrial Fiction of Charlotte Elizabeth Tonna," in *Nineteenth Century Fiction*, 25 (1970) 152-173. Author of "Frances Anne Kemble and her Southern Diary, 1838-1863," in *British Champions of the American Negro*, Ada Nisbet, editor.

KATE MILLETT, Department of Sociology, Bryn Mawr College. Author of *Sexual Politics*. An advisor for the Source Library of the Women's Movement (Source Books Press). Sculptor and film-maker.

M. JEANNE PETERSON, Lecturer in History, Indiana University, Bloomington. Author of a study of kinship, status, and social mobility in the mid-Victorian medical profession.

HELENE E. ROBERTS, Curator of Fine Arts Photographs and Slides, Fine Arts Library, Fogg Museum, Harvard College Library. Author of "British Art Periodicals of the Eighteenth and Nineteenth Centuries" in *The Victorian Periodicals Newsletter*, July 1970; *American Art Periodicals of the Nineteenth Century* in the ACRL Microcard Series (No. 141); and "The Knight Errant, Pre-Raphaelite Influences in America," in *The Dartmouth Library Bulletin*, Winter 1963.

ELAINE SHOWALTER, Assistant Professor of English, Douglass College. Editor of *Women's Liberation and Literature*, contributor to *Women in Sexist Society*, author of articles on nineteenth-century and contemporary women writers.

ENGLISH SHOWALTER, JR., Assistant Professor of French, Princeton University, Author of a study of French fiction in the eighteenth century.

ERIC MILTON SIGSWORTH, Professor of Economic and Social History, University of York, England. Author of *Black Dyke Mills, Modern York* in the *Victorian County History* and of many essays and articles on economic and social history.

PETER N. STEARNS, Chairman and Professor of History, Rutgers University. Author of *Revolutionary Syndicalism and French Labor* and other studies in working-class history. Managing Editor of the *Journal of Social History*.

JANE W. STEDMAN, Professor of English, Roosevelt University. Author-editor of *Gilbert Before Sullivan* and of "The Genesis of *Patience*," in which the surviving fragment of the "Rival Curates" draft of *Patience* was first published. Author of articles on Dickens, the Brontës, the Victorian stage, opera, and Victorian comic journalism.

MARTHA VICINUS, Editor of *Victorian Studies* and Assistant Professor of English, Indiana University. Author of articles on popular and working-class culture in the nineteenth century.

TERENCE JOHN WYKE, Lecturer in Economic and Social History, University of York, England. Author of a study of the history of prostitution and venereal disease in Victorian England.

Index

Academy, Royal, 46, 48, 50, 51, 56, 57, 60, 63, 65, 72, 75-76
Acton, William, 39, 63, 78, 91, 217, 218, 220; quoted, 80, 82-83, 84, 87, 89, 160, 162-163, 222
Addams, Jane, 150-152, 228; *Democracy and Social Ethics*, 151; *Newer Ideals of Peace*, 151
All the Year Round: quoted, 90
Allan, James MacGrigor: quoted, 40
Anderson, Elizabeth Garrett, 42-43
Army and Navy *Reports*, 93, 94, 221
Army Sanitary Commission, 89, 219-220
Art Journal, 50, 55; quoted, 56, 60
Athenaeum, 26; quoted, 53, 56, 60
Attwood, William, 22
Awakened Conscience, painting by T. Brooks, 65; by R. Redgrave, 65
Awakening Conscience, painting by W. H. Hunt, 63-67, 72, 73

Barnett, Alice, 31, 32
Barracks and Hospitals Sanitary Commission *Report*, 89-90, 220
Baxter, Charles: *The Sisters*, 45, 46, 48, 53; Pl.1, 47
Bell, Florence, 102, 104, 106, 109
Bergson, Henri, 150
Besant, Annie, 39, 163-164
Booth, Charles, 101, 103, 111
Bradlaugh, Charles, 39
Brandram, Rosina, 30, 31, 34, 35
Breakfast Time — Morning Games, painting by C. W. Cope, 55
Brennan, Maggie, 21, 27
Bridge of Sighs, by T. Hood, 73
British and Foreign Medico-Chirurgical Review, 220, 221; quoted, 84, 88-89, 94

Brodie, J. L.: *The Last Resource*, 52
Brontë, Charlotte: *Shirley*, xi; *Jane Eyre*, 3, 210; *Villette*, 211
Brooks, Shirley, 21
Brooks, Thomas: *Awakened Conscience*, 65
Brough, Robert, 22, 23, 25
Brough, William, 22, 24
Brown, Ford Madox: *Take Your Son, Sir*, 73-75; Pl.10, 74
Bryce, James, 150
"Bumboat Woman's Story," by W. S. Gilbert, 21-22
Burgoyne, John, 20
Burnand, F. C., 23, 26
Butler, Josephine E., 95-96, 97, 98
Byron, H. J., 21, 22

Carlyle, Thomas, 125
Chadwick, Edwin, 93
Chalon, A. E., 45
Clarke, Edward: *Sex in Education*, 41-42
Cobbe, Frances Power, 5, 8, 13, 208
Collins, Wilkie: *Armadale*, 7; *No Name*, 10, 15
Colquhoun, P., 78
Comte, August, 140, 143, 150, 153, 154
Contagious Diseases Acts, 77, 87-88, 91-99, 216-217, 221-222
Cope, C. W., 50, 52; *Breakfast Time . . .*, 55
Cushman, Charlotte S., 20-21

Dafforne, J., 60
Darwin, Charles, 142, 143, 229; *Origin of Species*, 140
Dickens, Charles, xi, 21, 22, 26, 212, 213, 219; *Bleak House*, 31; *David*

Index

Quiller-Couch, Arthur, 36

Index

Tupper, J. L., 50

Under a Dry Arch, painting by G. F. Watts, 62
Utopia Limited, by W. S. Gilbert, 35

Vanity Fair, by W. M. Thackeray, 3, 7, 15, 210
Vestris, Lucia E., 20, 22
La Vivandière, by W. S. Gilbert, 27, 213; quoted, 28-29

Walker, Frederick: *The Lost Path*, 63
Wallas, Graham, 152
Ward, Lester, 150
Wassermann, August von, 98
Watts, George F., 56, 76; *Found Drowned*, 62, 72; *The Seamstress*, 62, Pl.5, 61; *Under a Dry Arch*, 62
Webster, Thomas, 50
Wedding Card — Jilted, painting by J. E. Millais, 53; Pl.3, 54

Weismann, August, 141, 144, 228
Wells, H. G., 152
Western Daily Mercury, 218; quoted, 97-98
Westminster Review, 78-79, 217; quoted, 82, 90-91, 92, 93
Whitehorne, J. C., 78; quoted, 86
Whore's Catechism: quoted, 168
Widdicombe, Henry, 22-23
Wilde, Oscar, 122
Williams, Alfred, 117-118
Wilton, Marie, 22, 26, 27
Winterhalter, Franz: *The Royal Family*, 50-51
Woffington, Peg, 20, 22
Woman's Mission: Companion of Manhood, painting by G. E. Hicks, 48-50; Pl.2, 49
Wordsworth, William, 129
World, 31

Zeublin, Charles, 150